9/0150167

THE BATTLE FOR THE
ARDENNES

THE BATTLE FOR
THE ARDENNES

John Strawson

Disease
By desperate appli
Or not at all.

B. T. Batsford Ltd   London

© John Strawson 1972
First published 1972

Printed and bound in Great Britain by
C. Tinling & Co. Ltd
Warrington Road, Prescot, Lancashire

for the publishers

B. T. Batsford Ltd
4 Fitzhardinge Street, London W1H 0AH

ISBN 0 7134 1174 0

CONTENTS

ACKNOWLEDGMENTS

I would like to thank Mr Peter Kemmis Betty for his initial suggestions about this book and for his subsequent advice. There are innumerable accounts of the Ardennes battle, and I have found generally speaking that the shorter they are, the better they are. Single chapters like Chester Wilmot's in *The Struggle for Europe* or Major Ellis's in the *Official History* (which give at once the feel and the essentials of what happened) are, I believe, to be preferred to immensely detailed histories in which both the sequence of events and their significance tend to be obscured by the sheer volume and complexity of military operations described. I must nonetheless acknowledge my debt to these painstaking and meticulous narratives even though I may shun their example. Yet these two very different sorts of book, the analysis and the synthesis, so to speak, may be said to have one thing in common—their reading public. Each is designed primarily for the serious student of military history. If this distinction between the two and my preference for the one are supportable, by what right does another volume dedicated to events in the Ardennes now appear? My answer is this. Because of the unique nature of these events, by virtue of having such a battle at such a time with such consequences, it may be defensible to seize upon it as a climacteric moment in the struggle between Hitler's and the Allied armies, and— by showing broadly what transpired, by commenting on it, by discussing those in positions of command, in short by setting the whole affair in its proper historical context—hope to furnish some entertainment for the general reader.

My thanks are due to the following authors and publishers for permission to quote from the books named: Alistair Borthwick, *History of the 5th Battalion, The Seaforth Highlanders,* William Blackwood and Sons Ltd; Arthur Bryant, *The Lion and The Unicorn,* Collins; Winston S. Churchill, *The Second World War,* Cassell and Co. Ltd; H. Essame, *The Battle for Germany,* Batsford; Charles de Gaulle, *Salvation 1944–46,* Simon and Schuster; *The Story of the 23rd Hussars,* published privately by Members of the Regiment; D. H. Lawrence, *The Ship of Death,* Martin Secker; Fred Mackenzie, *The Men of Bastogne,* David McKay Co. Inc.; Fred Majdalany, *Cassino, Portrait of a Battle,* Longmans, Green and Co.; R. J. B. Sellar, *The Fife and Forfar Yeomanry, 1919–1956,* William Blackwood and Sons Ltd; Chester Wilmot, *The Struggle for Europe,* Collins.

Acknowledgments

I am grateful to the following for their invaluable assistance in getting books of reference for me: Mr John E. Garrod, Librarian of the SHAPE Military Library, and his Assistant, Petty Officer Henning Fechner; Miss Phylis Boldra, Librarian of the SHAPE Community Library, and her Assistant, Miss Janine Arnault; the staff of the Ministry of Defence Library (Central and Army).

I wish to thank Corporal W. Davis and Corporal D. Parry, both of the Royal Air Force, for their patience and industry in deciphering and typing my manuscript. Corporal Parry also gave me a great deal of help with the index.

The author and publishers wish to thank the following for permission to reproduce photographs: Associated Press for figs 4, 7 and 8; Imperial War Museum for figs 6 and 9–30; Süddeutscher Verlag, Munich for figs 1 and 3; Ullstein Bilderdienst for fig 2; US Signal Corps for fig 5.

THE ILLUSTRATIONS

THE MAPS

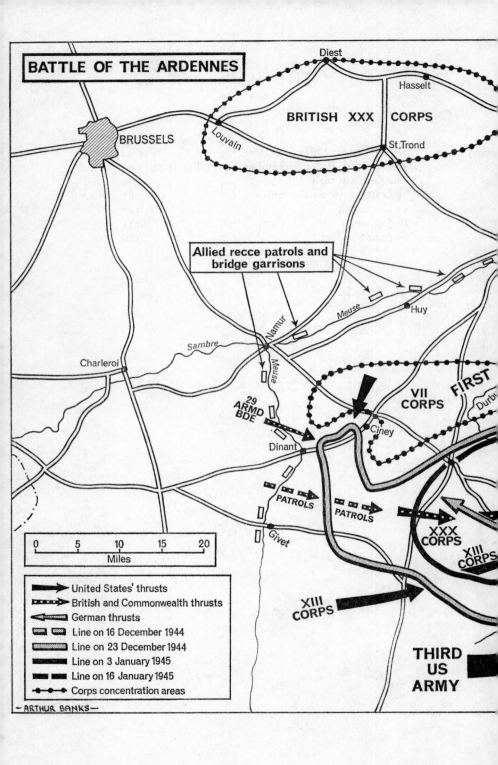

BATTLE OF THE ARDENNES

Diest

Hasselt

BRUSSELS

BRITISH XXX CORPS

Louvain

St.Trond

Allied recce patrols and bridge garrisons

Namur

Meuse

Huy

Sambre

Meuse

Charleroi

29 ARMD BDE

Ciney

VII CORPS

FIRST

Durbi

Dinant

PATROLS

PATROLS

XXX CORPS

XIII CORPS

Givet

XIII CORPS

THIRD US ARMY

Scale

0	5	10	15	20

Miles

▶ United States' thrusts
▶ British and Commonwealth thrusts
◀ German thrusts
▬ Line on 16 December 1944
▬ Line on 23 December 1944
▬ Line on 3 January 1945
▬ Line on 16 January 1945
●━● Corps concentration areas

~ ARTHUR BANKS ~

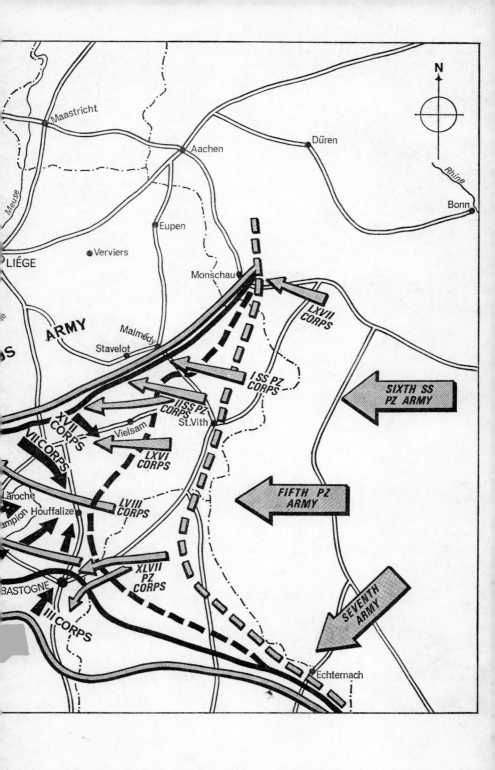

Prologue

---

*The essential matter of history is not what happened
but what people thought or said about it.*
Maitland

When we repeat the maxims of our great men of action, we
savour them not only for their inherent truth or wit, but also as
being characteristic of the men themselves. There must be few
soldiers whose maxims outnumber Napoleon's and it is perhaps
with one of his own and two others about him that this point may be
illustrated. 'Men are never attached to you by favours', observed
the Emperor, and yet, more than any other great national military
leader, he showered favours on his subordinates. Like Antony,
crowns and coronets walked in his livery, he dropped realms and
islands from his pocket as plates. Of course, he made sure that he
dropped them into the right hands. The Bonaparte family did
uncommonly well for crowns and coronets. The marshals had
little to complain of with their batons, their dukedoms and their
principalities. Even professional turncoats like the reptilian
Talleyrand and the sinister Fouché did not go unrewarded. The
common soldier or simple *bourgmestre* might look to become a
member of the Légion d'Honneur or enjoy the exquisite distinction of having his ear pinched. There was no shortage of
favours under Bonaparte. And as long as his star went on shining,
men were attached to him. But when the game went wrong, the
men went too.

That they went so far and so fast was due in large measure to
the efforts of Wellington, and one of his pronouncements during
the battle of Waterloo revealed the man absolutely. 'Damn the

fellow,' he said when he saw that Napoleon's tactics were mere
massed artillery together with Ney's head-on cavalry attacks, 'he
is a mere pounder after all.' In this comment lay not just contempt
for the *grand homme de guerre* who had once revolutionized warfare
and yet who now could not be bothered to manoeuvre properly
or to conform to the basic rules of fire and movement with
infantry and artillery. There was also chagrined recognition that
the Emperor's contempt for him, Wellington, as a general, was
such that he assumed victory would easily be his without resort to
the elementary military rules of the day. There was to be no
compliment paid to the sepoy general's otherwise widely
acclaimed skill in defence. Ironically enough, the mere pounding
might have done the trick had it not been for the coalition of the
Prussian and British armies.

Had Foch forgotten this when he maintained that the First
World War had robbed him of much of his veneration for
Napoleon because the Emperor had had to fight only coalitions
and that any reasonably efficient general could defeat a coalition?
Whether he had forgotten or not, we must allow that Foch was
certainly alive to the point that he himself had led a coalition of
armies to victory over a single and supremely efficient, warlike
nation. Foch's most celebrated saying also concerned his First
World War activities: '*Mon centre cède, ma droite recule, situation
excellent. J'attaque!*'*

In the winter of 1944, Hitler's right—if we can so classify the
Eastern front—was certainly more or less continuously in retreat.
His centre—if the West Wall may be taken as a protective shield
to the very heart of his industrial power—had been on the point
of giving way, but had been patched up. Hitler did not have the
Gallic touch to call the situation excellent. Most of his memorable
maxims were borrowed from his hero, Frederick the Great. But
he did reject the idea of remaining on the defensive. His decision
was the same as Foch's. '*J'attaque!*' In doing so, he again res-
embled Frederick, for he took comfort in hatred. 'The implacable
resentment with which his enemies pursued him,' wrote Macaulay of the Prussian King, 'though originally provoked by his
own unprincipled ambition, excited in him a thirst for vengeance
which he did not even attempt to conceal.' Indeed he maintained

---

* My centre is giving way, my right is in retreat; situation excellent. I shall
attack!

in 1761 that he would die content if only he could inflict on others a portion of the misery he himself endured. Such was Hitler's sentiment. Yet his position in 1944 was not a tenth part as bad as that of Frederick at the beginning of 1762. When Hitler talked of the fragility of the Allied coalition and that its destruction would turn the tables for him in the same way that the falling apart of the Allies in 1762 had for Frederick, he was not merely guilty of the most absurd exercise in make-believe. He was forgetting the history of Prussia. In comparing what happened to Frederick with what might happen to himself, he was ignoring the point that the death of the Czarina Elizabeth of Russia on 5 January 1762 did not merely remove one of the King's enemies. The enemy actually changed sides for a time and fought for him. All Russian conquests were returned to Prussia. Hitler's far-fetched hopes were tantamount to believing that in January 1945, Stalin, shall we say, would die and be succeeded by someone who would instantly call off the Red Army and send a few of its mighty contingents to hammer the Western Allies, or alternatively that the American and British armies would suddenly call it quits, leave Hitler in possession of Western Europe and allow him to have it out with Soviet Russia, face to face. For Frederick did not just have the benefit of initial Russian aid and later neutrality. Sweden withdrew from the war, then France, and finally Austria and Saxony made peace. 'It seemed mysterious at the time', observed Nancy Mitford, 'that Frederick who was really beaten to his knees, should have got away with such huge rewards as Upper and Lower Silesia and Glatz.' Who could have foreseen such a reversal of fortune? Are there other comparable snatchings of chestnuts out of the fire against all the odds?

The Trojan Horse perhaps, Agincourt, the Armada, Plassey, the Battle of Britain? All these were remarkable for the triumph of the few over the many. But the circumstances and the options of late 1944 were very different. Accurate forecasts of things to come are the more impressive simply because they are made before the event. On 21 October 1944, anniversary of Trafalgar, there appeared in the *Illustrated London News* an article by Arthur Bryant, in which he made it clear that there could be no chestnut snatching by Hitler, that it was only a question of time before Germany broke. But his thumbnail sketch of the prelude to a final act was forbidding:

For a few days at the end of August and beginning of September, it looked as though the very obstinacy with which the Germans had stood to their guns in the Normandy *bocage* would prove their undoing, and that the surge of British and American armour northwards and eastwards would pour unimpeded over the Siegfried Line into the Reich. But though nearly half-a-million prisoners were taken, the hard core of the German Army survived. Fighting close to its bases, while the victorious Allies raced forward at the end of elongated supply-lines and with inadequate port facilities behind them, it was able to hold before the Rhine. . . . The Germans are fighting desperately. The war they have twice in a quarter of a century loosed on the world is moving slowly and remorselessly into their own land. Millions of young Nazi braves—the fanatic blond savages whom Hitler and his henchmen have been schooling for battle for the past decade—are struggling to avert the inevitable. Beside them—terrified by the bludgeon and the hip-gun of a police state—the dregs of the barrel are fighting too: old men from the factories, *embusqués* from offices and theatres, half-starved prisoners from the East, quislings and criminals, cripples and convalescents. And the arch-criminals, for whom all this bloody endeavour and sacrifice is being made, are breathing threats of new destructive weapons to mangle, torture and annihilate mankind, and are spurring on their scientists to evolve some suicidal devilry which will either save them at the eleventh hour or bring the pillars of the reeling globe crashing down on their own and the victors' heads.

Optimists are to be found both in military camps and on the race course. Despite this sombre prospect neither Allied nor German military cliques were without those who tried to look on the bright side. If the Allies were tempted to draw reinforcement from hope, their enemies gained resolution from despair. And such was the seesawing of events during the week before the last Christmas of the war, that hope and despair changed sides a dozen times before the reinforcement of the Allies became more, overwhelmingly more, than a match for all the resolution the Germans could muster. There has been much controversy about the overall strategic effect of the Ardennes offensive. At the very moment when it was to all intents and purposes over—that is, in the second week of January, *after* Hitler had chucked away his last reserves of men and machines, the British war cabinet had come to the conclusion that the war could not be expected to end before 31 December 1945. Within ten days and as a result of the gigantic Russian offensive which had met with such startling and immediate success, they revised this opinion, and began to talk of the war's being over by mid-April. It is the shadow of the Ardennes battles on the whole strategic canvas of the war in Europe which is subject still to as great a variety of interpretation as Hamlet's cloud—camel, weasel or whale. Was Hitler's final crack at blitzkrieg a weasel or a whale? Apart from all the death and the destruction, did it matter? Did it make any difference? Was it a major strategic event or merely the last death throe of a doomed Third Reich? If the essential matter of history really is what people think and say about what happened, then there are plenty of essentials for us to contemplate about the events in the Ardennes some five months from the end of the struggle for Europe.

I
Eagle's Nest, December 1944

If it does not succeed, I no longer see any possibility for
ending the war well. ... But we will come through. A single
breakthrough on the Western front! You'll see! It will lead to
collapse and panic among the Americans. We'll drive right
through their middle and take Antwerp. Then they'll have lost
their supply port. And a tremendous pocket will encircle
the entire English army, with hundreds of thousands of
prisoners. As we used to do in Russia.
Hitler to Speer, November 1944

If the student of military history wished to examine a battle in
which most of the mistakes of high command were made on
both sides, a battle moreover during which both armies in a
matter of weeks practised all four phases of war—advance,
attack, defence and withdrawal—he could hardly do better than
study the Ardennes in December 1944. Yet it is not only for these
conformities that the battle continues to attract our attention. It
was remarkable also for its incongruities. On the one side, for
example, the forces engaged were directed by the inflexible and
tyrannical whim of a single man who had rejected all acknowledge-
ment of military realities and whose subordinates, however
conscientiously they may have carried out his orders, had no
faith in them. On the other side, command was exercised by a
triumvirate, divided in opinion and loyalty, grossly unequal in
experience and competence, strained by controversy and misunderstanding, weakened by inadequacies of resources in relation to
tasks, compromised by a sterile strategy, and united only by an
alliance of convenience and a common determination to end the
war quickly. What happened in the Ardennes in December 1944
and January 1945 has been the subject of many books, some of
which have given an almost blow-by-blow account of the battle

from both sides. So detailed a record is not the purpose of this volume. Rather it is to *discuss* the battle, to set so climacteric an event in the course of the war on the Western front in its proper strategic context, to observe the multitudinous mistakes of high command, and to examine the furious controversies which the offensive gave rise to. But to do this without seeing what really happened at the front line, *was eigentlich gewesen ist*, would be wrong. Those who did the actual fighting must have their say as well.

This extraordinary battle was the last fling of a Wehrmacht sorely tried. In the past the Wehrmacht had done some fearsome things—crushed Poland, broken France, turned England out of Europe and threatened the key to her Empire, destroyed millions of Russian soldiers and overrun millions of Russian acres—it had in fact conquered all Europe's armies, and brought its Supreme Commander to within an ace of *Weltmacht,* world power. Now the Wehrmacht was being conquered itself and meanwhile was grimly defending the frontiers of the Third Reich. But a defensive strategy, however prolonged it might be, had no appeal to the Führer. By the autumn of 1944, Hitler's strategy had degenerated to that of Mr Micawber. One of his favourite, one of his constantly recurring phrases throughout an unparalleled career, a phrase which characterized his tendency to oversimplify all problems, had been—'There are two possibilities'*. In 1936 he had told Albert Speer that there were two possibilities—to win through with all his plans, or to fail. If he won, he would be one of the greatest men in history; if he failed, he would be 'condemned, despised and damned'. There were two possibilities for him again in the autumn of 1944. Either the war against Germany on three fronts, east, west and south, would in some way be disrupted because of the mounting tension and discord between Russia, England and America, so that something might be rescued from the threatened ruin of the Thousand-Year Reich. Or the war would continue on all three fronts and Germany would be destroyed. In contemplating this second alternative, Hitler's nihilism knew no bounds. 'If the war is to be lost, the nation will also perish. This fate is inevitable.' Given this alternative Hitler's strategy was one of doom. Failure, however, was not yet to be

* One of Hitler's secretaries, Fräulein Schröder, would make fun of this phrase even in his presence. 'There are two possibilities,' she would announce, 'either it is going to rain or it is not going to rain.'

anticipated. The message which Hitler gave to his generals on
11 and 12 December 1944, respectively five and four days before
launching the Ardennes offensive, was in effect—screw your
courage to the sticking place, and we'll not fail. Everything was
to be done to facilitate and hasten the crack-up of the alliance
against Germany.

War, Hitler declared on these two consecutive days, with purpose but not originality, was a test of endurance. Endurance
must continue as long as there was hope of victory. But endurance
by defensive means alone was not enough. It was by offensive
action that the enemy's confidence must be destroyed. The idea
that the defensive was stronger than the offensive did not hold
good. The defensive might wear down an enemy, but it must
always be followed by a successful offensive. 'From the outset
of the war therefore I have striven to act offensively whenever
possible, to conduct a war of movement and not to allow myself
to be manoeuvred into a position comparable to that of the
First World War.'

Military arguments for resuming the offensive and for dismaying the enemy by persuading him that he could under no circumstances succeed were accompanied by underlining the fragility
of the coalition which they were facing. The Grand Alliance
against Germany was fraught with contradictions—capitalists in
league with Bolshevists, imperialists hand-in-hand with anti-
imperialists, Russia and Great Britain, so long in competition
with each other for control of the Near and Middle East, once
more at loggerheads over the Balkans and the Persian Gulf,
the United States eager to inherit and enjoy England's imperial
legacy—the whole thing was rotten and ready for dissolution. It
would have been an unusual lecture if Hitler's historical hero,
Frederick the Great, had escaped mention. He did not. The
seventh year of the Seven Years War may have brought all
Prussians save one to a state of despair. One man's steadfastness,
however, carried the battle through, but only because he waited.
'One must await the moment.' Politically therefore the time was
ripe. Nor were the military signs inauspicious; the balance of
power was by no means as unfavourable as it might appear. The
Americans had lost a quarter of a million men in less than a
month. It was perhaps true that the Luftwaffe was less powerful
than the Allied Air Forces, but on the ground the enemy was
outfought. The enemy might have more tanks, but the German

ones, even though fewer, were better.* All in all therefore now was the time. And he, Hitler, 'like a spider sitting in the middle of his web' watching the antagonisms of his enemies grow stronger, would strike. 'If now we can deliver a few more heavy blows, then at any moment this artificially bolstered common front may collapse with a mighty clap of thunder. . . . Wars are finally decided by one side or the other recognizing that they cannot be won. We must allow no moment to pass without showing the enemy that whatever he does, he can never reckon on capitulation. Never! Never!'

It was thus that Hitler chased political chimeras while subjecting the hard military facts to a less critical analysis. It was not that the military facts were unknown to Hitler. It was simply that they were disregarded. This disregard must have come less easily to the generals who attended the Führer's lecture in his bunkered headquarters near Bad Nauheim in Hesse with its legendary Wagnerian title, *Adlershorst*—Eagle's Nest. The very circumstances under which the lecture was given and the physical condition of the lecturer could have done little to reassure those who had been chosen actually to deliver these heavy blows to the artificially bolstered common front.

By December 1944 Hitler was a physical wreck. The years of living in underground bunkers, of subjecting himself to a routine of almost uninterrupted work, the strain of ceaseless responsibility and maintaining his granite will intact, the eccentric hours and diet he kept, his refusal to rest or to take exercise—however strong his constitution may have been to start with, such treatment could not but take effect. Together with the various drugs administered by the sinister and repulsive Dr Morell, it had reduced him to a state which Manteuffel, one of the principal commanders of the Ardennes counterstroke, described as that of an old and broken man. He stooped and shuffled, his face was pasty and puffy, his voice quavered, his hands trembled, one leg dragged behind him as he walked, a film of sheer exhaustion seemed at times to cover and cloud his eyes. Yet in spite of the game going wrong on all fronts, in spite of what perhaps had an even more powerful effect on his physical condition than all the purely physical degeneration, that is to say the

---

* This at least was true. The German Panther and Tiger tanks had a better combination of fire power and armour than the standard Allied tank— the Sherman.

psychological effect of a mission frustrated, all his hopes turned to disappointments—two things seemed to be unchanged. One was his will-power, the other his continued ability to impose this will on others. Only a few months before his harangue to the generals, he had in a rare moment of self-pity admitted that had his attempted assassination succeeded, it would have been a release from worry, sleepless nights and great nervous suffering. He was nevertheless grateful to Destiny for letting him live. If there were not an iron will behind it, the battle could not be won. He lived only for the purpose of leading the fight.

It had always been Hitler's custom before the start of a great campaign to summon the senior officers taking part in it down to the level of divisional commander and give them a pep-talk. On this occasion the method of their introduction into the room where Hitler spoke must have done as little to illustrate his confidence in them as what he had to say could have done to inspire theirs in him. They were unceremoniously stripped of all their weapons and brief-cases even before reaching Eagle's Nest. Once arrived there by bus, they descended into the bunker between rows of SS watchdogs. Major-General Fritz Bayerlein, who commanded Panzer Lehr Division in the battle, was so mesmerized by the menacing SS guards, one of whom stood behind each general's chair, that he refrained even from putting his hand in his pocket for a handkerchief lest they should suspect him of reaching for a gun. Such was the atmosphere in which Hitler delivered the preface to the last of his great offensives. Yet so animated did the Führer become during his two-hour speech that Manteuffel judged most of the generals present to be more than simply convinced of their Commander-in-Chief's being in far better condition than he really was. The speech, coming as it did from the one man who kept control of all strategic operations, gave them a picture of the enemy's overall situation, and in this respect modified to some extent their apprehensions about shortages of resources. Thus the circumstances for the attack were made to seem less inauspicious than they had feared. As Hitler had indicated to Speer, with his references to driving straight through the American front and rounding up the English army, the Ardennes offensive was to be one more great manifestation of blitzkrieg. Were the military conditions that prevailed on the Western front in December 1944 fitting for the conduct of one more blitzkrieg by the Wehrmacht?

In some respects they were. The principles of blitzkrieg were
surprise, speed and concentration. All three were interdependent.
Speed was only made possible by surprise and concentration.
Surprise itself was achieved principally by concentration and
speed. Concentration could only reap decisive results if in
conjunction with speed and surprise it tore open the enemy's front,
penetrated deeply behind it, paralyzed opposition, and led to a
battle of annihilation. Suddenness, violence, *blitzartig schnell*—
these were the very nuclei of blitzkrieg. But there was something
more. Once this violent all-destroying thrust had got going, it
must never stop until the battle was won. If it halted, it would be
found, checked and attacked. To maintain momentum, night
and day, was everything. The forces engaged must penetrate
ever deeper, ever broader, and so bring about the absolute
disruption of enemy positions, reserves, headquarters and
supplies. The key to it was a never-ending flow of mixed panzer
groups constantly supported and supplied by the fire power
and transport aircraft of the Luftwaffe. Thus the two indispensable
agents of blitzkrieg were still Panzer and Stuka. Nor should it be
forgotten that each was helpless without fuel.

Hitler had collected 28 divisions, eight of which were panzer
divisions, for Operation *Herbstnebel* (Autumn Mist—codename for
the Ardennes offensive), and as it transpired this force was
directed against a part in the Allied front where General Bradley
had deployed only four divisions over 75 miles. What is more the
Allies were unaware that a major German offensive was imminent,
indeed were agreed—on this if on nothing else—that it was out
of the question. So that surprise was guaranteed. Concentration,
locally, was overwhelming. Speed, to start with, was therefore
equally certain. But there were two fatal flaws in the framework
of the battle. Two ingredients of blitzkrieg were from the very
start missing in the necessary quantities. One was the Luftwaffe;
the other was fuel. In repeating one of his greatest mistakes in
the Russian campaign, hopelessly overestimating the capabilities
of his own resources, Hitler had already taken one step to
compromise the chances of this last desperate enterprise. Would
he make the other great mistake too, and comparably underestimate the capabilities of his enemy? It is when we consider
this point that we are brought face to face with Hitler's fascination
for the Ardennes in general and for his first great success there in
particular. 1940 and 1944—*Sichelschnitt* and *Herbstnebel*—did the

two have anything in common? Were there in fact any grounds, other than those of intuition, for Hitler's returning to the scene of his greatest triumph? Or was it to be compared with Napoleon's recalling the sun of Austerlitz when there would never be another Austerlitz, or anything like it?

In 1940 for *Sichelschnitt,* Cut of the Sickle, the Wehrmacht deployed about 90 divisions (excluding those in general reserve), rather fewer than the number which the Allied Commander-in-Chief, Gamelin, had to defend France and Belgium. But of the German divisions 45, including seven panzer divisions, were concentrated in von Rundstedt's Army Group A to smash through the Ardennes and swarm over the Meuse between Dinant and Sedan. It was this main thrust which turned the battle into what Rommel called 'a lightning tour of France'. Army Group A's operations were paralyzingly successful. Starting on 10 May 1940 the German panzers quickly passed through the Ardennes, crossed the French frontier on 12 May and were over the Meuse next day. It was fittingly enough Guderian, the panzer leader *par excellence,* and his Corps which, expanding this crossing into a 50-mile gap, exploited it in an exact practical demonstration of all that he had claimed for his tactical theories, reaching the Channel ports a week later and cutting the Allied armies in two. There are perhaps two things to remember about this unique battle which, as Alan Bullock has reminded us, achieved for Hitler in four weeks what the Imperial Armies of Kaiser Wilhelm II had failed to achieve in four years. First that the Allied forces were generally speaking ill-prepared, ill-deployed, ill-equipped and ill-led. Moreover the French will to fight was, as Hitler himself divined, low. No wonder the French Army was, in Vercors' phrase 'smashed to pieces, cut to shreds by the tanks, nailed to the ground by the enemy's Stukas'. The second point is that even in a battle of movement such as the world had not seen before, the Wehrmacht had plenty in hand to preserve what is the key to all battle-winning—balance. They had plenty of reserves, plenty of supplies and plenty of flexibility in interpreting the exact form in which operations would develop. At the same time the plan itself commanded plenty of confidence and there was plenty of will-power behind and throughout the machine. Most important of all perhaps Hitler's grip on the military machine was at its most effective—he was backing his mainly sound strategic intuition with all the granite-like determination at his disposal, yet not interfering too much in the day-to-day lower-level operational decisions which only the field commanders could properly make.

One further point might be added before we look at the conditions prevailing in 1944. In spite of all his visionary ideas about the conduct of future tank battles, Liddell Hart had argued just before the start of the Second World War that, because of broad numerical equality with the West in place of the three-to-one superiority needed for successful attack, the Germans would never attack the Western front. Such an attack he considered could end only in stalemate. 'If we can credit the German Staff with a sense of realities,' he wrote in 1939, 'the possibility of serious German offensive in the West becomes more than doubtful.' However often a historian may do so, history rarely repeats itself. Yet in 1944 whether the German Staff were allowed to have a sense of realities or not, the possibility of a serious German offensive was not merely doubted by the Western Allies. It was dismissed as absurd.

In 1944 the similarities with 1940 and the differences from it were equally marked. It was true that the area of both operations was the same and that in each case the crossing of the Meuse was critically important; it was true that the basic idea of each battle was comparable—striking strongly at a weak central point, splitting the Allied armies in two and rolling up the northern half; it was true that the main blow fell twice not on the British Army but on their Allies, and that between the commanders of these Allied armies there was something less than unqualified confidence; it was true that some of the Hitlerian tricks of Trojan Horse operations with German troops dressed in other than German uniforms and disruptive parachute operations were common features; the responsibility for making the big push was even given to the same man, von Rundstedt, for each battle; it might indeed be argued that, whatever the doubts felt by the middle-piece commanders of the Wehrmacht, at the very top and among the assaulting troops, something like the same spirit of fanatical enthusiasm and certainty in victory prevailed; what had been called the *drôle de guerre* of 1940 was perilously close to being reproduced when we remember that the American troops positioned in the Ardennes looked upon it as almost a rest area; and when Sitzkrieg suddenly burst into blitzkrieg something like panic re-entered Belgium and France as the German panzers pushed aside or went round what opposition there was.

Yet, in spite of all these incidental resemblances, however striking they may have appeared to be, the two battles were as different as chalk from cheese, as different as Trafalgar was from Jutland. In the first place there was the question of Allied morale and will-power. Five years of war might nearly have exhausted the resources of the British; it had not daunted their spirit. Three years of war might have put a strain on even American material and manpower; it had not changed their unbounded confidence in victory. American reaction to a set-back was perhaps typified by Patton's comment when the gravity of the Ardennes situation was beginning to be appreciated by the Allied High Command in conference at Verdun on 19 December: 'Let the —— —— go all the way to Paris'; then they would 'cut 'em off and chew 'em up'. As we now know, uncoordinated and heroic resistance by small United States units at the beginning of the battle was to have a major influence on its outcome. The United States Army in 1944 was in no way to be compared with the French Army in 1940. There was also the question of numbers. As we have seen, in 1940 von Rundstedt's Army Group A had 45 divisions. Flanking him were von Bock with 29 divisions in the north and von Leeb with 17 divisions in the south. But there were no fewer than a further 45 divisions in OKH reserve. It was roughly speaking a demonstration of the old British tactical formula—two up and one in reserve. Von Moltke's great and enduring maxim that no plan could survive contact with the enemy held no terrors for the German commanders in France in 1940. From the very outset of *Sichelschnitt,* the Wehrmacht retained inherently two of the traditional battle winning factors—balance and adaptability.

In the winter of 1944, miraculous as the scraping up of 28 divisions (including no fewer than eight panzer divisions), with a further six available for an attack in Alsace, had been, the miracle needs to be set against the fact that there were no substantial reserves. In other words, if we are dealing with German numbers alone, Hitler had but a fifth of the strength for the Ardennes offensive that he had had for the battle of France. And whereas in this latter battle he had one division up his sleeve for every two committed, for the second Ardennes offensive he had but a handful. Yet the Allies' strength in North West Europe was only some 70 divisions, and deployed as they were over a front of 600 miles, making ready for attacks north and south of the weakly held Ardennes Sector, they too seemed to be lacking in reserves.

There were perhaps two other major differences which should not be overlooked. Although in his tirade to the generals Hitler had promised that the Luftwaffe would turn out in full strength (and he had in one of his more honest, wry asides conceded that Göring's promise of 3,000 fighters was more likely to mean 1,000, if that, say 800), the fact was that the only real sign of German supremacy in the air either at the start of or throughout the operation was in the number of VI rockets which roared overhead as the panzers, assault guns and trucks moved into battle on the morning of 16 December. Indeed one of the prerequisites of any success at all was that the weather during the period immediately preceding the offensive and during its initial phases should be bad enough to prevent at first Allied air reconnaissance of the German concentrations, and then Allied interference with the advance itself. In short the Allied winter of discontent must not be turned into summer by a sun of any sort. Yet this very condition underlined further flaws in a plan which for any real dividends depended essentially on rapid, deep penetration. Given that the Ardennes is a piece of country with forested hills broken up by numerous and winding river valleys; given too that from the German point of view most of the principal roads through it run south–west; given finally that even in the campaign of four and a half years earlier with dry spring weather and virtual air supremacy, Guderian's Panzer Corps had not crossed the Meuse until 13 May—three days after the start of the campaign; given all that, was not to invite substantially smaller forces without proper air support to advance north-west and cross the country's grain in winter, to say the least of it, asking a lot? But there was nothing unusual about Hitler's doing this. The generals were used to being given tasks wholly beyond their resources. Nevertheless even such unlikely companions in arms as that levelling, trimming traditionalist of the Offizier Korps, von Rundstedt, and the faithful, favourite upstart, Sepp Dietrich, drew the line at the Führer's ultimate objective. 'Antwerp?' exclaimed the former. 'If we reach the Meuse we should go down on our knees and thank God—let alone trying to reach Antwerp!' Dietrich was no less scathing: 'All Hitler wants me to do,' he shouted angrily when he heard what the plan was, 'is to cross a

river, capture Brussels and then go on and take Antwerp!' And
this at the worst possible time of year, with deep snow, no chance
of properly deploying the panzers, with only a few hours of
light each day and an army composed of children and old sick
men. It just did not make sense. But like all the others before
them, protests to the Führer, when his mind was made up,
availed them not at all. Here was perhaps the final and most
fatal difference between 1940 and 1944. Hitler's control of the
Wehrmacht was absolute. There was no longer any consultation
or discussion. As Jodl, Operations Chief of OKW, put it: 'There
can be no arguments—it is the Führer's order.' Why, in spite of all
the professional advice that it was beyond his reach, was Hitler
so set on having Antwerp? It beckoned him for two reasons, the
first logistic, the second tactical.

As the Second World War reached its fifth year, Hitler, in
conference with some of his generals, made two things clear.
The first was that no matter what the cost the struggle would
continue. On 31 August 1944 he told Keitel, Krebs and Westphal*
that the time had not yet come for a political decision. The
moment for favourable political dealings came only when you
were having successes, not grave military defeats. But the time
would come when tension between the Allies would be so great
that their coalition would disintegrate. 'The only thing is to wait
for the right moment, no matter how hard it is. Since the year
1941 it has been my task not to lose my nerve, under any circumstances.' He would not lose it now and they would in any case
continue the battle.

It was one thing to say that the fight would go on, another to
say how. Yet the following day Hitler was precise in telling von
Rundstedt and Westphal what was to be done. The situation as
he saw it was that the Allies had no ports and their lines of
communication were already stretched to the limit. They would
have to halt sooner or later. That would be the moment to strike
back. Meanwhile all measures to fight a defensive battle on Germany's frontiers were to be taken. The principles which he
laid down for this defensive battle indicated his intention not
merely to stabilize the Western Front, but to stabilize it with a
view to regaining the initiative:

* Keitel was Chief of OKW, Krebs Chief of Staff, Army Group B and
Westphal Chief of Staff to Commander-in-Chief West (from 4 September
1944 von Rundstedt).

The Netherlands are to be retained; not an inch of German territory is to be abandoned; the Allies are to be prevented from using Antwerp and resistance is therefore to be kept up as long as possible at the mouth of the Scheldt; the Allied air bases are to be held as far as possible from the heart of Germany, and the Ruhr and Saar are to be protected.

However unreal these principles might have been, for a defensive strategy based on holding everywhere without adequate reserves was bound to be sterile, Hitler had at least put his finger on one of the Allies' main strategic set-backs—lack of ports sufficient to sustain their logistic needs.

So conscious were the Allies of the deficiency that Eisenhower in his operational plans, after crossing the Seine, gave priority to the left or northern flank so that he could open the Channel ports and Antwerp as well as clear the bases from which V weapons were launched and also threaten the all-important Ruhr. Antwerp was captured on 4 September, and in the orders he gave Montgomery later that month, Eisenhower stressed that Antwerp must be opened 'as a matter of urgency'. Yet the difficulties of doing so and thus restoring to the whole of Eisenhower's command a proper line of supply were immense. In order to guarantee the use of Antwerp, the Scheldt would have to be cleared. The West Scheldt, leading from the North Sea to Antwerp, is in military terms dominated by Walcheren and South Beveland in the north and what became known as the Breskens pocket (east of Zeebrugge) in the south. The Germans held them all—with strong entrenched defensive positions. Early in October 1944 the Canadian 1st Army began their clearing operations. Stubbornness of the German defenders and difficulties encountered by the Canadians could hardly be better illustrated than by the fact that not until two months later, on 28 November, almost three months since the town's capture, did the first convoy enter Antwerp. Exactly one month earlier Eisenhower had underlined once more the critical importance of Antwerp in a directive to his commanders which stipulated that his Armies' main effort would be made in the north. The objects would be to defeat the enemy west of the Rhine, seize bridgeheads over it, capture the Ruhr and advance into Germany. There would be subsidiary operations in the Saar area and further south. The whole of this general plan was prefaced with the words—'*subject always to prior capture of the approaches to Antwerp'*. Hitler was thus not the only one to get his priorities right in this respect. The line of supply from Antwerp was not merely important for the Allies to be able to deploy their full strength and retake the initiative which the breakout from Normandy had given them. It was indispensable for the conduct of those offensive operations which would finish off the war.

There was therefore nothing wrong with Hitler's choice of objective. Only the resources available to achieve it were out of tune with his ideas. Yet as so often before when his imagination was fired by one of his own brainwaves, it ran riot. What a paradox that so often in Hitler's career as a War Lord, he broke the two fundamental rules of strategy—to choose the right objective and allot the necessary strength to ensure its realization —when he had all the cards in his hand, and then when the game was almost finished and his cards were few and far between and of insufficient seniority, he began at least to obey the master rule. For the idea itself could not have been better. As we have seen it was the last thing the Allies expected; the blow was directed at the weakest position of their front; interference with the functioning of Antwerp would have hit them hard. All this is militarily clear. So too is the political idea behind it all which Hitler obviously harboured. He cannot really have believed that the course of the war could be reversed by the intervention of a mere 30 divisions and the loss of a supply port. He might have imposed a check on the Western Allies; he might even have dislocated Allied plans to the point where their resumption of the offensive would be delayed until the spring. To recognize that what he was trying to do above all was to gain time, would have been to look reality in the face. And what might not time do for him? The new submarines to reverse his fortunes at sea, the new jet aircraft to recapture control of the air, more V weapons to break the spirit of Britain—if he could assure the Reich's integrity long enough to allow all these new weapons to enter the lists, what might not follow? Political compromise in the West, military stabilization in the East? Such imaginings are at least just supportable. But Hitler went further, and in confiding his hopes to Speer and others allowed himself to envisage another Dunkirk and the destruction of the entire British Army.

How different were the views of the generals required to carry out the offensive. When the plan was first made known to them on

24 October, von Rundstedt, Commander-in-Chief, West, was 'staggered'. It was at once clear to him that the forces available were wholly inadequate for so ambitious a plan with such distant targets. Although the whole battle became known as the 'Rundstedt offensive', it could not have been more completely misnamed. Rundstedt was not consulted. As the Field Marshal himself recalled—'it was planned in all its details including formations involved, time schedules, objectives and so on by the Führer'. The only troops he was allowed to move, he told Liddell Hart later, were the guards in front of his headquarters. Field Marshal Model, commanding Army Group B, felt the same. Always ready to stand up to the Führer, Model tried to substitute a more modest plan—'the small solution'—to drive the Allies back to the Meuse, take the main US supply base at Liège, and then see what might follow. Hitler predictably would have nothing to do with a plan, which even if successful could not turn the tables and dismay the Allies to the point where they might be prepared to negotiate. Manteuffel was more precise in his objections and put his finger on two of the plan's principal, practical flaws. One was that it depended essentially on rapid and major successes before the Allies could react and bring their resources to bear. Once this happened the flanks of the penetration would be so vulnerable as to endanger the entire operation. And there were insufficient reserves to protect them. Even this objection was in the realm of conjecture. The other was hard fact. Manteuffel judged—and told Hitler so—that five times more petrol was needed than the standard scales. In the event only one and a half times was collected, and even of this inadequate total, too much was kept too far back from the battle area.

In spite of all these drawbacks, the troops themselves were in high spirits, confident of victory, trusting still in Hitler's leadership and assurances. Only the higher field commanders knew that unlike 1940 this would be no manoeuvre with live ammunition'. Yet on 12 December at Eagle's Nest, Hitler insisted on likening the two occasions.

To act offensively against France and against England [in 1940] people thought lunacy, a crime, a Utopia, a hopeless undertaking. The course of events proved the opposite. We cannot today even imagine where we should have got, had we not then dealt with France. The objection may be made that there is a major difference between 1940 and the present situation. . . . But as regards relative strength there is little difference. . . . From the technical point of view the two sides are about equal. . . .

On the other hand, the Führer observed, in other respects things had changed enormously. They had in the past made war far from the borders of the Reich. Even now they were only back on the old frontier in places, elsewhere they were still far out from them. Above all, they were carrying on the war in a situation which offered every possibility of holding on provided they could eliminate the danger in the West.

It was here that Hitler drew attention to the second circumstance—second after the key question of time—which should have determined his strategy—space. Time and space! What soldier has not considered them in appreciating the situation? But here, as in so many other cases, the Führer got his priorities upside down. There was only one way in which he could hope to put time back on his side and that was by forfeiting space. Far from doing so, he elected not just to hang on to all the space which was robbing him of manoeuvrability, but to go bald-headed for more. He was so much blinded by obstinacy that this inconsistency went unnoticed. He chose rigidity in the East where he should have been flexible and plumped for flexibility in the West where he should have been rigid. Such topsy-turvyness could not promote security.

1   *von Rundstedt*

2   *Model*

3   *von Manteuffel*

4   *Dietrich*

5   *Eisenhower*   6   *Montgomery*

7   *Bradley*   8   *Patton*

2
Time and Space

For the first time in sixty-seven years we do not
have to fight a two-front war.
Hitler, November 1939

In the summer of 1944 Field Marshal Model, the Führer's fireman, was called upon to put out two very serious fires in quick succession, one in the East, the other in the West. There was need for a good fireman in each place, for by the end of July the Eastern front was in tatters, and just as a Russian breakthrough there had cut off great numbers of German divisions and destroyed many more, so on the Western front a breakthrough by United States forces was threatening to repeat the pattern. To such a nadir of inability to control events had Hitler's strategy of holding everywhere at all costs brought him.

'Space is one of the most important military factors,' the Führer had told Jodl early in 1943, 'you can conduct military operations only if you have space.' In 1943 Hitler had so much space to play with, in Africa, in Russia and in the Balkans, quite apart from those unthreatened areas to the West and South of *Festung Europa*, that he could afford to give up a little here and there; he could conduct what he called strategical operations for the sake of gaining a little time, in short to buy time with space. But space, like time, must have a stop, and even though time for him had not quite come to a stop on 20 July 1944, space outside the frontiers of Germany almost had. What is more time had been purchased at so high a price in soldiers and weapons that when the moment arrived for defending the Reich itself there were hardly enough to go round. The relative importance of time and space, therefore, could only properly be calculated by reference to the most critical—

c

given broad parity of weapons and skills in using them—of all factors in a military confrontation—actual strengths of the opponents. So reckless and ill-judged had Hitler's calculations been that he had flung away the strength he needed in order not to be overtaken by space, without the consolation of having gained the benefits of time for which this strength had been sacrificed.

Witness first the Eastern front, and the absolute squandering of Army Group North. In the spring of 1944 some 50 divisions were tied up in defence of Estonia, Latvia and Lithuania. At this time before the great Russian offensive of June 1944, Hitler could have done two things fundamental to the conduct of successful defence. He could have shortened the front by as much as 300 miles and added to the number of divisions to argue the toss with the Red Army by as many as 30. A double dividend was at hand. Hitler refused to grasp it. His reasons were twofold: to abandon the Baltic states to Russia might interfere with the supply of Swedish iron-ore and certainly would interfere with the plans for training in that part of the Baltic the new U-boats which he hoped would do so much. Here was focused the curious relationship of time and space. He had to have time to bring the new U-boats into action, therefore hung on to one area of space in which to work them up. As a result he forfeited both time and space. For by protecting a subsidiary flank in such strength, he left insufficiently protected the vital centre. Such misreading of priorities is difficult to reconcile. It was like shielding your horse's flank from a sabre cut when the enemy's lance was about to pierce the armour at your own throat. And the result produced the tactical absurdity that, after the Russians' successful thrust of June and July, the Germans were required to hold an even longer line with far fewer forces than those which the Red Army had already penetrated. Many times in the past Hitler had demonstrated that mobility was everything—the gigantic, terrifyingly swift, deeply penetrating, all-annihilating blow which cut through static thinly-held linear defences and proved so decisively 'the superiority of free operations'—this had been his doctrine, the doctrine of blitzkrieg, and he had often heard Guderian expound the antidote—mobility to meet mobility, rapid counterpenetration by mixed fast-moving panzer teams of all arms which would seal off and destroy the *Schwerpunkte* before they could cry havoc in sufficient width and depth. Now mobility had gone, he had resorted to the strategy on which he had poured scorn.

He was trying to petrify the front line, and as a result he was about to get some of his own former medicine.

The Russian offensive of 22 June 1944 against the German Army Group Centre, timed to assist the battles of Normandy and thus rub home, as Hitler himself had put it, the absolute folly of fighting on two fronts, employed no fewer than 118 infantry and 43 tank divisions. Not surprisingly the German front disintegrated. In July Minsk, Pinsk, Grodno, all fell to the Red Army which threatened even East Prussia. But Model, the Führer's fireman, had saved something from the wreck* left him by his predecessor, Busch.

One of the main reasons for Model's being able to do anything at all when he took over on 28 June was that he did not obey Hitler's orders to the letter. He brought not merely a new style of leadership and new tactical methods based on mobile defence to Army Group Centre, but the fact that Hitler trusted him completely—even more so when Model was the first to send him a telegram vowing loyalty after the failure of the 20 July plot— brought a different and easier relationship into being between the Army Group HQ and Führer HQ. Yet if Model was able to stop the rot in the Centre with what he had—the remnants left him by Busch—what might he not have done with an extra 30 divisions from Army Group North?

Model held this command for a mere six weeks. On 16 August Hitler summoned him to take over from von Kluge as Supreme Commander West. The reasons were part military, part political. Militarily Model had shown his worth to Hitler, particularly in defensive battles. Manteuffel, a shrewd judge, considered Model a 'very good tactician, and better in defence than in attack'. Besides his rough and ready manner, his touch of divining what troops could do in any given situation and what was beyond them, appealed to Hitler. Perhaps this was what allowed Hitler to tolerate Model's uncompromising manner towards himself. But apart from all these considerations of sheer competence, on 15 and 16 August it was loyalty to the Führer which weighed most heavily with Hitler for as he put it himself: 'August 15th was the worst day of my life.'

* 'No greater crisis than the one we've had this year in the East could be imagined', Hitler later observed. 'When Field Marshal Model arrived Army Group Centre was nothing but a yawning gap. It was more of a gap than a front and finally it became more of a front than a gap.'

He was referring not to the military disasters which were overtaking his armies in the West, largely as a result of his own direction. He was referring to his fear that von Kluge had been planning to surrender these armies to the Allies. The situation was grave enough without this. On 25 July, after Montgomery's offensive *Goodwood* had pinned down the bulk of the German panzer strength in the eastern part of the Normandy bridgehead, the Americans under Bradley and Patton broke through in the western part. Patton's armoured columns swept eastwards and the German armies were threatened with encirclement at Falaise. Now was the moment to temper valour with discretion and withdraw these armies east of the Seine to fight again another day. Just the contrary was what the Führer decided to do. He ordered von Kluge to counter-attack the American corridor through Avranches and Mortain. What is more, from his East Prussian HQ at Rastenburg Hitler did not simply say what was to be done. Ignorant of the local situation, above all of the crippling influence of Allied air power, he laid down exactly how it was to be done. Blumentritt, von Kluge's Chief of Staff, recorded that the plan, made from large scale maps of France and without the benefit of any advice that von Kluge and his subordinates might have had to offer, came to them in the greatest detail, showing which divisions were to be employed, which routes they were to advance along and which objectives were to be taken. That the attack failed was a matter of course. It was stopped and overwhelmed by Allied air power. When General Warlimont, Jodl's deputy in OKW Operations Staff, explained to Hitler on 8 August what had happened and expiated on the enormous difficulties of operating under the stifling effects of Allied air supremacy, adding that the counter-attack's failure certainly was not because of poor preparation, the Supreme Commander's reply revealed him at his most petulant, perverse and self-deluding—'the attack failed because Field Marshal von Kluge wanted it to fail'.

A week later on 15 August, not only did the Allied landings take place in the South of France—far too late to influence the battle for Normandy*—but von Kluge, visiting the front, was out of touch with his headquarters for twelve hours. It was this

---

* 'The landing had been planned in order to distract German strength from the north. Postponement destroyed its purpose. ... It was now the landing in the north which distracted the Germans from the south.' (A. J. P. Taylor.)

which led Hitler to believe that von Kluge was trying to make contact with the enemy in order to negotiate a surrender. Throughout his career Hitler was adept at finding good reasons for justifying a course on which he had already made up his mind. Having made up his mind in this case that von Kluge was bent on treachery, he was not slow to find reasons to fit in with all the other developments which might be related to his *idée toute faite*. It was only by chance, by accident he argued, that von Kluge's plan of surrender had not come off. 'It's the only way you can explain everything the Army Group did; otherwise it would all be completely incomprehensible.'

So von Kluge was dismissed, and Model was summoned to take over on the Western front. Each had something to report to the Führer. Von Kluge committed suicide on his way back to Germany. His farewell letter acknowledged the Führer's unparalleled leadership and applauded his iron will in conducting the gigantic battle, but urged him to concede that Providence might be more powerful still and therefore to show his true greatness by putting an end to the hopeless struggle. Model's message, delivered after he had extracted what he could of the German Army in the West across the Seine, was more matter-of-fact. The best part of 20 infantry divisions together with some 2,200 tanks and assault guns had been the price of hanging on in Normandy. By anchoring the 7th Army in a position where it could no longer react to the storm about to engulf it, Hitler had ensured that the Falaise battle would devour two-thirds of its strength. Not Model nor anyone else could reverse the odds. Yet Hitler, even four months later, was talking of striving always to conduct a war of movement. In the summer of 1944 he had broken all the rules. He had forfeited both military strength and space without gaining enough of the commodity which in his view was most indispensable to him—time. He had contravened the lesson which he himself had demonstrated so convincingly—that armoured forces can only operate with real success when complemented by air power. Worse still, he had continued with the dreadful process of putting the blame for his own mistakes on others. Above all he had squandered both in the East and the West the reserves he needed to fight the most important battle of his career, the battle for Germany. No wonder, as Speidel put it, the floodgates were creaking.

It was not likely that Hitler would recognize the military

realities. On the very day of the Falaise battle, 19 August, he began
to sow the seeds of the Ardennes offensive. Jodl's diary for that
day records the Führer's refusal to be dismayed and his intention
to regain the initiative at the very first moment that it might be
possible:

> 19 August. The Führer discussed the equipment and man-
> power position in the West with Chief of OKW, Chief Army
> Staff and Speer. Prepare to *take the offensive in November* when
> the enemy's air forces can't operate. Main point: some *25
> divisions must* be moved in the next one or two months.

If this were to be done there would be two requirements—
stabilization of each front, and then the creation of a strategic
reserve. It proved much easier to halt the Western Allies than to
slow down the Red Army. Hitler's War Directives for August
and September 1944 are concerned almost exclusively with the
construction of defensive positions in the south and west. The
Directives are not concerned solely with military matters or
addressed solely to military commanders.

> The system of positions for the defence of the Home theatre of
> war [reads one of them] will be completed by a call-up of the
> civil population for total war. This is only possible by means of
> a political leadership conscious of its responsibilities. The
> great success which can be achieved by the employment of the
> masses in this way has already been shown in the East.

In other words foreign slave labour organized by Nazi Gauleiters
would build defensive walls for the German Reich. This would
be done in Northern Italy, the Apennine positions and the so-
called Alpine Approaches; the West Wall would be rebuilt and
put in a state of defence; the North Sea coast would be fortified
and strengthened. In each of these directives clear distinction is
drawn between the Army and the Party. There is little doubt as
to where Hitler places the principal reliance. The orders are to
Bormann, the 'Brown Eminence, sitting in the shadows', since
April 1943. Secretary to the Führer, the man closest to him for the
longest period, in the end Party Minister, although his power did
not survive that of his master. Yet in the autumn of 1944 Bormann
was still in control of the great machinery of the Nazi Party and
through him went orders to his own chosen Gauleiters—'new
men, younger, more energetic, more fanatical men who owed

everything not to the impersonal Party . . . but to Bormann himself'.

In a directive dated 24 August 1944 overall responsibility for the West Wall, the Siegfried Line, was given to the Gauleiters. Grohe, Reich Commissioner in Belgium and Northern France, was responsible for the lines Scheldt-Albert Canal to the West of Aachen; other Gauleiters were responsible for the line of the Moselle and for the Vosges position. The Chief of Army Equipment and the Replacement Army, Himmler, was charged only with the purely military tasks. Sectors belonging to military commanders would be adapted to those of the Gauleiters. Details of construction—anti-tank obstacles, defences in depth, strong points—the soldiers could get on with; but while the military authorities employed in the work would remain under normal Army command, they would '*be bound by Gauleiters*'. Orders for the construction of the West Wall were complemented by instructions for its actual defence. Five years to the day after the declaration of war by England and France, Hitler's direction to Commander-in-Chief West begins with an admission that the initiative has been forfeited:

> Our own heavily tried forces, and the impossibility of bringing up adequate reinforcements quickly, do not allow us at the present moment to determine a line which must be held and which certainly can be held.

But it quickly goes on to stress the need for gaining as much time as possible so that new formations can be raised and brought up to the West ready for counter attack. Therefore on the right flank and in the centre, the Army would 'dispute every inch of ground'. On the left flank Army Group G was to assemble a mobile force—whose main task, after it had protected construction work, would be 'to deliver a concentrated attack against the deep eastern flank and rear positions of the Americans'. In other words defence only in order to be able to attack. It was a point to which Hitler was constantly to return during the coming months—his determination to attack and start once more a war of movement.

Paradoxically the whole question of whether the Siegfried Line could be prepared, manned and held in sufficient strength depended on whether or not von Rundstedt (re-appointed as Commander-in-Chief West on 4 September, the day Antwerp

fell) could *prevent* the battle's becoming fluid again. His charter
was to stop the Allies on the line of the Albert Canal, the Meuse
and the Upper Moselle. By 6 September, however, two days after
von Rundstedt's re-appointment and the day after he actually
resumed command, the Allies had already established bridgeheads
over the Albert Canal and the Meuse. Moreover only by committing in a series of local attacks the very armoured forces which
Model had been gathering for a major counter-stroke was the
line of the Upper Moselle being successfully held.

'Six weeks!' von Rundstedt announced next day. It would
take six weeks to put the Siegfried line in order. To conduct a
successful defensive battle while this was being done, he would
need at least an additional ten infantry divisions and 2,000 tanks.
Needless to say he did not get them. Nevertheless in spite of
American forces crossing the Meuse on 8 September, actually
reaching German soil on 12 September, and advancing across the
frontier to the south of Aachen, and in spite of Montgomery's
bold attempt to open the gap into Northern Germany by seizing
the road bridges over the Meuse, the Waal and the Rhine respectively at Grave, Nijmegen and Arnhem, the German defences
held. This was not because of some great feat of tactical genius by
von Rundstedt, however well he may have supervised the battle
and however bravely and skilfully the German soldiers may
have fought. It was that the Allies neglected to take this particular
tide at the flood. Contradictions of Allied policy and failure to
stick to the master rules of conducting war—absolute clarity of
purpose and relentless concentration on that purpose—must
bear a heavy responsibility that this came about. For that the
Allies possessed the strength to break through the Siegfried Line
in September 1944, when we remember that 75 miles of it in
Belgium was held by a mere eight battalions, is as certain as
anything ever is in military affairs. What they would have done
thereafter is another matter. Speidel, Chief of Staff Army Group
B, was in no doubt:

> The halting of the Allied pursuit was a German variation of
> the 'miracle of the Marne'. Had the Allies held on grimly to the
> retreating Germans they could have harried the breath out of
> every man and beast and ended the war half a year earlier.
> There were no German ground forces of any importance that
> could be thrown in and next to nothing in the air.

General Blumentritt and General Westphal, who were successively Chief of Staff to Commander-in-Chief West, held the same view. But it could only have been done if the Allies had concentrated their forces and their purpose in Belgium. By not doing so they allowed Hitler to do exactly the same thing in reverse.

So much for the Western front for the moment—what was happening in the East? If Hitler ever recalled that his historical hero, Frederick the Great, once observed that there would always be more to lose than to gain by war with Russia, we have no record of it. But as to its truth, by the autumn of 1944 the Führer could hardly have been under any delusions. On the Eastern front space was disappearing without saving much of the other precious commodity—time. Although, as we have seen, Model had pulled things together on the Central Front in Poland, the Red Army had occupied Rumania and had advanced into Yugo-slavia and Hungary. The British had re-entered Greece after an absence of some three and a half years. In November Hitler had finally left East Prussia and returned to Berlin. By then the Wehrmacht was doing its best to stem the Russian advance on the Danube. Meanwhile the pattern of building fortifications in the West and South was being repeated in the East. Slovakia had been fortified and in December, whilst the Russians were besieging Budapest, Bratislava was declared to be a fortress. Declarations, however, were not enough. The whole of Europe had been declared a fortress too. Its violation had been almost complete. Except for Italy where the skill and resolution of Kesselring held firm on a winter line north of Rimini–Florence–Pisa, only the Reich was left. And, it almost went without saying, all the fortified lines protecting the Reich would be held at all costs. 'The war will decide,' Hitler told the Wehrmacht in an order about command arrangements issued on 25 November, 'whether the German people shall continue to exist or perish. It demands selfless exertion from every individual. Situations which have seemed hopeless have been redeemed by the courage of soldiers contemptuous of death, by the steadfast perseverance of all ranks, and by inflexible, exalted leadership.'

It seemed that the Führer's own exalted leadership had produced the first of the two requirements implicit in his statement of 19 August which Jodl's diary had taken note of—stabilization of all fronts. What was to be done about the second and equally indispensable requirement? Could 25 divisions be moved to the

West quickly enough to resume the offensive at a time when 'fog, night and snow' would furnish the Wehrmacht's Supreme Commander with a 'great opportunity'?

'As winter and the invading Armies closed in upon them,' wrote Chester Wilmot, 'the German people and their armed forces rallied to uphold the rule of the very man who had led them to the brink of ruin.' If the rally were to be effective, Hitler would need both men and machines, both new divisions and the weapons to equip and support them. Notwithstanding the Allied strategic air offensive and by resort to desperate appliance, Albert Speer, Minister of Armament and War Production, succeeded in rearming the Wehrmacht for one more offensive. In September 1944 for example more single-engined fighter aircraft, (the actual number was 3,031) were produced than in any other month of the war; in the same month nearly 170,000 rifles, 27,000 machine guns, 1,000 anti-tank guns, over 2,000 mortars and 1,500 other guns together with 321,000 tons of ammunition left the factories; the figures for tanks were equally remarkable—in the three months preceding September, some 2,500 Tigers, Panthers and Mark IVs were delivered, although Allied air attacks reduced this figure by roughly half during the following three months. What is more, critical though the oil situation was, the lessening of Allied bombing against oil refineries—because of bad weather, not bad policy—together with the harshest economy both within the Wehrmacht and for civil consumption enabled the German stocks to be preserved at a level, which allowed the continued conduct of a defensive strategy and the assembly of enough reserves to make an offensive theoretically possible in 1944. 1945 could look after itself.

The tools therefore existed. As for the men, Himmler,* Commander-in-Chief, Home Army, had raised no fewer than 25

---

* In his harangue to the Gauleiters at Possen on 3 August 1944, Himmler had let his imagination and self-delusion alike run away with him: 'We are going to raise a new army, 30 or 40 panzer divisions and same number of regular infantry divisions. We shall be tireless in organizing and training them from the last boot button to political indoctrination. From anti-tank fighting to ability to spend the night in the open in a temperature of minus forty.... In addition there will be 12 SS Panzer divisions and 30 European divisions, which, as you saw on the Narva, can fight with great dash. Then when weariness is gaining a hold on the other side, will come the time to talk of peace. A new army, fully ready to fight, will give the Führer the arguments and the triumphs which will allow him to dictate the peace.'

Volksgrenadier divisions. Into them went the last reserves of German manpower. For more than a year Speer and Goebbels had been trying to persuade Hitler of the absolutely overriding need for measures totally to mobilize the nation. Eventually, after the assassination plot of 20 July 1944, Goebbels had been appointed Reich Commissioner for Total Mobilization of Resources for War. With his customary ability, thoroughness and energy, Goebbels set about it. Between August and October he produced over half a million men for Himmler's new divisions. The measures themselves were necessarily draconian. Industrial workers were combed out of factories, the Kriegsmarine and the Luftwaffe were heavily drawn on, the call-up age itself was reduced to 16. These reinforcements for the German Army were not only substantial in quantity. The quality of many of them was precisely that most needed by Hitler—young, fit, fanatical Nazis. Furthermore their training was put into the hands of battle-hardened experts and the bulk of the new weapons and equipment went, not to replace losses at the front line, but to these newly raised divisions. When we consider that as well as this remarkable total of 25 new *Volksgrenadier* divisions, a dozen panzer or panzer grenadier divisions were refitted in the West alone, we can see that the second of the two requirements for regaining the initiative was well on the way to being realized. What is more the 6th Panzer Army had been newly created on 13 September 1944 and was made up, apart from *Volksgrenadier* divisions, parachute units and special forces, of no fewer than four SS panzer divisions. All in all Germany managed to raise roughly some 40 divisions between September and December 1944—not as many as Himmler had promised, but enough for Hitler's purposes. At last he had a strategic reserve again. The only question which now remained was exactly where, when and how to use it. Before we examine the plans which Hitler's staff began to make and perfect, we should perhaps put the whole question into its strategic context, that is of the general balance of power and the critical inter-dependence of sea, air and ground operations.

In October 1944 the Wehrmacht—on paper—totalled more than 10 million men, three-quarters of which were in the Army and Waffen SS alone; the Luftwaffe was about two million strong; the Kriegsmarine some 700,000. Of the seven and a half million in the Army, however, less than half actually belonged to the field army. Roughly two million were on the Eastern Front and about

700,000 on the Western Front. 'The Front', General Horrocks had once observed, 'is a very small club.' With numbers such as these even the 'Front' in the German Army was quite a large club, but the trouble was that geographically as opposed to humanly, the Front was so huge. Halder accused Hitler of refusing to acknowledge any limit to possibility and of scattering formations of the German Army from the North Pole to the Libyan Desert. By the end of 1944 the Libyan Desert was far behind him, but the Wehrmacht still had substantial numbers of divisions in areas where they could no longer influence the decisive battle area—the Central Fronts encircling Germany itself. Thus 30 German divisions were cut off in Courland and Memel, a similar number were in Hungary and Austria, rather fewer in Italy, 17 in Scandinavia, 10 in Yugoslavia. If Napoleon had strung out the Grand Army between Cadiz and Moscow and so broken his own supreme rules of concentration of force and singleness of aim, Hitler was running him a close second. In the really critical areas, the Wehrmacht deployed about 75 divisions in the West and about 130 in the East.

The other side of the coin was very different. Whereas the German strength represented the last scrapings of the barrel, Allied strength in 1944 and 1945 was still growing. British and American fighting numbers rose from some 14 million in mid 1943 to nearly 17 million a year later. The number of divisions at Eisenhower's disposal almost doubled itself between October 1944 and the end of the war in Europe. And the Red Army seemed to be inexhaustible. In Poland and East Prussia alone, while the Germans had deployed 75 divisions, the Russians, according to Stalin, had 180 divisions. Nor was this all. At sea and in the air, the Allies were virtually supreme.

Curiously enough it was the relentless interdependence of air, sea and ground operations and the respective priorities which Hitler gave to each that had resulted in a Wehrmacht deployment doomed to defeat by reason of these very priorities. On the one hand Hitler was determined to hang on to the U-boat bases in the Western Baltic so that by creating another fleet of new submarines he could turn the tables on the Western Allies at sea. On the other hand neither the German Navy nor the Luftwaffe could satisfactorily protect these bases if the Eastern Baltic fell into Russian hands. Therefore 30 to 40 divisions were tied up to protect the means of attacking the Western enemy from falling into the hands of the Eastern enemy. To this level had the strategy of the man—who firstly would never fight on two fronts and secondly would be supreme in the air—fallen. Caught in the toils of his own special and wholly unreal picture of the situation, hanging on everywhere, refusing to give up space before time ran out, grasping at straws on the flanks while leaving the vital centre too weakly defended, having lost all strategic balance and almost all capability of calling the tune, he yet held Wehrmacht, Party and people in thrall and still talked of recapturing the initiative in the West.

If necessary we'll fight on the Rhine [Hitler had declared on 31 August]. It doesn't make any difference. Under all circumstances we will continue this battle until, as Frederick the Great said, one of our damned enemies gets too tired to fight any more. We'll fight until we get a peace which secures the life of the German nation for the next 50 or 100 years and which above all, does not besmirch our honour a second time, as happened in 1918. . .

If there were to be a chance of Hitler's realizing these ideas, all would turn upon the precise use to which he now put the last reserves of men and material which he had under his hand. What exactly would he do?

3
Wacht Am Rhein— Watch on the Rhine

The first blow is half the battle.
Oliver Goldsmith

As so often before, in contemplating the strategic action to be taken, there were for Hitler two possible courses—to attack in the East or in the West. In the past when he had made use of the uncanny *Fingerspitzengefühl*—the intuitive and instinctive fingertip feeling that now was the moment to do this or that or to do nothing at all—he had known how to wait. He had explained it all to Rauschning years before:

> No matter what you attempt, if an idea is not yet mature you will not be able to realize it. Then there is only one thing to do: have patience, wait, try again, wait again. In the subconscious the work goes on. It matures, sometimes it dies. Unless I have the inner, incorruptible conviction: *this is the solution,* I do nothing.

In December 1944 Hitler returned to this point when he reminded the generals who were to fight the Ardennes battle for him that it was necessary to await the moment. Now the moment was almost upon them. When had the Führer out of an inner incorruptible conviction decided that the plan he was about to execute was the solution? We should perhaps remember first that the *Fingerspitzengefühl* that Hitler had spoken of to Rauschning ten years earlier had by 1944 been replaced by distrust and hatred of all about him. While the 'hardest man in centuries' retained his

will-power until the end, what previously had been a hardness
able, in spite of its misuse, to withstand the shock of fortune
and take arms against even the most mountainous seas of trouble,
had degenerated into mere indifference to or worse actual pleasure
in the infliction of suffering. What formerly had been one of his
strongest cards, the use of bluff and surprise, had lapsed into
self-delusion and simple dishonesty. 'He often lied without
hesitation', wrote Guderian of Hitler after the 20 July plot, 'and
assumed that others lied to him.' Hitler had always advocated
the telling of lies. And if you were going to lie, they must be big
lies. *Mein Kampf* was very eloquent and specific here. 'In the big
lie there is always certain force of credibility . . . the grossly
impudent lie always leaves traces behind it.' In fabricating one
more colossal untruth, therefore, the idea that a ground offensive
of any sort in December 1944 could alter the course of the war,
Hitler seemed to have shared what he would have called the
primitive simplicity of the masses, and swallowed his own huge
lie.

Even he, however, could not deceive himself to the extent of
believing that an attack in the East could help him. No quick or
decisive victories were to be won there. Frontages were too
wide, distances too great, the logistic means, particularly fuel,
to deal with such vast expanses of terrain were simply not to be
had, there were no dramatic objectives whose capture would
dismay the Russians, besides the Red Army itself was simply too
large and strategically too elusive to yield up the sort of prize
he had in mind. It was the initiative he wanted, the initiative
at any price, the initiative almost for its own sake, so that events
would once more be subject to and controlled by his will-power,
without any reasoned strategic objective, the initiative to gain
time, to deploy the new weapons, to create a situation in which
'one of our damned enemies gets too tired to fight any more'.
Only in the West could this be done—against the British and
Americans, less hardy than the Russians, uncomfortable allies
anyway, with shorter routes to more compelling objectives, less
fuel required and plenty to lay hands on. The West it must be.
It was the last turnabout of a never-ending series of turnabouts.
Hitler's war offensives had begun with the lightning but limited
requisition of *Lebensraum* in the East; then he had turned West
and another foe had been erased, *ausradiert*; then back again to
the East for the greatest battle in world history; now finally

West once more for another breakthrough, another blitzkrieg, another and this time utterly conclusive Dunkirk.*

On 16 September 1944, almost exactly a month after his pronouncement on 19 August about moving 25 divisions to the West in the following months, and the day before the Allied airborne assault at Arnhem and Nijmegen, the Commander-in-Chief of the Wehrmacht made clear to Guderian, Keitel and Jodl† at Wolfsschanze, Führer HQ at Rastenburg in East Prussia, that his ideas had matured, that his conviction as to *the* solution was absolute: 'I have just made a momentous decision,' he declared. 'I shall go over to the counter-attack, that is to say here [pointing to a map] out of the Ardennes with the objective—Antwerp.' Nine days later, when the British 1st Airborne Division's withdrawal from Arnhem was under way, Hitler instructed Jodl to get on with the detailed planning. Jodl's responsibilities at OKW were not confined to the execution of the Führer's day-to-day decisions. He was an exceptional member of the Staff in two other respects. First it was with Jodl that Hitler would discuss *ideas*. Secondly it was Jodl who would convert an agreed concept into an actual military plan. It was such planning that he began on 25 September for the Ardennes offensive. By 8 October he submitted to Hitler not one, but five plans.

None of these plans was in keeping with the general directive that Hitler had already given to the staff. Determined as he had been all along on achieving a major victory, Hitler was 'thinking big'. He favoured the Ardennes for two reasons—the area was thinly held by the Americans and its sheer nature, heavily wooded, and difficult for large scale manoeuvre, would yield the additional advantages of affording concealment from Allied airpower and by limiting movement would demand the deployment of fewer divisions. Also by striking near the junction of the American and British armies—such junctions being always the most difficult at which to coordinate defence and to produce powerful counter-action and reserves—he might drive a giant wedge between them, not simply in the immediate military consequences but in their very leadership and political harmony. Furthermore

* In a signal to the CIGS (Sir Alan Brooke) during the first critical days of the Ardennes battle, Montgomery, after describing the action he was taking, added: 'We cannot come out through Dunkirk this time as the Germans still hold it.'

† Guderian became Chief of Staff after the July plot; Keitel and Jodl were still respectively Chief and Operations Chief of OKW.

9 *German soldier in the attack*

10 *The Ardennes 1944*

Antwerp, a great prize in itself, seemed to be within reach. If it were to be reached, if the Allies could be split and the British armies encircled, not only would threats to the indispensable Ruhr be expunged, but the whole strategic situation in the West would be transformed. What might not then transpire? Thus Hitler's outline instructions on which the staff were to base their detailed planning contained a number of features which persisted right up until the offensive was finally abandoned. There was no doubt about the tenacity with which Hitler would stick to his own ideas once they were formed. '*This is the solution*.' Nor was there any doubt that he, like so many commanders before and since, made the plan first and then arranged consideration of the various 'factors' affecting it so that they conformed. The principal features which survived all critical examination and all protests by the generals who were to execute the plan were these: the attack would be made by two panzer armies, with infantry formations blocking the flanks, through the Ardennes between Monschau and Echternach to seize bridgeheads over the Meuse between Liège and Namur with the ultimate objective of capturing Antwerp; the British and Canadian armies would then be *ausradiert,* utterly annihilated in the area north of Antwerp—Liège—Bastogne; maximum support by artillery, rockets and the Luftwaffe would be provided; secrecy and tactical methods would be so arranged as to ensure two of the absolute prerequisites of success—speed and surprise. Like Oliver Goldsmith, Hitler believed in the efficacy of the first blow*. This much stayed unchanged. The actual day of the offensive and the precise numbers and organization of divisions to be employed were subject to alteration.

It is curious, knowing Hitler as he did, that Jodl in presenting on 8 October the five plans which he had worked out, included not a single one close enough to Hitler's grand concept likely to satisfy him. Indeed three of them were in the wrong area and far too limited in every way. Operation *Luxembourg,* directed against the front of the US 3rd Army (commanded by Patton) was a

---

* It may be doubted whether Hitler was familiar with one of English literature's most celebrated, yet anonymous, jingles made use of by Goldsmith in his *Art of Poetry on a New Plan*:

> For he who fights and runs away
> May live to fight another day;
> But he who is in battle slain
> Can never rise and fight again.

Or that even if he had been, he would have paid it much attention.

D

twofold attack from central Luxembourg, and Metz to capture
Longwy; *Lorraine* was a similar sort of operation also to destroy
part of Patton's army, with two thrusts directed on Nancy from
Metz and Baccarat; further south still, *Alsace* was an envelopment
against part of the French 1st Army and consisted of two attacks
from Epinal and Montbéliard directed on Vesoul. Not surprisingly
Hitler would have nothing to do with any of these proposals.
Too much like the limited counter-attacks with which he had
been trying to stabilize the Western front in September, too
unpromising strategically, totally lacking in opportunism as far as
turning the tables on the Allies was concerned, the only point
of interest here is that such unlikely propositions were made at
all. Yet if they had not been, if the entire Western front had not
been subjected to analysis and suggestion, Hitler would perhaps
have wanted to know the reasons why.

Jodl's other two proposals, however, were quite different. To
start with they were in the north, the area on which Hitler had
his eye. Secondly they were more dramatic. Operation *Holland*
was a single *Schwerpunkt* from Venlo, west of the Ruhr, directed
on Antwerp. *Liège–Aachen* was a pincer operation, one army
driving north-west from Luxembourg and then turning north to
meet the other one which would be launched south-west from
the area of Aachen. It was a synthesis of these two ideas which
led to the actual plan—*Wacht am Rhein,* defensive in nomenclature
and designed to mislead friend and foe alike. For Hitler was
quick to grasp at a solution which approximated so closely to
his own ideas. Jodl was ordered to get on with the preparation
of a more comprehensive directive which would form the basis
of further planning procedures. At this point Hitler had neither
consulted nor taken into his confidence the generals who were to
be responsible for executing the operation. This was not long to
be delayed, but before we see the eccentric way in which it
was done—emphasizing the very antithesis of true confidence and
cooperation between commanders at all levels, one of the basic
requirements for the successful conduct of war, we would do well
to examine the concept itself.

Liddell Hart's view was that it would have been a brilliant
brain-wave if Hitler had still had sufficient military power to give
it a fair chance of success. This is not a far cry from von
Rundstedt's pronouncements. On the one hand von Rundstedt
maintained that all the conditions necessary for the success of the

operation were lacking; on the other hand he later called the operational idea a stroke of genius. Neither of these views will quite do, as they have permitted execution of the operation to colour the concept. Major Schramm, a professional historian who kept the war diary at OKW headquarters, is more circumspect. 'Systematic re-examination confirmed', he noted, 'that the area selected by the Führer actually was the most promising on the whole Western front.' When he wanted to make use of it, Hitler's *Fingerspitzengefühl,* his strategic grip, his *Vorhersehung,* to say nothing of his continued and astonishing grasp of military detail, did not forsake him. His concept of an offensive was fundamentally sound. In spite of all the mistakes made by him and others on the German side before, during and after the battle, this —the idea itself—was not one of them. It is when we come to the actual conduct of the battle, and see him making all the same errors of judgment which marred his handling of the African, Russian and Normandy campaigns, the same refusal to face facts, to acknowledge that the enemy too had some freedom of will, decision and manoeuvre, the same stubborn insistence on reinforcing failure instead of success, the arid reluctance to complement his own granite determination with the improvisations of others—that we see once again why Hitler was so frequently and furiously at odds with his generals.

Apart from Keitel, Jodl and the others at OKW, the first two generals who were to learn what Hitler had in mind were not, as might have been expected, the two principal commanders concerned, von Rundstedt, Commander-in-Chief West, and Model, Commander Army Group B, but their two Chiefs of Staff, respectively, Westphal and Krebs, who were to pass on what they learned to their commanders. On 24 October they were ordered to report to Wolfsschanze in East Prussia. They were in for several surprises. They were first required to sign a paper pledging themselves to absolute secrecy—on pain of being shot if the plans leaked out. After this unpromising start they were informed of substantial reinforcements which were to be transferred to the Western front during the coming weeks. Finally Hitler briefed them on the secret operation itself—*Wacht am Rhein*—to be carried out by Army Group B.

The purpose of the attack, explained the Führer, to his two flabbergasted subordinates was to destroy all Allied forces north of the line Antwerp–Liège–Bastogne. There would be two phases—first push to the Meuse and over it; second capture Antwerp. What was to happen after that remained no doubt as so many other decisions had in the past, 'locked in the impenetrable bosom of the Führer'. The broad allotment of troops to Army Group B was that there would be three Armies, 5th and 6th Panzer Armies for the main thrust and 7th Army to guard the southern, open and, intrinsic to a north-western hook, much longer flank. The total number of divisions to be made available, the Führer went on, was 30—18 infantry and 12 panzer or mechanized, but of this number Commander-in-Chief West would have to field three and six respectively from his own already overstretched resources. 1,500 aircraft including 100 of the new jets were to be available and Keitel had promised over four million gallons of fuel. Timing was not yet certain, but Hitler mentioned two dates—20 and 25 November. These dates had nothing to do with detailed calculations as to preparation. They were plucked, as it were, from the sky, since the meteorologists, responding to the Führer's demand for an estimate of a period of bad weather and poor visibility to reduce the effectiveness of Allied air forces, had come up with this period.

It was this point of timing together with the view that Hitler's objective, Antwerp, hopelessly outran resources, which were to be the principal concerns of Westphal and Krebs. After all, the earlier date was less than a month away. The objections they put forward to Hitler himself were understandably moderated by enthusiasm for the idea. The forthcoming reinforcements were of course extremely welcome. Equally so was the general notion of undertaking an offensive once more. What worried them was the situation that might develop between then and the start of the offensive. Would there in fact be adequate forces on the day, would the Luftwaffe live up to its promises of being able to support the ground forces? Panzer attacks in the face of enemy air superiority were profitless enterprises. Air protection was therefore a necessary prelude to an advance of such proportions. Would all these conditions prevail?

Krebs and Westphal were only touching on the objections which their commanders were bound to point to. No sooner were Model and Rundstedt aware of what the Führer had in mind than they bent all their not inconsiderable energies to modifying it. They were no doubt aware that attempts to change Hitler's mind had not met with startling or immediate success in the past, but nevertheless they tried. Before submitting a draft detailed plan for the first phase of the operation, there was a good deal of rapid consultation both within and between von Rundstedt's and Model's headquarters. Von Rundstedt and Westphal were not slow to put their fingers on the concept's weaknesses— insufficient resources to reach the ultimate objective of Antwerp, the difficulties of flank protection for so extensive an advance which might lead merely to the commitment of all the German strength to maintain a salient, in other words the rapid deterioration of a designed breakthrough into a holding operation (in this respect von Rundstedt's *Vorhersehung* was more acute than the Führer's); then there was the whole question of what the Allies would do at a time when the Western front was nothing if not precarious. Having discussed the impracticability of the operation on the grounds of space, von Rundstedt proceeded to do the same with regard to time. There simply was not enough time to prepare for so elaborate an offensive. Von Rundstedt's alternative plan, codename *Martin,* far more consistent with actual resources, far more limited in distance and obeying the basic blitzkrieg rule of concentrating heavily for a breakthrough on a narrow front, was for two thrusts by the 5th and 6th Panzer Armies. The main *Schwerpunkt* with an axis Bütgenbach–Werbomont would aim to cross the Meuse north of the line Huy–Antwerp; a subsidiary thrust from Roermund would join the main one near Liège. In other words a limited but powerful attack, properly protected by the 15th Army in the north and 7th Army in the south, to seize crossings over the Meuse, destroy Allied forces caught in the pincer and then see what exploitation might be possible.

In conjunction with Krebs, Field Marshal Model, at his head-quarters came to similar but not identical conclusions. Hitler's big thinking was too big. 'This plan hasn't got a damned leg to stand on.' Model's ideas were put together in the Army Group B plan *Herbstnebel*—Autumn Mist—and the eventual codename for the actual offensive. Even more anxious to concentrate and much concerned about the Allied threat in the Aachen area, Model advocated a single thrust at the Meuse with the break-through between Lützkampen and the Hürtgenforst. The aim would be to envelop the enemy east of the Meuse in what was called the Aachen salient and then think again. Model's plan also kept more divisions in reserve than *Martin*.

On 27 October both these plans were discussed by the five

commanders most concerned—von Rundstedt and Model together
with the three Army commanders—Dietrich, 6th Panzer Army,
von Manteuffel, 5th Panzer Army, and Brandenberger, 7th Army.
What a mixture they were! Von Rundstedt, symbol of the Old
Guard, the very model of all that was best in the Offizierkorps
with strategic and tactical professionalism of the highest order,
infinite experience both in Russia and the West, an absolute
contempt for all forms of amateur strategists, yet not prepared
to break with the Führer. Von Rundstedt's ideas of conducting
war in the West at that time were simple—hold on, improve
defences, create reserves, indulge in limited counter-attack, but
above all do not throw away the last remaining strength with
which to influence the battle for Germany. Model, as we have
seen, was a card of a very different sort. Without the traditional
Army background, devoid of social grace, a Nazi, no great
strategist, but a superb tactician, a man of tireless energy, a master
of improvisation, bold in attack, resolute in defence, whose stocky
and bustling figure was constantly seen about the battlefield,
never hesitating to disagree with superior or subordinate alike,
rough and ready, never one to despair, and never afraid to stand
up to and argue with Hitler. He would promise anything, act
first and ask permission later—the best possible method of out-
flanking the Führer's interference. He would send reports to
OKW, and write on them that they were to be submitted to the
Supreme Commander 'in the original'. He would agree to do
what the Führer required only so long as the advantages of doing
so outweighed the disadvantages. But it was not simply his
origins and his methods that appealed to Hitler. It was his record
of success as well. The two senior commanders therefore were as
different as they could be. The three Army commanders—Dietrich,
von Manteuffel and Brandenberger—were equally so.

The son of a Bavarian butcher, Sepp Dietrich had had a remarkable career. He joined the National Socialist Party as early as
1928, was soon a hard core member of the SS, was in personal
control of the SS guard battalion which proved so useful in
eliminating SA rivals during the Röhm putsch and later commanded the SS Panzer Division Leibstandarte Adolf Hitler.
He was Hitler's man first and last. In the Normandy battles he had
commanded the 1st Panzer Corps. His post-war comment on the
Falaise disaster was to the effect that there was only one person to
blame for so stupid and impossible an operation—'that madman

Adolf Hitler'. But in the autumn of 1944 he was still the Führer's obedient servant. A leader and trainer of undoubted ability, he lacked a formal military education, but to some extent this was compensated for by his experienced and clever Chief of Staff, Kraemer. General Hasso von Manteuffel was almost the complete antithesis of Dietrich. An aristocrat, a cavalryman, scion of a Prussian military family, a panzer soldier of drive, originality and courage, at forty-seven he was young even by wartime standards to command an Army. He was to have a major influence on the tactical handling of the forthcoming battle. Indeed had he been given *carte blanche,* it might have been a far greater success than it turned out to be. Third and last of this unlikely trio, Brandenberger was a sound professional soldier with neither the swashbuckling bravado of Dietrich nor the cynical cleverness of Manteuffel. He figures little in the great accounts of Hitler's battles. Consistent with this lack of spectacular achievement, his role in the offensive was a subsidiary one, to provide a defensive flank guard to the south.

These five men met and considered what best to do. The result was compromise. Model agreed to adopt a good many of the features of von Rundstedt's plan and put them into a new Army Group B proposal which would be submitted to OKW. This submission of the Small Solution, however—to drive back and destroy the Allied armies which had breached the Siegfried Line at Aachen, re-establish themselves on the Meuse and capture Liège—was marginally preceded by the arrival at von Rundstedt's headquarters of Hitler's written instructions for the Big One.

On 1 November Jodl sent Westphal the order which was endorsed in Hitler's own handwriting '*Nicht abändern!*' 'Not to be altered'. By this was meant that neither the operation's aims nor the organization of the armies for it nor the final objective were to be changed. The plan in essence was in fact no different from Hitler's original idea. The three armies were to attack between Monschau and Echternach. In the north Dietrich's 6th Panzer Army was to strike the principal blow, cross the Meuse at Huy and Andenne and then push on to capture Antwerp; Manteuffel's 5th Panzer Army was to advance in the centre through Namur and Dinant to Brussels; Brandenberger's 7th Army in the south would cover that flank. Various subsidiary operations were designed to support the main one, and half a dozen divisions, mostly mechanized, would be in reserve. At this time, 25 November was still the date on which the attack was to be launched. Jodl followed up the written instructions by visiting the headquarters of Army Group B on 3 November. He was subjected to the combined protests of von Rundstedt, Model and von Manteuffel.

While agreeing with the Führer's concept of an offensive, they argued once more that the proposed plan was far too ambitious. In his restrained account of what happened Manteuffel summed up his and his colleagues' main apprehensions in one sentence: 'They expressed doubts whether the numbers, equipment, arms, mobility and supplies were sufficient to sustain an attack over a front of something like 125 miles under winter conditions, and then to hold the western flank sufficiently long to encompass the destruction of the 25-30 divisions it was hoped to encircle.' Here in a nutshell is the reason—however brilliant the idea itself had been—that the Ardennes offensive could not possibly succeed against enemies who were prepared to fight back. And Manteuffel had not even mentioned the absolute inequality of air power which the two sides could deploy. Once again the Small Solution was explained to Jodl, its advantages underlined, its chances of success elaborated. Finally Model and Manteuffel again committed their arguments to paper. During the course of the discussions Jodl made it clear that he was certain that anything short of the Führer's own plan would be unacceptable to him— not so much on grounds of military reasoning, but simply because any modified plan could not possibly have the political effect of obliging the Western Allies to throw in their hand. It could do no more than delay defeat. Desperate sorties from beleaguered garrisons, ran Jodl's argument, had in the past done more than delay the moment of surrender. They had raised the siege. By resorting to extreme measures therefore something might still be saved from a Germany besieged. Jodl's written reply on 4 November, after he had returned to OKW, to the written arguments of Model and Manteuffel was uncompromising: 'The Führer has decided that the operation is unalterable in every detail.'

In fact as November advanced and December began two important details of the operation were altered. One was its timing; the other its tactical execution. D Day was postponed largely because preparations were simply not proceeding fast enough. Concentrations could not be completed in time for 25 November. The attack was put off until 7 December, then postponed three days, then another three days; finally 16 December was fixed upon. The second of the two changes—tactical handling —was far more interesting and its main exponent was Manteuffel. His arguments were put forward in the Reichskanzlei on 2 December 1944—a mere two weeks before the offensive began— during a final attempt by himself, Westphal, Dietrich and Model to persuade Hitler to alter the objective of the attack and the very concept itself. Before we examine this conference, it will be well to remember to what condition Hitler had brought himself when discussing military affairs during the months after the 20 July plot. Guderian's report is perhaps the most succinct and revealing:

> Hitler's mistrust now reached extremes and the miracle of his survival gave him greater faith than ever in his mission. He shut himself up in his bunker, engaged in no further private talks, and had every word of his conversation recorded. He lost himself more and more in the realm of the imagination which had no basis in reality. Every free expression of opinion and every objection to his frequently incomprehensible views evoked an outburst of rage on his part. He lost his capacity to listen to a report to the end. His criticisms became stronger, and his actions more drastic, with every passing day. He felt that he alone had the right to hold opinions upon which decisions would be based. He was convinced that he alone possessed clear perception concerning all fields of human activity. Accordingly, he condemned generals, staff officers, diplomats, government officials and towards the end even Party and SS Leaders as armchair strategists, weaklings and finally as criminals and traitors.

That being so it was no surprise that even all the stubborn arguments of the quartet who reported to him, failed to change the Führer's mind about the basic aims and organization of the battle. What is surprising is that Manteuffel did succeed in impressing on Hitler that some fairly fundamental changes in the tactical handling of the all-important first blow were not merely sensible, but so necessary as to require an immediate overhauling of the orders.

Model's objections to the basic plan were simply brushed aside. Hitler was riding on a high wave of confidence and optimism. There might be shortages of material, there might be some unpreparedness on the part of the assaulting units, it might well be that the actual air support forthcoming on the day would be less than what the Luftwaffe had originally undertaken to produce, it might even be that a number of decisions as to exactly what would be happening on other sections of the Western front were still to be taken—all of this might be so. But victory was assured; always provided his plan was carried out. Any smaller, modified solution was no solution at all. No fundamental changes were to be made in the strategic concept, the organization of divisions into armies, the allotment of objectives—and that was that.

Yet when Manteuffel pointed out that having an H-hour as late as 11 a.m., to be preceded by a three-hour bombardment of all known enemy positions along the assault frontage, would have the effect firstly of alerting the enemy that this might be the start of something big, secondly of subjecting the assault forces waiting in their concentration and forward assembly areas to the counter-bombardment of enemy artillery, to say nothing of air attack if the weather permitted flying, Hitler listened. What Manteuffel was after was that the offensive should get off to a good start, that the tactical operations up to the Meuse should at least not be marred at the outset by bad planning which would forfeit all advantage of speed and surprise. 'The first blow is half the battle!' What happened if and when they got to and over the Meuse could look after itself. The essential changes that Hitler agreed to were that H-hour should be moved forward to 5.30 a.m. with a much shorter artillery bombardment, only 45 minutes, to be directed on American headquarters, communication centres, gun areas, likely counter-penetration positions; the bombardment itself to be preceded by the infiltration of special storm battalions from each division. Searchlights used as artificial moonlight would help them forward. All this should mean a quick penetration of enemy positions still at night, and maximum daylight hours for the exploitation by the following-up panzers. In talking to Liddell Hart after the war, Manteuffel summed up the views he gave when telling Hitler that it was impossible to carry out the offensive in any other way than the one he, Manteuffel, proposed if they were to have a reasonable chance of success:

'At 4 p.m. it will be dark,' I explained to the Führer. 'So you will only have five hours after the assault at 11 a.m., in which to achieve the breakthrough. It is very doubtful if you can do it in the time. If you adopt my ideas, you will gain a further five and a half hours for the purpose. Then when darkness comes I can launch the tanks. They will advance during the night, pass through our infantry and by dawn the next day they will be able to launch their own attack on the main position, along a cleared approach.'

Manteuffel's ideas found their way into the final plan. There was one other point that Manteuffel made to Hitler. It was that in his view when the time came for the Americans to react to the German offensive, they would be likely to counter it from the Sedan area towards—Bastogne. It was at Bastogne that the important roads in that area all converged. How different might have been the outcome of the German attack if Hitler had seized on this point with half the zeal he took up Manteuffel's other ideas. Yet had any of the principal Allied commanders been privileged to hear Manteuffel make his point, they would have been utterly sceptical about the likelihood of such a requirement. For their minds were moving along very different lines.

4

Allied Discord

Unanimity is almost always an indication of servitude.
Charles de Rémusat

On 15 September 1944 General Eisenhower wrote a letter to his two principal subordinates, Montgomery, commanding 21st Army Group and Bradley, 12th Army Group, which outlined his ideas about future Allied strategy and asked for their views. His ideas suggested that they would soon be in possession of the Ruhr, the Saar and Frankfurt and advocated a rapid thrust to Berlin either via Hannover or Leipzig or both. 'It is my desire', the letter stated, 'to move on Berlin by the most direct and expeditious route, with combined US-British forces supported by other available forces moving through key centres and occupying strategic areas on the flanks, all in one coordinated, concerted operation.' The final point made in the letter was that timings and strengths of the various thrusts could not yet be decided. To one of Eisenhower's subordinates, one who did not lack ideas of his own, all this added up to the very strategy which he considered to be the wrong one—a broad front advance. He was therefore quick to take up the Supreme Commander on a number of points. If Hitler was the Supreme Commander who thought he knew better than his subordinates, Montgomery was the subordinate who knew he knew better than his Supreme Commander.

In his reply Montgomery's two main arguments were first that the logistic resources available simply would not allow *all* Allied Land forces to advance both simultaneously and quickly, secondly that since time was the 'vital factor . . . what we have to do, we must do quickly'. In short, a proper, master plan must be made now. He therefore proposed two possible courses of action. One, the preferred plan, was for his own 21st Army Group plus the 1st US Army (together making three armies of 28 divisions) to seize the Ruhr and thence Berlin, that is by making use of the shorter, northern route together with the advantages which Allied sea power could wrest from the ports there; the second plan was for Bradley's 12th Army Group (also of three armies) to advance by Frankfurt and central Germany on Berlin. Whichever Army Group was chosen would have the bulk of administrative support —in short a single thrust in strength with maximum logistic resources. 'It is my opinion', Montgomery wrote, 'that three Armies are enough if you select the northern route, and I consider that from a maintenance point of view, it could be done.' Three Armies! There has been a good deal of discussion as to whether Montgomery's proposal would have succeeded. In spite of Allied air strength, when we remember the superiority of strength normally necessary for a major strategic offensive on land to succeed, say two or three to one at a minimum; when we remember too that Hitler was about to undertake an offensive himself with no less than three armies also totalling 28 divisions and that his offensive was defeated within two weeks; when finally we contemplate what might have been the fate of a Montgomery single thrust, if it had been greeted not only by the counter-penetration capability of the 5th and 6th Panzer Armies, to say nothing of the other newly raised *Volksgrenadierdivisionen* and all the formations already in the line or in reserve, but also by the Luftwaffe aircraft scraped together for Hitler's offensive, we may doubt whether Montgomery would have got to Berlin and may perhaps be thankful that on this occasion his eloquence was unable to prevail. Yet at first it seemed that it had, for in his reply Eisenhower expressed almost complete agreement. This agreement did not however modify Eisenhower's actual plans to the degree Montgomery desired, for whereas the former was still thinking of a final and perhaps single thrust on Berlin *after* the capture of the Ruhr, the Saar and Frankfurt, Montgomery was arguing for a strategy which would first capture the Ruhr or Frankfurt and then go for Berlin.

A week after Eisenhower's first letter, a number of decisions were taken at Supreme Headquarters Allied Expeditionary Force. In distinguishing between presently planned operations—

seizing the Ruhr and breaking the Siegfried Line—and future ones—the final advance on Berlin—it was agreed that for the latter, the advance deep into Germany, another principal northern port was indispensable and that for the former, present operations, the main effort would be that of 21st Army Group supported by US 1st Army to encircle the Ruhr. Yet there was no question of relegating the other parts of the front to mere containing activity. Bradley's 12th Army Group was to continue to push towards Cologne and Bonn and if possible seize crossings over the Rhine there *and* be prepared to attack the Ruhr from the south should logistic resources prove to be adequate. Most important of all—although not at this time emphasized as such—21st Army Group was to 'open the port of Antwerp as a matter of urgency'. Meanwhile 6th Army Group—the formation which had landed in southern France in August 1944—was to move on towards Strasbourg and Mulhouse, an operation which could be undertaken with its own logistic supplies through Mediterranean ports. Thus we can see that none of the conditions which Montgomery had stipulated as being necessary to Allied strategy was present.

Indeed his own orders to 21st Army Group after the withdrawal from Arnhem reflected his persuasion that a step-by-step policy was the only realistic one. 2nd Army's main task was to gain contact with the Ruhr, and secure bridgeheads over the Rhine— 'then we can decide on a plan for further action'. The 1st Canadian Army was to finish off its operations to enable the Allies to use Antwerp, Boulogne and Calais. Montgomery emphasized what had been agreed at Eisenhower's conference of 22 September, that the opening of Antwerp was 'absolutely essential before we can advance deep into Germany'. As we have seen this operation was not an easy one. Antwerp, although captured on 4 September, was not operating until 28 November. It is curious that while all the higher commanders seemed to be unanimous in recognizing the overriding need to clear Antwerp for Allied use and kept on reiterating this need in their directives and orders, more actual drive was not forthcoming to see that the operation was given the priority it demanded. It is not enough for you to give orders— so runs the military maxim—you must then ensure that they are carried out. Somehow neither Eisenhower nor Montgomery nor the British Admiralty nor even that great strategist, Churchill, put their finger on this critical point early enough. They might have done well to cast the same envious eye on it as had Hitler.

Yet on 4 October the CIGS, Field Marshal Sir Alan Brooke, noted in his diary that instead of going for Arnhem, 'Monty . . . ought to have made certain of Antwerp in the first place'. The truth was that Montgomery had his eye on two balls—Antwerp *and* the Ruhr—instead of one, the vital one. Uncharacteristically, he gave priority to a tactical gamble instead of a logistic necessity. No advance without security had long been his doctrine, by which he meant tactical and logistic security. For once he chose to ignore it. Even after Arnhem Montgomery did not seem to have got his priorities quite right. On 9 October he issued another directive which emphasized the three factors which had most influence on the situation at that time. These were: first the Nijmegen bridge-head had to be strengthened, secondly the enemy must be pushed to the east of the Meuse, and thirdly, Antwerp must be opened up quickly. All these were to be done before 2nd Army could be launched towards Krefeld and the Ruhr. We may note that Antwerp figured as the third factor. On the same day Montgomery received a signal from Eisenhower which gave it a very different precedence, and included these sentences:

> I must emphasize that I consider Antwerp of first importance of all our endeavours on entire front from Switzerland to Channel. I believe your personal attention is required in operation designed to clear entrance.

Even this appeal did not cause Montgomery to modify his orders. A subsequent letter from Eisenhower, however, which reached Montgomery on 15 October, did. This letter, in answer to one of Montgomery's on the question of command in Western Europe, was a model of clarity and precision, particularly so as regards Antwerp.

> I do not know the exact state of your supply, but I do know what a woeful state it is throughout the American and French forces extending all the way from your southern boundary to Switzerland. By comparison, you are rich! If you could have a similarly clear picture of that situation you would understand why I keep reverting again and again to the matter of getting Antwerp into a workable condition. I have been informed by the Chief of the Imperial General Staff and by the Chief of Staff of the United States Army that they seriously considered giving me a flat order that until the capture of Antwerp and its

approaches were fully assured, this operation should take precedence over all others. . . . However, all this [the Arnhem operation] serves merely to re-emphasize *now* the importance of that port to our future operations.

This was enough for Montgomery as far as the question of Antwerp went. He replied that all energies and efforts would be directed to opening the port, and a new directive to 21st Army Group made this plain. Operations for this purpose would therefore be given absolute priority over all others. On this point then Eisenhower and Montgomery saw eye to eye, indeed always had seen eye to eye. It was only in the execution of an agreed intention that priorities wavered. Montgomery's *Memoirs* subsequently admitted to a bad mistake in that he had underestimated the difficulties of opening the Antwerp approaches. 'I reckoned that the Canadian Army could do it *while* we were going for the Ruhr. I was wrong.'

The ultimately far graver question of command, however, was one in which the two did not see eye to eye. They agreed to differ. It was a matter which was to loom large in the Ardennes battles but two months away.

Eisenhower's directive of 28 October 1944 (modified later on 2 November) which we referred to in the first chapter, and which gave his general plan 'subject always to prior capture of the approaches to Antwerp', was in essence a continuation of the broad front strategy. The main effort was to be in the north— the enemy west of the Rhine were to be defeated, bridgeheads over the river to be secured and an advance deep into Germany was to be made. But additionally operations to destroy the enemy in the Saar, secure crossings over the Rhine there and advance from there, together with aggressive action on the southern flank also to destroy the enemy west of the Rhine, were to be conducted. By studying the further details of how this directive would be carried out it is now possible to identify an Allied weakness of both deployment and command which the coming German offensive tried to turn to its advantage. There were to be three phases. In the first, dealing with the enemy west of the Rhine, the formations *north of the Ardennes* belonging to Bradley's 12th Army Group would advance to the Rhine, while 21st Army Group having opened Antwerp would do the same; the second phase called for bridgeheads over the Rhine; during both phases

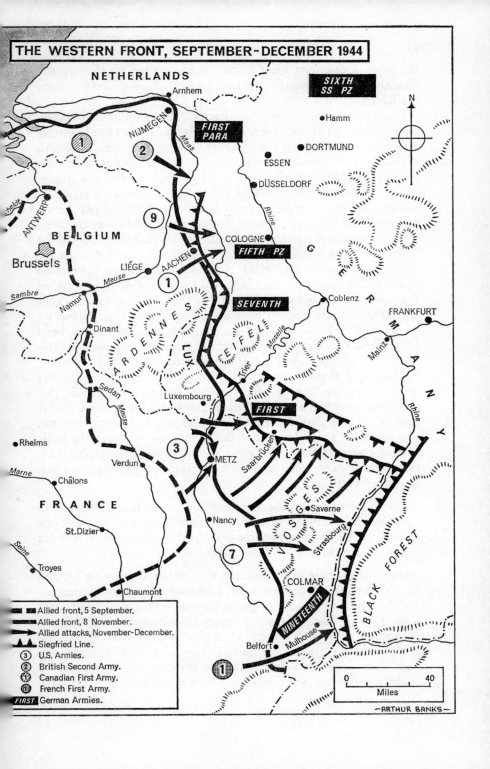

THE WESTERN FRONT, SEPTEMBER-DECEMBER 1944

NETHERLANDS

Arnhem

SIXTH SS PZ

Hamm

NIJMEGEN

FIRST PARA

DORTMUND

Maas

ESSEN

DÜSSELDORF

①

②

Scheldt

ANTWERP

⑨

Rhine

G

BELGIUM

COLOGNE

FIFTH PZ

Brussels

LIÉGE

AACHEN

①

Meuse

Namur

Sambre

SEVENTH

Coblenz

FRANKFURT

Dinant

ARDENNES

LUX.

EIFEL

Moselle

Mainz

R

Sedan

Meuse

Luxembourg

Trier

FIRST

M

Rheims

③

Verdun

METZ

Saarbrücken

Rhine

A

Marne

Châlons

Nancy

V O S G E S

Saverne

N

St.Dizier

⑦

Strasbourg

Y

Seine

Troyes

COLMAR

BLACK FOREST

Chaumont

NINETEENTH

Belfort

Mulhouse

①

N

0   Miles   40

Allied front, 5 September.
Allied front, 8 November.
Allied attacks, November-December.
Siegfried Line.
③ U.S. Armies.
② British Second Army.
⑪ Canadian First Army.
⑪ French First Army.
FIRST German Armies.

~ARTHUR BANKS~

Bradley's formations *south of the Ardennes* were to capture the
Saar and Rhine crossings; the final phase to be the advance from
the Rhine.

Exactly one month after this directive, that is on 28 November,
Eisenhower and Montgomery conferred at the latter's headquarters
at Zonhoven. Few of the directive's aims had been realized.
Although the Americans had captured Aachen, the attack to the
north of the Ardennes had not even got half way to the Rhine.
South of Aachen the battle of the Hürtgen Forest—a tactically
sterile one—cost Bradley 33,000 casualties. Patton's 3rd Army,
south of the Ardennes, was more successful. Metz was captured
on 22 November. Further south still 1st French Army reached the
Rhine near the Swiss frontier on 20 November and the 7th US
Army took Strasbourg on 23 November. Yet these operations
south of the Ardennes were intended to be subsidiary to those in
the north. It seemed in the event that things had gone the other
way round. In expressing his disappointment to Eisenhower on
28 November, Montgomery pointed out that there had been
insufficient concentration of force in the north where the main
effort was supposed to be. He also returned to his old argument
for having a single commander north of the Ardennes. A letter
to the Supreme Commander two days later reiterated his dis-
satisfaction with the October plan, expressed his opinion that it
had failed and that the Allies had suffered a strategic reverse.
A new plan, which 'must not fail', must also observe the basic
rule of concentration. The letter included one paragraph which
especially touches the subsequent command problems of the
Ardennes battle.

> The theatre divides itself naturally into two fronts: one north
> of the Ardennes and one south of the Ardennes. We want one
> commander in full operational control north of the Ardennes
> and one south.

Montgomery therefore suggested that either Bradley or himself
should have this full operational control north of the Ardennes,
and declared that it was the spring campaign that must be planned
now. He held himself ready to meet Eisenhower and Bradley at
Maastricht on 6 or 7 December. Before we see what transpired
there we may perhaps note that Montgomery's oft-iterated point
that there were two fronts in the theatre, one north of the
Ardennes and one south (and it was an argument not fundamen-

tally contradicted by Eisenhower and Bradley as the deployment of Bradley's Army Group with its principal strength deployed either side of the Ardennes made clear), ignored one glaringly obvious fact—that there was a third front—*the Ardennes itself.*

The Deputy Supreme Allied Commander, Air Marshal Sir Arthur Tedder, was also present at Maastricht when Eisenhower, Bradley and Montgomery discussed future strategy, and he recorded, together with the main points of discord, those where the three commanders were in accord. Very briefly, the latter were that pressure on the enemy must be kept up through the winter and the Rhine reached if possible; that to cut all the Ruhr off from the rest of Germany was the primary object of future strategy, that the main attack would be north of the Ruhr and therefore be for 21st Army Group to do with a strong US Army under command. The question of what sort of supporting attack should be made south of the Ruhr was not decided. On the other hand Eisenhower clearly ruled that the inter-Army Group boundary would be the Ruhr itself and not as Montgomery wanted it to be—the Ardennes. There is one curious discrepancy here. Eisenhower was willing enough to place a strong US Army under Montgomery's command; he agreed that operations against the Ruhr were to be split into those in the north by 21st Army Group and in the south by 12th Army Group; all were agreed that the Ardennes was a difficult area for operations. Yet Eisenhower's reason for choosing the Ruhr as the Army Group boundary was that 'we did not propose to operate in the Ruhr itself'. All the more reason, we might suppose, for giving it to one commander and thus ensuring proper coordination and tight command and control. We need not follow the later controversies of what strategy should be pursued further than to say it provoked a letter from Churchill to Roosevelt, which moved Roosevelt hardly at all, and provoked also a note from the Chiefs of Staff to Churchill emphasizing the key point of the whole argument—that whereas in theory Allied strategy which had been endorsed by the Combined Chiefs of Staff was that the main effort of advancing into Germany should be made in the north, in practice as it appeared to many, particularly the British, there was to be a two pronged advance, one north, one south. It was to some extent this very problem and the Allied deployment which reflected it which made the German attack when it came so much more of a surprise and so much more difficult to cope with in a tidy, coordinated fashion. For on one matter the Allies were firmly agreed—the Germans could not, would not fritter away their newly created reserves in mounting another offensive. One other curious result of the Maastricht conference was a statement that the operation to cut off the Ruhr would be designed amongst other things to oblige the enemy to fight. It is always militarily sound to destroy the enemy's forces in battle if you wish to impose your will upon him. But a plan designed to make the Wehrmacht fight, in the West in December 1944, knowing as we do what Hitler had in mind, strikes an ironic note.

The Allies knew all about the newly formed Sixth Panzer Army. But it was in their interpretation first of its technical capability, second of German intentions that their intelligence staff faltered. Capability and intention! How often we hear these phrases today on the lips of amateur and actual strategists alike. Different weight is given to each according to whatever argument needs to be put forward at that particular moment. The intention of hostile powers, interpreted as peaceful, usually takes precedence over their capability, which may be overwhelmingly strong, in the minds of those politicians charged with promoting retrenchment. Capability, a reality, weighs more heavily than intention, a guess at best, with the soldiers charged with promoting security. To underestimate either is a dangerous game, more so than to overestimate both. Yet it was the former game that the Allies played. A SHAEF Intelligence Summary of 12 November, for example, greatly underestimated the capability of 6th Panzer Army:

> Formidable though it is, this Army is incapable from lack of size and of gasoline, of staging a true counter-offensive. It is capable still, if given a little more time, of staging a spoiling attack of considerable power, and if an opportunity offers, both it and the attendant risk might be taken. However, the Army's most obvious use is in counter-attack, if and when and wherever a determined Allied thrust towards the Rhine Province develops.

21st Army Group Intelligence Staffs held comparable views. 6th Panzer Army was thought of as a formation for resting, re-equipping and re-training panzer units which had been withdrawn from the fighting. The Panzer Army's capability actually to take the field as an operational formation was thought to be 'open to doubt'. How different was the real state of affairs! Within a matter of weeks of this estimate, 6th Panzer Army had four crack panzer divisions fully up to strength, two other élite divisions, 12th Volksgrenadier and 3rd Parachute, and a further three infantry divisions.

Having got the reality wrong, the actual capability of German reserves, and this was not difficult to do, the Allies proceeded to go even further astray with the guess, their intended use, and with far less excuse. For some years now the Supreme Commander of the Wehrmacht, Adolf Hitler, had given the world a continuous and convincing demonstration that he was a War Lord who gave the orders, that he and he alone called the tune. How else was it possible to explain the history of Europe during the preceding ten years? Reoccupation of the Rhineland, the Anschluss, the smashing of Czechoslovakia, the invasion of Poland and the outbreak of war itself, the battle for France, the attack on Russia, Stalingrad, Tunisia, Normandy—these were not moves in a reasoned strategic programme, but the violent impulses of a man whose will-power could see no limit to military capability. Hitler's intention? It was to erase his enemies, destroy all who opposed him, use force whenever, wherever and however he could. 'We may be destroyed, but if we are, we shall drag a world with us—a world in flames.'

Yet von Rundstedt's re-appointment as Commander-in-Chief West, and his moderate conduct of affairs on the Western front in September, October and November of 1944 had lulled the Allies into the extraordinary misconception that he, Rundstedt, was actually in charge of the conduct of operations. 'The war from the military side', read a 21st Army Group Intelligence report, 'would now seem to be in the hands of the soldiers, a change making the enemy easier to understand but harder to defeat.' An odd statement, when, in spite of all Hitler's disastrous policies from 1942 onwards, we remember that it was he who insisted against the advice of most of the soldiers on both the military plans which defeated most of Europe and the political certainty that most of his enemies' will to resist was low. Von Rundstedt, the report went on, was unlikely to risk the Panzer reserve forward of Cologne–Bonn except in conditions where a quick counter-attack could take an Allied thrust off balance and put paid to their offensive prospects for the winter. 'To disrupt our winter cam-

paigning would be a gain worth many risks. To lose 6th Panzer
Army in the doing of it would be a disaster perhaps irreparable. . . .'
This misjudgment by 21st Army Group Intelligence Staff of who
really held the military reins is particularly strange when we
recall that at the time of von Rundstedt's reinstatement in
September 1944 they had made a comment which was as realistic
as it was racy. It made the point that bringing back the Old
Guard indicated a desperate situation for whose further deterioration the Old Guard could then take the blame. Much more
important it went on to say that the appointment would make no
difference since 'the task of Commander-in-Chief in any German
theatre has degenerated to that of local Chief of Staff to Hitler'.
12th Army Group Intelligence Staff misjudged the situation in
almost identical terms. Little did they know the Führer who was
prepared to gamble all on a single throw.

Information on the movement of 6th Panzer Army to positions
behind the front of the Aachen sector was interpreted by the
Allies as a German reaction to what they, the Germans, must
have regarded as the area most gravely threatened by the Allies.
Changes in deployment of the Luftwaffe, in order to give more
support to the German armies in the field and less to the strategic
defence of the Reich, received comparably short shrift. Capability
and intention were again misread. It might be observed that to be
deceived by others is one thing; to persist in self-deception is
another. We are put in mind almost of Moltke's point that when
the enemy has three courses of action he will choose the fourth.
In any event the Allies were unanimous in one consideration.
There would be no German counter-offensive. This unusual
unanimity did not spring, as de Rémusat's generality implies,
from servitude; rather the reverse—from over-confidence in their
superiority and obsession with their own plans to the exclusion of
the enemy's.

Even rumours failed to dispel illusion or to induce caution.
Early in December 1944 German movement on the Ardennes front
was observed and there was talk of an attempt by the German
armies to recapture Antwerp. But in spite of crediting 6th Panzer
Army with five panzer divisions, 1st, 2nd, 9th, 2nd SS and 12th
SS, the 21st Army Group estimate of 3 December judged the
rumoured drive on Antwerp to be beyond von Rundstedt's
potential. With this estimate von Rundstedt himself would have
agreed wholeheartedly.

5
Preparations

Loyalty implies loyalty in misfortune; and when a soldier
has accepted any nation's uniform he has already accepted
its defeat.
G. K. Chesterton

Purely in numbers of divisions the German and Allied forces
opposing each other on the Western front early in December 1944
were almost identical. Von Rundstedt was accurately credited by
the Allies with 64 divisions. Eisenhower had 65. On the German
side Army Group H in the north contained 11 divisions; Army
Group B under Model had 25; in Army Group G further south
there were 21; seven were thought to be in reserve and were
unlocated. Eisenhower's divisions were also disposed in three
major commands—nineteen in Montgomery's 21st Army Group,
29 under Bradley in 12th Army Group and in 6th Army Group
commanded by Devers, a further seventeen. In the critical central
sector where the Ardennes offensive was to be launched, Bradley
was very weak. Only four divisions and a few reconnaissance units
were positioned on a front of 65 miles, for his two major concentrations to the north and south of the Ardennes were deployed
for offensive operations directed respectively on Cologne and the
Saar. The truth was that Bradley dismissed or ignored the likelihood of a German attack in that area. His subsequent comment—
'we were not unmindful that in 1940 Hitler had broken through
this same unlikely Ardennes front to overrun France' and that
he had knowingly taken a calculated risk—simply does not ring
true. A risk yes, but not a calculated one. His reference to 1940,
however, reminds us of Alistair Horne's comment on the deployment of the Allied armies in the spring of that year—strong in

the north to counter a German advance through Belgium, a powerful southern flank based on the Maginot Line to protect the frontier between the Reich and the Third Republic, weak in the centre opposite the Belgian Ardennes. 'What a standing temptation the spectacle of this line, then, so weak in the centre, might present to an opposing Captain of audacity and genius.' The circumstances of 1944 reproduced the temptation and the audacity, but the genius had long since been used up.

'Forward to and over the Meuse' was to be Hitler's watchword for the attack. To reach the Meuse alone would mean an advance of some 30 to 60 miles depending on which part of the front and which attacking formation we are thinking of; from Liège to Antwerp was a further 65 miles as the crow flies—more like 100 miles by any sensible route; Brussels too was about 40 miles beyond Namur. This was to be no limited advance. And then the country at such a time of year in spite of all that the panzer columns so powerfully supported by the Luftwaffe in the fine dry weather of May 1940 had shown, was not conducive to rapid movement of tracked and wheeled units, particularly if they were to be opposed in an area ideal for defensive tactics. 1914 and 1940 had been summer route marches. Repetition of so mathematical a descent on the Meuse was hardly to be expected in the fogs and bogs of winter. Although we talk always of the Ardennes offensive, we should not forget that the country we are talking about composed both the Eifel and the Ardennes.

The Eifel range of hills is situated between three rivers—the Rhine, the Moselle and the Roer. Most of the Eifel is in Germany and therefore at the time of Hitler's offensive was still in German hands. But two of the Eifel's features of particular importance during the forthcoming battle were in Allied hands—the Schnee Eifel, a high ridge near St Vith, covered with trees, and Hohes Venn, a marshy wooded plateau east of Liège. In general the Eifel is forested, with a good road network to serve the numerous villages. The Ardennes, which lie to the west of the Eifel, are roughly between Aachen, Sedan and Luxembourg. Their northern part is more open and rolling, the southern part more wooded and bisected with sharp ridges. This area too had plenty of roads. As Model himself was to observe, the battle of the Ardennes would be a battle for those roads and therefore more particularly for road junctions, two of the more critical being St Vith and Bastogne.

At the time when the Führer was delivering his harangue to the generals on 11 and 12 December, final arrangements for assembling and concentrating the assault forces were under way. By 11 December 7th Army's divisions were all there, although some adjustments of actual locations would be needed before the attack itself. 5th Panzer Army still lacked one of its panzer divisions which did not in the event arrive until after H-hour. 6th Panzer Army on the other hand was complete with all its panzer strength. Assembly was one thing, concentration for the operation another. Three nights—for all final movement to attack positions was to be done under cover of darkness—were still needed before everything would be ready. Hitler kept as tight a hold on these preparatory moves as on the rest of the planning. None of the assaulting Panzer Armies' troops were to be allowed forward of an Army Group B base line, 12 miles from the front, until Hitler himself gave the order. Movement forward was thus secret, gradual and controlled. On 12 December troops were given their warning orders for final assembly; by the next day the leading elements of all units were to have closed up to the Army Group base line; during the nights of 13 and 14 December the infantry and panzer divisions, the artillery and rocket batteries moved further forward again into allotted areas near the front according to their role in the coming operation; on the night before the attack started, 15 December, the assaulting units finally fitted into their forming-up places for the advance itself. Briefing of the troops as to the details of the attack also took place that night, although the formation commanders, quite apart from Hitler's own briefing at Adlershorst, had been put into the picture a week before. All was now ready.

This is not to say that everything was perfect, but when we consider what had been done we can have only admiration for the way in which it was done. Of course everything had not gone exactly according to plan. Things never do in war—or even in peacetime manoeuvres. No order, however simple, concise, clear and foolproof it may appear to be can ensure that an officer in command of a transport column does not misread his map and take his convoy down the wrong road and thus meet another convoy with consequent traffic tangles, loss of temper and waste of time; no logistic machine is so perfect that some deliveries of the wrong commodity to the right place or the right commodity to the wrong one do not take place; no radio message is not subject to distortion in content and interpretation as it passes from one headquarters to another; no repair and recovery system combined with the most experienced drivers of tanks and trucks will see to it that some do not break down or slither off a muddy track and get bogged in the adjacent ditch. But in spite of all that might have gone wrong, very little did. The great bulk of Hitler's three assaulting armies were deployed properly—in their correct assembly or attack positions, grouped with their supporting units, supplied with the immediately necessary fuel, ammunition and other supplies—*on time*. The great rules of deploying an army ready for a forthcoming attack are designed to guarantee the maximum amount of simultaneous action by as many components of that army as possible. For example the reconnoitring of an exact concentration area by those responsible for laying it out and guiding the troops in may be done at exactly the same time—but 50 miles further forward—as the troops and vehicles for whom the area is being prepared are moving towards it, so that when they arrive, everything is ready. Similarly, orders may be given to key commanders while subordinate commanders are bringing up those troops for whom these orders are eventually intended. All is designed to save time and preserve security. When such drills are perfected, the commander of, say, an infantry battalion, having given the correct instructions, may set off to see his superior commander knowing that the next action he is to fight will be in a certain area, confident that by the time his troops reach that area, he will not only have received his orders, seen the ground over which he is to fight, given his own orders out to his company commanders, but that they too *and their subordinates* will all have had the opportunity and time to have seen and understood what it is they are to do and to have prepared for it, so that the whole battalion crosses the start line on time with the best chance of success open to it.

If we multiply this problem several hundred times, compound it with the reflection that security had to be absolute in order not to arouse Allied suspicions, make it yet more difficult by acknowledging that the Allies' almost total air supremacy confined movement to the hours of darkness, movement moreover yet further hampered by Allied bombing of rail and road communications, then we may begin to have some idea of what the Germans were up against. The grouping and regrouping involved, when so many of the assaulting formations had first of all to be relieved, taken out of the line, withdrawn for reinforcement, re-equipment, training and briefing, then sent back towards the line to their assembly positions and finally moved into the actual attack, presented staff problems calculated to dismay even the most experienced and cool-headed of the great German General Staff. So that to have done it all, to be ready to cross the start line on time, in good order with something like 200,000 soldiers and all their accompanying paraphernalia of kit, weapons, vehicles and supplies was something like a miracle of organization, which perhaps only the Germans with their genius for discipline, thoroughness, foresight and attention to detail would have been capable of.

Nor was this the whole story. It had to be done in such a way that the Allies—whether we are thinking of their forward patrols, their air reconnaissance, their intercept radio organization or their ubiquitous and industrious Intelligence staffs—were not a jot wiser. That the Germans succeeded absolutely is not just to argue that the Allied Intelligence Staffs and the Allied Commanders, obsessed as they were with their own plans of attack and confident that the Wehrmacht was too close to the breaking point ever to stage another full scale offensive, simply closed their eyes, ears and minds to what was evident or deducible. It is to say that the German measures of security in every sense of the word—guarding the secret, patrol policy, deception, radio discipline, movement, artillery programmes and general pattern of behaviour from the front line itself to the rear administrative and command areas—was a feat remarkable in the annals of war. We should not even confine our admiration to what was happening in the immediate sector opposite the Ardennes.

The logistic build-up for such an ambitious affair—even though that achieved fell short of full requirements—was formidable. In order to muster all the sinews of war—ammunition and fuel, the guns and tanks which these commodities would supply, the men to drive and shoot them—the Wehrmacht cast its net far and wide, from the most northern group of Hitler's armies in Scandinavia to the most southern in Austria and Northern Italy. Something short of five million gallons of fuel was moved, somewhere between ten and twenty thousand tons of ammunition. Most of it was moved by train, and even at this late hour, the German railway service—all the bombing of bridges and rolling stock, all the smashing of marshalling yards (an undertaking which figured so consistently and to some ears so unconvincingly in Allied wartime communiqués) notwithstanding—was so efficient in repair and maintenance that they managed to keep the flow of supplies and men and machinery under way. Had the efficiency of Hitler's organization for the preparation of his great offensive been matched in its execution by comparable drive and improvisation, plus sheer skill at overcoming all obstacles no matter how numerous or complex, there might have been another story to tell.

While Hitler was perfecting his plans and preparations, and, in spite of the fact that his drive to put every possible man and machine into this last gamble had starved the Eastern front and robbed the Reich of its dwindling reserves, was riding on a wave of optimism, Churchill was undergoing one of his infrequent descents into gloom. He wrote to Smuts on 3 December that the Allies had suffered a strategic reverse on the Western front, and gave it as his view that to attack along the whole front was a mistake. 'A far greater mass should have been gathered at the point of desired penetration.' There would be at least one more full-scale battle before the Allies reached the Rhine in the north. He would try this and that, but in view of the American preponderance of troops, 'it is not as easy as it used to be for me to get things done'. Delay in Italy, reverses in China, a coming general election, national bankruptcy—all added up to 'a horizon overrun with clouds'. The Prime Minister repeated his apprehensions to President Roosevelt a few days later. On the Western front they had failed to achieve the strategic objectives which the armies had been given. Everywhere there was disappointment and frustration. Churchill urged further top level meetings, if not between themselves at least between the Combined Chiefs of Staff and Eisenhower. Roosevelt, while conceding that progress was slow, shared neither Churchill's disappointment nor his view of the need for immediate consultation.

The differing realism of these two political leaders was reflected by that of their field commanders. Eisenhower, while concerned that his armies were overstretched, was confident that his policy of attacking wherever possible was the right one. Enemy casualties were twice as high as American ones. The American armies could certainly not sit still and do nothing until further reinforcements arrived to make certain of a successful offensive. The Supreme Commander was nothing if not generous in his assumption of responsibility for the weakness of the Ardennes position. Easy as it would have been, he subsequently wrote, to have moved over to the defensive and thereby be secure everywhere, instead of concentrating his forces for the two offensives, north near the Roer dams, south bordering the Saar, and continuing with these offensives as strongly as possible, it was his own decision for the latter course which was responsible for the startling success of the first week of the German December attack. If there were any blame to be distributed by the historians later, it should be reserved, he claimed, for himself alone.

This loyalty to Bradley, while admirable in itself, distorts the picture, for it was Bradley who had soothed Eisenhower's anxieties about the dangers of a German counter-attack. Bradley's argument was, first that the flanks of any attacking force would become intolerably vulnerable to interference from north or south, second that the German supply problems would never allow them to reach the Meuse, third that their own air force could quickly turn the tables. The facts were, however, that the offensive when it came was not initially stopped by air power or supplies or interference from the flanks. It was stopped by the stubborn, piecemeal and improvised defensive fighting of the American units in the paths of the Germans and by the Germans' own failure to reinforce success or seize the supplies which were there for the taking. In his book Bradley writes of his astonishment when the attack started that von Rundstedt should have chosen 'so unremunerative an objective'. In discussing the inherent risks of his Ardennes deployment before the offensive started, he had, it seemed, discussed the matter with Middleton, Commanding US VIII Corps which manned this sector, and had declared that in the Ardennes the Germans could not attain any of the proper purposes of an attack. They could neither capture a worthwhile objective nor destroy US forces, because there were few forces there and no great industrial or other strategic objective. A curious argument, since it might be supposed that a scarcity of US forces would make them easier to overwhelm and thus enable a distant objective to be reached.

'Even if the German were to burst through all the way to the Meuse,' he told Eisenhower, 'he wouldn't find a thing in the Ardennes to make it worth his while.' In fact Bradley went one stage further and told the Supreme Commander that if the Germans were to come out of the Siegfried Line and fight in the open, it would be to the Allies' advantage. All this has a somewhat hollow ring about it when we recall that in the event Bradley's Army Group was so surprised and thrown so much off balance by the attack, that he himself lost all grip of the battle and forfeited half his command before the offensive was checked —principally because of ad hoc counter-penetration action by his own subordinates.

Patton's contribution to the affair, before the active attack got under way, was typical of the man's extraordinary coalition of hardness, showmanship and sentimentality, and was, if we may allow ourselves the same indulgence as those who believed in the Angels of Mons, ultimately the most effective. On 14 December he blew for his chaplain. 'Chaplain, I want you to publish a prayer for good weather. I'm tired of these soldiers having to fight mud and floods as well as Germans. See if we can't get God to work on our side.' The prayer itself which had been required by Patton to assist 3rd Army's breakthrough to the Rhine in the Saarguemines area, was not actually issued until his Army was engaged against the southern flank of the Ardennes bulge.* It called upon the Almighty to restrain the immoderate rains and to grant fair weather for battle in order to crush the oppression and wickedness of the enemy. As we shall see, his prayer was answered.

Amid all this extravagance, Montgomery's pre-battle reflections —based on what he wrote and said *at the time*—are a model both of restraint and of strategic foresight. We have seen in his exchanges with Eisenhower recorded in the last chapter what were his principal arguments for concentration somewhere or other. Montgomery's summary of their differences made it clear that these differences were profound. Indeed it was not a difference at all. It was a contradiction. Montgomery was convinced that the Allied resources must not be split. Eisenhower was determined to split them. Montgomery insisted that, to get the command arrangement right, he should be in charge of all forces north of the Ardennes, Bradley in command to the south. Eisenhower left Bradley in command of his forces both north and south of the Ardennes. Montgomery pleaded that to do two things

* As the German penetration bulged out into the Allied positions, the whole affair became known as the Battle of the Bulge.

inadequately would simply ensure that both failed. Eisenhower decided that the two things would be done. In short, Montgomery maintained that, in spite of the current strategy's having failed, it was to be persevered with as if it had not failed. Thus for the Allies there was general agreement to differ.

On the other side of the hill there was general agreement to agree—with the Führer's wishes. But the fundamental problem was the same. Subordinate commanders were being required to persist in a strategy which they regarded as bound to end in failure. On 10 December Hitler with his Staff arrived at Adlershorst, Eagle's Nest, his headquarters for the battle. He had come to 'help'. On the same day Westphal, von Rundstedt's Chief of Staff, expressed the view that, if the Meuse were not reached by the third day of the offensive and if possible bridgeheads over the river secured, the whole plan could be considered to have failed. Jodl disagreed and argued that five or six days could be allowed for this first phase. As we have seen, on the following two days Hitler treated his commanders to an estimate of both the political and military positions in which they found themselves. He declared that both were favourable. 'We are now carrying on the war from a situation which gives us every possibility of holding out and sticking it through, particularly if we can eliminate the danger here in the West.'

The reaction of those chosen to do the eliminating varied in detail but not in essentials. After Hitler's lecture was over, von Rundstedt, it is true, attempted to speak up for the generals' loyalty, and in spite of his real beliefs, announced to them in the Führer's presence that they could not fail because they were staking their last card. Yet in reality he took little more than a nominal and formal interest in the operation. 'He was expected,' said Blumentritt who was his Chief of Staff before Westphal, 'to carry out the offensive in a mechanical way in accordance with the Führer's operation orders . . . without being able to interfere in any way himself.' His attitude was best summed up by a gesture that Westphal recalled. 'Just before the offensive was carried out Hitler and Rundstedt met and Hitler said to Rundstedt, who had put forward his objections: "I think I am a better judge of this than you are, Field Marshal. I have come here to help you." Rundstedt turned on his heel and walked away.' Model's view of the thing, however often he reiterated his loyalty to Hitler and the plan, was contained in a conversation he had with Colonel von der Heydte who had been chosen by the Führer to command a parachute operation to assist 6th Panzer Army's advance by securing bridges or road junctions in their path. In talking over the matter with Model on 12 December, von der Heydte gave his parachute drop a ten per cent chance of success. Model's reply was that since the entire offensive had no greater chance, the attempt must be made. The offensive, he maintained, was the last remaining option for concluding the war favourably. If therefore they did not make the most of it, only certain defeat faced their country. Von der Heydte's next conversation was with Dietrich, commanding 6th Panzer Army, at Münstereifel, only a few miles to the south of Model's head-quarters. Model might be rough and ready. Dietrich was more so. He at first refused to give von der Heydte a mission until he knew what the parachute force could do; he then disclaimed all pretensions about being a prophet in estimating the location and likely reaction of United States reserves, adding that behind their front line there were nothing but 'bank clerks and Jewish hoodlums'; finally when asked for carrier pigeons, he shouted that he was not running a zoo and that if he, Dietrich, could lead an entire Panzer Army without pigeons, surely von der Heydte could command a mere battle group without them. Far more revealing than this exchange was the mission that General Kraemer, Dietrich's Chief of Staff, did in fact give to the parachute force. The primary task presupposed that 6th Panzer Army would seize Liège or the bridges over the Meuse to the south of Liège, *on the first day of the attack.* Heydte's force would therefore be required to drop before dawn on that day about eight miles north of Malmedy to secure bridges in the Ambleve river or Amay area on the following morning. Heydte also obtained the necessary coordinating instructions to ensure that his operations and those of Skorzeny did not clash. The optimism implied by these instructions was not shared by the other Panzer Army Commander, von Manteuffel. Whilst consoling himself with the thought that perhaps Hitler really did have intelligence about the enemy, which in spite of all appearances to the contrary augured well for the operation, and leaving aside the big picture, as a commander it was with his own shortage of troops and equipment that he was principally concerned, together with the all-important question of *speed* in reaching the Meuse. 'I imagined', Manteuffel observed later,

11 - 12 *German troops attack*

13 *US prisoners move into captivity as panzer advances*

that Hitler must realize that a rapid advance would not be possible under winter conditions ... but from what I have heard since it is clear that Hitler thought the advance could go much quicker than it did. The Meuse could not possibly have been reached on the second or third day as Jodl expected. He and Keitel tended to encourage Hitler's optimistic illusions.

Before we see how these illusions turned into delusions, we will do well to remind ourselves first what the essentials of the actual plan were, second that, as Moltke observed, no plan survives contact with the enemy. The plan as modified by actual availability of forces on the day was broadly this. Three armies containing seven panzer and 15 infantry divisions, were to attack on a frontage of 50-60 miles between Monschau and Echternach. 6th Panzer Army with nine divisions, including 1st and 2nd SS Panzer Corps (of four panzer divisions) was to make the main effort, cross the Meuse near Liège at Huy and Andenne and drive on to capture Antwerp and the line of the Albert Canal; this advance was to be supported by the parachute operations of von der Heydte and by Skorzeny's Trojan Horse troops. 5th Panzer Army in the centre with eight divisions, including 2nd and 116th Panzer and the Panzer Lehr Division, would advance to and cross the Meuse between Namur and Dinant, then turn northwest to Brussels. 7th Army of five divisions was to guard the southern flank by putting out a line of infantry divisions from Luxembourg to Givet. In addition to these 22 divisions, Hitler had hoped to have about nine divisions in reserve, but in the event he had more like four. The artillery support would include nine artillery corps, and seven *Werfer* or mortar brigades plus the guns already deployed in the line. Later in the operation 15th Army in the north would assist by protecting 6th Panzer Army's northern flank. Finally Army Group H would cooperate in destroying what was left of the Allied armies in the north.

As for mere numbers nearly a quarter of a million German troops with about 700 tanks and supported by 2,000 guns would be attacking about 80,000 Americans with about 250 tanks and roughly 500 guns. Two of the basic ingredients of blitzkrieg, therefore, would be on parade. Concentration was there; surprise was there. All would turn on the third ingredient—speed. And this in turn would be determined by a fourth element fundamental

F

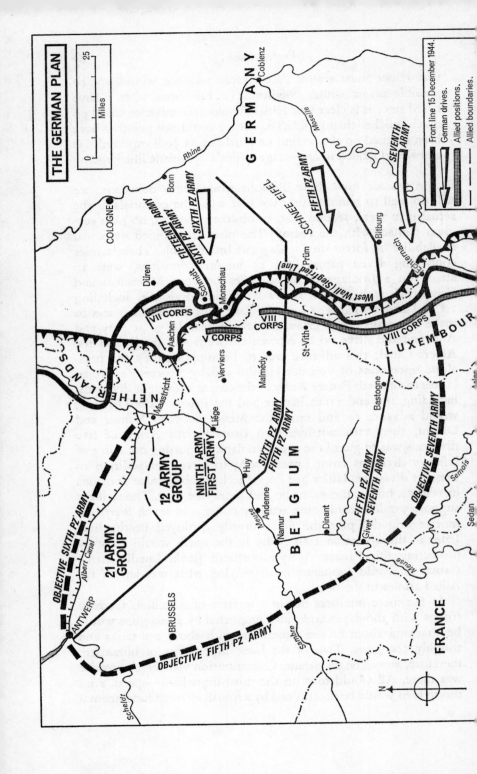

THE GERMAN PLAN

Front line 15 December 1944.
German drives.
Allied positions.
Allied boundaries.

25
Miles
0

GERMANY

Coblenz

Rhine

Moselle

SEVENTH ARMY

Bonn

FIFTH PZ ARMY

SCHNEE EIFEL

Bitburg

COLOGNE

SIXTH PZ ARMY

FIFTEENTH ARMY

Prüm

Echternach

Düren

Schmidt

Monschau

West Wall (Siegfried Line)

VII CORPS

Aachen

V CORPS

VIII CORPS

St-Vith

VIII CORPS

LUXEMBOURG

NETHERLANDS

Maastricht

Verviers

Malmédy

Liège

Bastogne

OBJECTIVE SIXTH PZ ARMY

Huy

SIXTH PZ ARMY

FIFTH PZ ARMY

OBJECTIVE SEVENTH ARMY

NINTH ARMY
FIRST ARMY

12 ARMY
GROUP

Meuse

Andenne

Semois

21 ARMY
GROUP

Namur

Dinant

FIFTH PZ ARMY
SEVENTH ARMY

Givet

Sedan

BELGIUM

Albert Canal

Meuse

ANTWERP

BRUSSELS

Sambre

FRANCE

OBJECTIVE FIFTH PZ ARMY

Scheldt

N

to the whole concept—flexibility, the keeping of an open mind, readiness to reinforce success anywhere it appeared, the ruthless searching out and exploitation of weak spots, the turning of initial penetration into a flood of panzer teams which would drive on relentlessly to disrupt and dismay the enemy's command posts, gun positions, reserve and supply areas. Yet although speed of a sort was with the Germans for a day or two, flexibility was not. It was wholly absent, was indeed expressly forbidden by the Führer's own handwritten '*Nicht abändern*', his insistence on sticking to the detailed pre-planned programme. His fixed idea—that 6th Panzer Army would be the spearhead, no matter what contact with the enemy revealed, and that 5th Panzer Army would, come what may, be the subsidiary thrust—was fatal to the enterprise. With flexibility chucked away, speed quickly forsook the assaulting armies. Once this was so and the panzers began to flounder either because of shortage of petrol or because of an abundance of opposition, the field was lost.

The actual battle is best considered first as a whole and then piecemeal, rather than as a continuous and comprehensive story. For it was extremely complex, or, as Montgomery put it, one of the trickiest battles he had ever handled—not that he did in fact handle it until the Germans had already so mishandled it that from their point of view, it could no longer be won.

In a summary of the battle it is the activities of the two Panzer Armies which matter, for these were the assaulting formations with the most distant objectives. In some respects it appeared that 6th Panzer Army had the easier task, at least to start with. Its initial objective, the Meuse, was nearer, its front narrower and its strength greater. There were five infantry divisions with which to break through the American lines between Rötgen and Losheim and four SS panzer divisions fully up to strength and of unquestionable skill and dash to exploit to the Meuse and beyond. In the way of their advance was one of the two features referred to earlier—the Hohes Venn, high, wooded and swampy. Dietrich, or rather Kraemer, who did all his thinking for him, estimated that four days would be needed actually to have established bridgeheads over the Meuse. Broadly speaking the plan was for the main effort to be made in the south of Dietrich's sector at the Losheim Gap. 3rd Parachute, 12th and 277th Volksgrenadier Divisions would make the hole, through which 1st SS and 12th SS Panzer Divisions of 1st SS Panzer Corps (very much formations

of the Führer for the former was Leibstandarte Adolf Hitler and
the latter Hitler Jugend) would drive to the Meuse either side of
Liège; 2nd Panzer Corps would then take on the advance to
Antwerp; meanwhile 67th Infantry Corps attacking further north
near Monschau would protect the right flank. Manteuffel's 5th
Panzer Army had a broader front, fewer divisions and further
to go to reach the Meuse. On his front too was not only the
other difficult feature mentioned earlier, Schnee Eifel, but also the
two critical road centres, St Vith and Bastogne. Manteuffel's
intention was that von Lüttwitz, commanding 47 Panzer Corps,
which contained both 2 Panzer and Panzer Lehr Divisions, would
cross the Our south of Dasburg, seize Clerf and Wiltz, drive on
to Bastogne, and so to the Meuse south of Namur. Meanwhile
Krüger's 58 Panzer Corps which contained only one panzer
division, the 116th, was to cross the Our further north, take
Houffalize and push on across the River Ourthe to the Meuse
north of Namur. The Schnee Eifel itself (which was held by
106th US Infantry Division) would be dealt with by the 66th
Infantry Corps, under General Lucht, who would also capture
St Vith and so help to protect 5th Panzer Army's right flank.

This was the outline plan. The battle itself may be conveniently
divided into three general parts: first the initial German attempt
to reach the Meuse on 16-20 December; next further German
advances plus the struggle for St Vith and Bastogne from 20
December to Christmas Day; last from Christmas Day until
Hitler called off the offensive on 8 January, a period when the
last desperate German efforts were made, and the Allied counter-
attacks got under way, resulting in Army Group B's defeat and
retreat. It is with these three broad divisions that the next three
chapters will deal.

On the evening of 15 December the Führer telephoned to
Model. His final decisions had been made, he told the Field
Marshal. Everything in the way of preparation had been done to
ensure the operation's success. Now it depended on leadership
and the actual conduct of the battle. It was therefore up to Model
and his subordinates. Even while making this point Hitler did
not fail to add that Dietrich's Panzer Corps must not get involved
in fighting along the northern flank or get confused with the
action of 66th Infantry Corps to the south. Freedom of action
was all. Yet it was precisely this freedom that Hitler had already
denied and was to persist in denying his subordinates. Further-

more Dietrich must have priority in the use of roads. If his, Hitler's, instructions were followed properly, a major success was assured. Indeed everything pointed to victory. Model duly passed on these instructions to Dietrich.

Herbstnebel, Autumn Mist, was about to start. The season of mists had long since arrived and was, as Hitler had predicted, staying put. The fateful year of 1944 was mellow indeed. For Hitler and the Wehrmacht, would it be fruitful too?

6

Autumn Mist—
The First Four Days

Now it is autumn and the falling fruit . . .
The grim frost is at hand . . .
And death is on the air like a smell of ashes!
Ah! Can't you smell it?
                                    D. H. Lawrence

What is a battle like? It is a question which most soldiers ask
themselves when they know that they are about to be committed
to one. The answer, of course, depends largely on your positioning—both in time and in space. That is to say, whereas in Wellington's day it was just possible for a single man during a single day
to view an entire field of battle and comprehend its development
simply because it was so confined in both time and space, a modern
battle is an epilogue to the operations which have just preceded it
and a prologue for those still to come, in a theatre of operations
moreover which may embrace a complete continent. The modern
battle is just too large and too long to be thus comprehended—
until long afterwards. Even then its exact nature and course are
not always readily identifiable. Rather it is a campaign which
forms a coherent whole. Yet each campaign has its phases.
Overlord which lasted almost a year can be roughly divided into
five—the battle for Normandy, the autumn stalemate, the
Ardennes counter-offensive, closing up to the Rhine, and the
overrunning of Germany. Such a broad division might have some
meaning for those concerned with command and staff work at the
high level—Corps, Army and above. For those in divisions, above
all for those in the units which do the actual fighting, the mosaic
has a far less disciplined pattern. For them, the infantryman, the
tank crew, the sapper, the gunner, the signaller and the truck
driver, there are a series of uncoordinated and unforgettable

periods of intense excitement, discomfort, activity, apprehension and sometimes triumph. While most of them might on reflection agree with Rosenstock-Huessy's point that three-quarters of a soldier's life is spent in aimlessly waiting about, it is the other quarter which they remember, with advantages. The great secret of getting through a battle without having to undergo disagreeable moments of introspection is to be busy, so busy thinking of what to do, how to do it, how to make sure it is done and then actually doing it, that there is little time for concern about oneself. But while such industry and commitment are easy at the level of almost any headquarters from battalion or regiment upwards, for those who pull the triggers, advance into hostile country, get the bullets and shells fired at them, make the critical low-level decisions which turn operation orders from mere pieces of paper or groups of words into reality, this total preoccupation with every minute of the night and day is less easy to accomplish. Even in the thick of a battle there is a good deal of aimless waiting about, or so it often seems.

When the layman reads or hears that such and such an infantry division has launched an attack on some point or other or that an armoured division has broken out and is conducting pursuit operations against enemy rearguards, he is apt to harbour a picture of massed infantry sweeping across open ground storming and taking all before them, or great phalanxes of tanks charging about with their guns belching flame and dismaying their adversaries into surrender or flight. It is not like that at all. A British infantry division in the last war had three brigades. An attack would probably be made by two of them, with the third in reserve. Each brigade in a comparable way would customarily despatch two of its three battalions in attack, and keep one in hand. So in turn would the battalions deploy their companies, the companies their platoons, and the platoons their sections. Each section, if it were up to strength (and few were after being in action for a day or two) contained 9 or 10 men. So that in terms of fighting soldiers, wielding rifles or light machine guns or grenades, and actually closing with the enemy, we are dealing with comparatively small numbers. The division's attack would be made with four battalions up, that is eight companies, 16 platoons, 32 sections— so that its leading echelon would contain only 300 men, out of a total perhaps of 20,000 in the division as a whole. A division would deploy in a comparable way if it were occupying a defensive position. This sort of arithmetic helps us to understand what Horrocks meant when he said that the front is a very small club. And it helps us to understand too—even though we may be talking of 20 divisions attacking and encountering a mere four or five divisions in defence—how small groups of determined soldiers can do great things on either side in a battle. In a similar way we should be aware that the sweeping forward of a panzer division may in real terms, particularly over country where the going is difficult, the roads and tracks few and far between, mean that only one panzer battalion, perhaps two companies in all, are in the lead. Of these two companies, only a handful of tanks will actually be able to make use of their basic tactical recipe of fire and movement to engage the enemy closely, and so overcome defences, knock out anti-tank guns, find and destroy artillery pieces, defeat the challenging tank destroyers and enemy tanks, and eventually open the door for the following up panzers to pour through and advance without fear of interruption. It was for this reason that during the European battles whether the axes of advance for Allied armour were in Italy, the *bocage* of Normandy or the hills and valleys of the Ardennes, there were times when a very few of the Germans' formidable Panther and Tiger tanks were able to prevent the advance of complete armoured divisions. So in reverse during the Ardennes offensive, it is necessary to put the total number of seven panzer divisions into perspective. The actual number of panzers which would confront the American defenders, because of the nature of the country and the nature of the defence which the Americans chose to conduct, was small in relation to the total available.*

And then as both Field Marshal Slim and Fred Majdalany have in their very different ways pointed out, the account of a battle as it appears in an official despatch or a newspaper report would be almost unrecognizable to the soldier who had taken part in the operation as an accurate description of what had happened to him. 'It comes as a genuine surprise to him', wrote the latter, 'to discover that the day the orders were changed three times in as many hours, and his unit eventually spent three days kicking their heels in a muddy farm area without a notion of what was

---

* In Italy when in August 1944 it was thought that the Gothic Line had been breached and the 1st British Armoured Division was 'launched' through the gap, only to come to a grinding halt within a single day, the launching initially took place on the frontage of a single tank—my own.

happening, he was a reserve being "poured in": it is difficult for Trooper Jones to grasp that on that unhappy morning when all but two tanks in his squadron were knocked out, he was part of a "great armoured breakthrough". It is no easier for a lonely platoon commander, recollecting in tranquillity a shambles in which his company commander dispatched him into the night without any clear orders about what he was to do, to realize that he was nevertheless an important contributor to a "three-point thrust".'

If the soldier and the junior commander have little idea of what is happening to themselves and their own unit, how much smaller still will be their understanding of what those units on the flanks are up to.* Small wonder, since the orders to all are constantly being revised to such an extent that if one wanted to point to a single feature of armoured and infantry battles during the Second World War which was consistent, uninterrupted and omnipresent, it would be the insatiable appetite of commanders at all levels for chopping and changing. This in turn meant delay—delay in making decisions, delay in transmitting orders, delay in preparing to obey them, delay in actually carrying them out. It was no surprise that the expectancy of danger was only partially mitigated by endlessly hanging about. Such is the nature of a battle.

If there was one thing that the troops of Middleton's VIII US Corps were expecting in mid-December of 1944, it was not a battle. Robert Merriam, who was there, called it a 'a ghost front, a phoney sector'. VIII Corps had four divisions, three infantry, 4th, 28th and 106th, each deployed forward holding some 25 miles of front, and 9th Armoured Division together with a reconnaissance regiment spread out to support the infantry. To Middleton's north was part of Gerow's V US Corps with two infantry divisions in the Monschau–Bütgenbach area of the Ardennes. This last sector was the only part of the Ardennes in any sense firmly held, for Middleton's total frontage, nearly 90

---

* I have always admired the answer given to me by the Commanding Officer of a New Zealand infantry battalion when, as his supporting armoured commander during one of the Italian battles, I asked him what the situation was. 'Fluid', was his succinct and accurate reply, a euphemism for 'No idea'. A few moments later I received over the radio one of the less encouraging messages I had during that particular battle from my own superior commander: 'Enemy SP guns moving towards you now. OUT.' My immediate and heated demand for the intruders to be engaged by the entire divisional artillery was ignored.

miles, was so broad that one of 9th Armoured Division's combat
commands was actually holding a position in the line, as was also
part of the reconnaissance regiment. He had therefore almost
nothing in reserve. What is more 106th Infantry Division, fresh
from the United States, had only taken over its positions in the
Schnee Eifel on 10 December. 9th Armoured Division was also
inexperienced while 4th and 28th Divisions had suffered heavily
in the Hürtgen Forest battles. In short, Bradley was using the
Ardennes to rest formations which had had a lot of recent
fighting and to introduce new ones to the rigours of war. If he
failed in the former purpose, he certainly succeeded in the latter.
Because of his frontage, Middleton had no proper system of
mutually supporting dug-in defensive positions in depth, but
rather a series of widely separated defended points strung out
along river lines, such as the Our, with large gaps between
them, gaps which often included the roads themselves.

Army Group B's estimate of Middleton's defensive system
was about right—no continuous main defensive position, but a
series of strongpoints throughout a depth of some five kilometres;
the strongpoints had plenty of hardware, tanks, anti-tank guns,
mortars, and units were mostly fully motorized; a few scattered
reserves of battalion group size were available to counter-attack.
Such a system of defence could not be manipulated as a whole in
accordance with some master plan. There was only one way in
which it could give an account of itself—uncoordinated fighting
by each strongpoint, and in the event this is what happened.

If therefore the US forces were materially at a disadvantage, in
respect of morale too—for the whole philosophy of the US Army
was one of training for powerfully supported, improvised and
speedy attack, not for dogged, patient defence—they were poorly
placed. Inactivity bred ill-preparedness. Merriam recalled riding
about in a jeep near the front line east of Wiltz a few weeks before
the battle started:

All was peaceful; farmers in the fields along the road were
ploughing for the winter fallow, and some were taking in the
last of the harvest, cattle were grazing lazily . . . we were
riding along the lip of a huge ridge, silhouetted in plain view
of an enemy not more than eight hundred yards away, guns of
the West Wall supposedly bristling behind every bush, and
nothing happened.

All was quiet on the Western front, and on 10 December 1st Army's Intelligence officer in referring to the quiet sector opposite VIII US Corps inferred that the German formations in the line there were being prepared for despatch to more active fronts. It would not be long, however, before this particular front was active enough to satisfy even the most ardent fighting man.

Whatever the state of mind of the American soldiers—and there was no doubting either their confidence in victory or their resolution in a fight—it hardly matched the exalted fanaticism of a young Nazi commander in 12th SS Panzer Division (Hitler Jugend) as expressed in a letter written to his sister on the night 15/16 December.

> I write during one of the great hours before an attack—full of excitement, full of expectation of what the next days will bring. Everyone who has been here the last two days and nights, who has witnessed hour after hour the assembly of our crack divisions, who has heard the constant rattling of panzers, knows that something is up. Some believe in living, but life is not everything! It is enough to know that we attack, and will throw the enemy from our homeland. It is a holy task. Overhead is the terrific noise of V1s and artillery, the voice of war.

His reference to the holy task was a reflection of von Rundstedt's Order of the Day when he had referred to the 'holy obligation to give everything to achieve things beyond human possibilities for our Fatherland and Führer'. Model complemented this order by claiming that no soldiers in the world could be better than those of Army Group B. Von Manteuffel's exhortation was more practical—'Forward double time'.

Before dawn broke on the morning of 16 December 1944 nearly 20 German divisions were on the move through the Eifel woods and mists towards Gerow's and Middleton's Corps. The noise of their movement was drowned by the V1s which roared overhead whilst at H-hour, 5.30 a.m., two thousand German guns began to shell the American positions all along the front. In spite of the fact the battle was to continue for a further three weeks, it was really decided in the first four days, that is to say it was determined by the spontaneous defensive action of Bradley's armies, no matter how little influence he himself may have had on it.

The principal thrust by 6th Panzer Army, except for the ad-

vance of one panzer group commanded by Colonel Jochen Peiper
of 1st SS Panzer Division as far as Stavelot and beyond to the
River Salm, was virtually defeated by the defensive action of US
V Corps at Monschau and Elsenborn, later reinforced by the US
VII Corps.

One of the most important initial objectives for the Germans
in the north, where the main effort was to be made, and which
as the crow flies was nearer to their final target of Antwerp than
any other, was the Elsenborn Ridge. It was an objective allotted
to the 277 Volksgrenadier and 12th SS Panzer Divisions.
Curiously enough this was the only area of the entire frontage
for the Ardennes offensive where, as it began, the Americans were
themselves conducting an attack. The US formations involved
were the 2nd and 99th Infantry Divisions, both part of US V
Corps. While 99th Division held the left part of the Ardennes
sector and was spread over about 12 miles of front, 2nd Division,
supported by one regiment of the 99th, had begun a drive directed
on the Roer Dams three days before the German assault started.
This unexpected concentration of US forces at one of the critical
shoulders of their planned advance was one of the many factors
which contributed to the German failure in that area. Equally
influential, although working for the Germans, not against them,
was the fact that immediately to the south, between the two
Corps, V and VIII, there was a hole in the US defending forces
which coincided almost precisely with the Losheim Gap—one
of the axes for 1st SS Panzer Division. With the exception of this
latter attack at the Losheim Gap, the German assaulting troops
were largely held. There was to start with a fatal lack of concentration on the part of the attackers—both of numbers and of their
sometime substitute, firepower. On the front of the 393rd and
394th US Infantry Regiments, prolonged infantry fighting and
heavy casualties on both sides did not yield the sort of result
which could allow the waiting panzers to push forward. The
3rd Battalion of 394th Regiment, for example, was positioned
near Buckholz, a mere two miles from the Belgian-German
frontier, and at breakfast time on 16 December while the men of
one company belonging to this battalion were about to eat their
breakfast, they suddenly became aware that they were being
attacked. A fierce fire fight broke out, the Americans fortunately
being able to call on the support of both mortars and tank destroyers, which together with the arrival of a fourth company effectively

stopped the German advance. Further north a battalion of 393rd Regiment was right up against the West Wall, deployed at the eastern end of a forest behind which ran the tactically important villages of Rocherath and Krinkelt—part of the Elsenborn Ridge. The combination of an extremely heavy German artillery bombardment with a cleverly timed assault by grenadiers succeeded in pushing the Americans back to a small perimeter further west, but there they held on. The movement forward from the Elsenborn Ridge itself by a reserve regiment of 2nd Division, and its later replacement there by another regiment from the 1st US Division meant not only that the 99th Division's front was holding firm, however precariously, but that in addition some depth was being given to the position.

All this had its effect. The tanks of 1st SS Panzer Corps were seriously delayed and Skorzeny's columns, designed to sow dismay everywhere and reach the Meuse bridges in order to hold them open for the panzers, simply could not get forward. All Hitler's talk of reaching the Meuse in two days was turning out to be the myth that von Rundstedt had predicted it would be. Already the roads behind the assaulting infantry divisions were becoming jammed with tanks and trucks. There had been plenty of violent fighting. But the two requirements inherent to successful breakthrough—substantial gaining of ground and a collapse of the defences—had not materialized.

Limited attacks by the 2nd US Infantry Division to the south east of Monschau, although their original design had to be abandoned, completely threw out of gear Dietrich's plans for establishing a hard shoulder on his right flank. Not only did some of his assaulting formations get pinned down in countering the unwelcome American attack, but this engagement itself further disrupted the movement of other formations, so that the strength available to General Hirtzfeld, commanding the German LXXII Corps, to overwhelm Monschau and seize villages astride the Eupen road was reduced to something like a quarter of what had been counted on. Nonetheless the 3rd Battalion of the US 390th Infantry Regiment, which was occupying a defensive position near Höfen, and a squadron of reconnaissance troops with machine-guns, supported by artillery, mortars and anti-tank guns situated to the north of Monschau on the extreme left of the Ardennes defensive line, were subjected to serious attacks by the assaulting troops of 326th Volksgrenadier Division. The German soldiers were courageous to the point of foolhardiness and suffered many casualties from point-blank machine-gun and anti-tank gun fire, as well as supporting mortars and field artillery. The 326th Volksgrenadier Division lost about a quarter of its fighting strength without gaining the ground which the battle had been all about. It was as unexpected a setback on the northern flank as it was to be on the southern, and far more grave since it was here in the north that the principal thrust was intended and here too that Hitler insisted on Dietrich's continuing to bang away until he had lost all the advantages of time, concentration and surprise.

In the extreme south 7th Army failed to reach its objectives and continued to fail. Brandenberger's Army was necessarily much weaker than the two Panzer Armies operating to the north. For the assault its two corps had only four divisions available, none of which were panzer divisions, indeed none of which, in spite of von Manteuffel's pleading, for he obviously wanted his left flank to be properly protected and screened, contained any tanks at all. Brandenberger had to be content with about 30 self-propelled guns and normal artillery support plus a number of special rocket launchers and 120mm guns. His right-hand or northern Corps, the LXXXV, contained two divisions. 5 Parachute Division's task was to advance to the left of Manteuffel's armoured columns and provide them with close flank security at Wiltz, Bastogne, and further west at Neufchâteau and Givet. 352 Volksgrenadier Division was to cross the Our, dispose of the American units in its path and then turn south to assist Brandenberger's other Corps, the LXXX, in establishing a major firm base for the southern shoulder. LXXX Corps had two Volksgrenadier Divisions, 212 and 276, and their initial attacks were to be across the Sauer at Echternach and to the south of Wallendorf.

Opposite 7th Army were elements of two US Infantry Divisions. In the north was the 28th, whose headquarters was at Wiltz and which had deployed the 109th Infantry Regiment opposite 5th Parachute and 352 Volksgrenadier Division; further south was 4th US Infantry Division, with its 12th Infantry Regiment deployed forward and supported by a combat command of 10th US Armoured Division. The German attacks and the American reaction to them were typical of the many mini-battles which took place elsewhere along the front—initial surprise and success by the attacking forces giving way to stubborn, improvised defensive action which took the steam out of the German advance. The 12th US Infantry Regiment, for example, stretched as it was over 10 miles—far too wide for any properly co-ordinated and mutually supporting defence in depth—had its companies strung out in the front line occupying the wooded hills and cliffs which overlooked the River Sauer between themselves and the Germans. Having suffered heavily in the sterile and costly Hürtgen Forest battles, well below strength, with much of their equipment under repair, they were looking forward to a period of rest and recuperation in this reputedly quiet sector of the front. Four days after they had taken over, the storm burst over them. Many of their outposts were quickly overrun by the Germans, but others, in spite of shortages of ammunition and supplies and in spite also of being out of touch with their superior headquarters, fought on from naturally strong positions, such as stone farm houses, and were greatly influential in slowing down and halting the enemy. The battle developed into a to-and-fro affair. The 423rd Volksgrenadier Regiment which had crossed the Sauer west of Echternach succeeded in reaching Berdorf and even Lauerborn, a village directly on the road between Echternach and Junglister, the latter being a major German objective on their way to the city of Luxembourg itself. The US reactions to these moves underlined both the deficiency of anti-tank guns which handicapped the German grenadiers and the steps they took to compensate for this de-ficiency. When the Commander of 4th US Division, Major-General Barton, despatched a small company group of infantry and tanks to retake Lauerborn and Berdorf, he succeeded with the former simply because the German grenadier troops there could not take on the American tanks. Yet in Berdorf by organizing a defence of bazooka/machine-gun teams, the Germans defeated the American counter-attack.

The Americans made excellent use of what artillery they had available. In spite of having lost all their former observation of the River Sauer because their forward positions had been over-run, with the aid of aerial observation officers in light aircraft they brought down heavy concentrations not only on the assaulting German infantry teams, and their immediately follow-ing up reserves who had crossed the river under the cover of darkness, but much more critically important on the German pioneer troops who were attempting to bridge the river itself and so allow the passage of the heavier supporting weapons, the assault guns and mortars, which could have redressed the balance of the American superiority of tanks. This in turn allowed the US infantry and tank teams to keep the Germans at bay and prevent their reaching the main US divisional gun areas near the tactically important Schlamm Bach feature some miles to the south-west of Echternach. Here were real illustrations of how widely separated elements of the same formation cooperated to make each more effective.

Between the 12th Infantry Regiment and the most southerly elements of the 109th Infantry Regiment of 28th US Infantry Division, was an armoured Infantry battalion, the 60th, belonging to 9th Armoured Division, and which included in its equipment a number of light anti-tank guns and howitzers. German battalions from 276 Volksgrenadier Division tried to outflank and surround the 60th Armoured Infantry Battalion, but the pattern was similar here to that further south. Skilful use of artillery, both on forward German positions and on the Sauer crossing places, help from the mortars and machine-guns of US flanking formations, particularly from the hills where 109th US Infantry Regiment had good observation over the battlefield, the throwing in of small parties of tanks, self-propelled guns and armoured cars to meet a local threat, and deploying the reserve infantry company in a counter-penetration role—all these measures enabled the 60th Armoured Infantry to hold on. It was an interesting example of how numerically inferior infantry units, by virtue of getting proper support from artillery and tanks were able to hold off superior numbers of infantry which lacked this very support. It was the same sort of story further north still when the 352 Volksgrenadier Division came up against the 109th US Infantry Regiment who succeeded in checking their advance in the area of Diekirch. The most northerly of 7th Army's attacks, too, those by 5th Parachute Division, had made disappointing progress.

There was in short no part of Brandenberger's Army which had succeeded in capturing its initial objectives. After four days the situation would not be much better, and 7th Army's front line would have reached only as far as from Waldbillig in the extreme south, some five miles into formerly Allied held territory, to the environs of Wiltz, a town which the Americans lost on the fourth day, about eight miles east of Bastogne.

East of Bastogne—think of it! Givet, the most western part of

14   *Peiper force*

15   *Defending US troops manhandle anti-tank gun*

16 *Knocked-out Panther*

17 *Stavelot petrol dump destroyed to prevent German capture*

7th Army's original objective is some 40 miles to the *west* of Bastogne. However unachievable that might have been, had the 7th Army done no more than establish themselves in some strength astride the Arlon–Bastogne road during these first four vital days —that is astride the very axis which Patton was later to use for his drive to relieve Bastogne—how different could have been the behaviour of those troops of von Manteuffel's Army, for whom Brandenberger was supposed to be providing flank protection, and how different would have been the task which Patton was later set. Had Brandenberger actually accomplished his primary mission, it might even have been the case that those first American reinforcements to be despatched to Bastogne—the elements of 101st Airborne Division and 10th Armoured Division—would have become entangled with 5th German Parachute Division, and resulted in the rapid fall of Bastogne itself.

But Brandenberger's failure meant that 5th Panzer Army's southern flank was never properly protected. American reinforcement of and holding of Bastogne was the result. Thus the faltering of a subsidiary attack marred the chances of a main one. Yet to start with, 5th Panzer Army had greater success than either of the other two.

In these first days they encircled the Schnee Eifel, opened the road to St Vith, crossed the Our and reached Houffalize. But the capture of St Vith and Bastogne eluded them. Moreover Army Group B's initial objective, the Meuse, was still 20-30 miles distant, and this after *four* days. There were two main reasons for the Americans' success in breaking the back of the offensive even before a proper defensive plan had been made to do so. The first was that individual commanders of the various key points in the Ardennes defences themselves showed both skill and tenacity in hanging on, despite supply difficulties and lack of overall direction, in blowing bridges, burning petrol dumps, blocking road positions and generally taking just the right sort of action to slow down the advancing panzers. The second point was that piecemeal though reinforcements might have been, they moved fast and in some cases to exactly the places which were to have a profound influence on the battle. For example, during the first four days Eisenhower ordered first two armoured divisions to intervene at St Vith and on the southern flank, then two reserve airborne divisions to Bastogne (only one of which got there), next two more divisions to reinforce Bradley's Army Group.

G

Meanwhile Patton's Saar offensive was cancelled and first one corps, then another, from his 3rd Army diverted to concentrate against the German advance. It is, however, not so much the moves in the game which are of principal interest, but rather the way they came about, that is to say the reasoning of the Allied commanders which gave rise to them. Similarly it is the reaction of the German commanders to their tantalizing glimpses of success mixed with a growing apprehension that the game was beginning to go wrong, even after only four days, which commands our attention.

On 16 December Bradley and Eisenhower were conferring at Versailles when first reports of the German attack reached them. Bradley at first judged it to be a spoiling attack to interfere with Patton's operations further south, but Eisenhower recorded his instant conviction that this was no local offensive. The immediate precautions they agreed on were to move 7th Armoured Division commanded by Hasbrouck from a rest area near Aachen, and 10th Armoured Division from Patton's Army. Hasbrouck's division went to St Vith where it became the rock on which the town's defences rested. One combat command of 10th Armoured Division made its way to Bastogne where it supported 101st Airborne Division in a defensive action which perhaps more than any other single one wrote finis to Hitler's hopes. These rapid and almost capricious reinforcements were decisive in influencing the further course of the battle. For before long and despite further advances by 5th Panzer Army, the Ardennes battle was to become the battle for St Vith and the battle for Bastogne.

It seemed therefore that the initial US decisions, however hapazardly they were arrived at, and however short they may have fallen of a comprehensive plan to defeat the German attack, were not faulty. Could the same be said of the German commanders?

As early as the evening of 16 December, von Rundstedt, in briefing Hitler at Adlershorst reiterated the pessimism he had shown throughout the planning stages by pointing to 6th Panzer Army's failure to make progress. He added that in spite of Manteuffel's success with 5th Panzer Army it was *already* too late to shift the main weight of the attack further south—a remarkable statement and obviously a false one, when we consider that this was exactly what was done some days later. What he should have said was that now was the moment to switch the

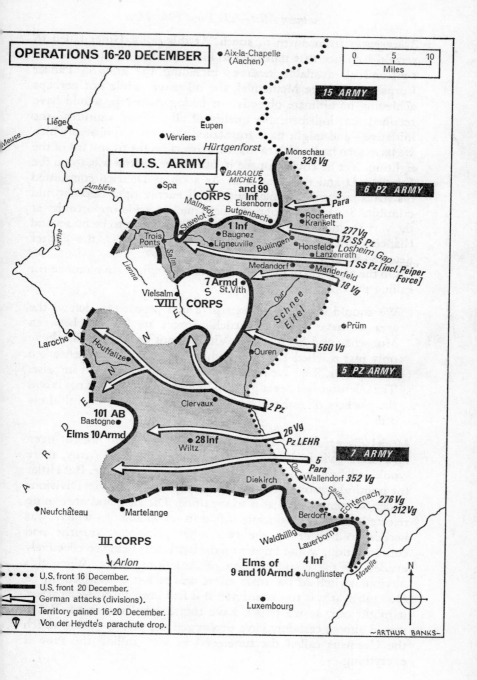

OPERATIONS 16-20 DECEMBER

Aix-la-Chapelle (Aachen)

0 ___ 5 ___ 10
Miles

Liége

Meuse

Verviers

Eupen

Hürtgenforst

1 U.S. ARMY

Monschau *326 Vg*

15 ARMY

Ambléve

Spa

BARAQUE MICHEL **2 and 99 Inf**

V CORPS

Malmédy

Elsenborn

Butgenbach

3 Para

6 PZ ARMY

Rocherath
Krankelt

Stavelot

1 Inf

Baugnez

Ligneuville

Buílingen

Honsfeld

Lanzenrath

*277 Vg
12 SS Pz*

Losheim Gap

1 SS Pz [incl. Peiper Force]

Trois Ponts

Salm

Medandorf

Manderfeld

18 Vg

Lienne

Vielsalm

7 Armd

St. Vith

VIII S E CORPS

Schnee Eifel

Our

Prüm

Laroche

Houffalize

N

Ouren

560 Vg

5 PZ ARMY

Clervaux

2 Pz

101 AB

Bastogne

Elms 10 Armd

28 Inf

Wiltz

26 Vg

Pz LEHR

5 Para

Diekirch

Wallendorf *352 Vg*

7 ARMY

Our

Sûre

Neufchâteau

Martelange

Berdorf

Echternach

276 Vg

212 Vg

III CORPS

Arlon

Waldbillig

Lauerborn

Elms of 9 and 10 Armd

4 Inf

Junglinster

Moselle

N

Luxembourg

- - - - U.S. front 16 December.
▬▬▬ U.S. front 20 December.
⬅ German attacks (divisions).
░░ Territory gained 16-20 December.
▽ Von der Heydte's parachute drop.

~ARTHUR BANKS~

Schwerpunkt from north to south. At this point Hitler failed to seize the chance that remained to him—if there and then he had switched all available reserves including the 2nd SS Panzer Corps to reinforce Manteuffel, the offensive, while not perhaps achieving its ultimate objective of taking Antwerp, would have retained that indispensable quality of all military ventures—the initiative—and might have forestalled the very US moves which we have seen had such a momentous effect on the to and fro of the fighting. Yet he could not see it. 6th Panzer Army was to be the *Schwerpunkt* and that was that. As soon as Dietrich committed his main strength, he maintained, all enemy opposition would crumble. So the great opportunist chucked aside opportunity at the very moment it beckoned to him. There were to be no second chances, although, self-deception being what it is, the Führer detected several.

On the night 18-19 December von Rundstedt again plumped for calling the operation off:

> We should abandon the offensive and prepare to defend the area we have gained. Dietrich's forces are held up between Monschau and Malmedy. St Vith has not been taken. We have only just reached Bastogne, which ought to have been taken on D plus 1. We have not made the most of our initial surprise. The offensive has never gathered speed, due to the icy roads and the pockets of resistance which forced us to lay on full-dress attacks.

Model disagreed and considered that if the main weight even now were switched to Manteuffel and 5th Panzer Army, there would still be a chance of a breakthrough to the Meuse. But Hitler for political reasons still wished to keep his SS Panzer Divisions under SS command, that is to say under Dietrich, and once more rejected the one principle of war—adaptability—which was needed to bolster up the two other principles, surprise and concentration, whose impact on the battle was being so effectively evaded by the counter-action of American forces. When this obvious switch of the main effort was at last authorized on 20 December, it was too late. Even if it had been authorized earlier, it might not, as we noted, have transformed the scene. But it would almost certainly have prolonged the period during which the Germans called the tune, and in war, calling the tune is everything.

This dichotomy of pulls between north and south which Hitler failed to resolve was paralleled by a similar dichotomy of command on the Allied side and on the same day—19 December. On that day Eisenhower had met Bradley, Devers and Patton at Verdun. As a result Devers' 6th Army Group was to take over part of Patton's front and enable Patton to divert another corps against the Ardennes bulge. Patton, never slow with plans for a counter-attack, planned to launch it only three days later on 22 December. But it was already clear to Eisenhower that *two* Allied battles were developing—one to the south of the German penetration, one to the north, 'When it became apparent,' the Supreme Commander subsequently wrote in his report to the Combined Chiefs of Staff,

> that General Bradley's left flank was badly separated from his right flank and the situation of his own headquarters, located at Luxembourg, limited his command and communication capabilities to the area south of the penetration, I realized that it would be impracticable for him to handle the American forces both north and south of the large salient which was being created. I therefore fixed a boundary running east and west through the breach in our lines, generally on the axis Givet–Prüm. . . . All forces north of the boundary, including the major part of the US First and Ninth Armies and part of the Ninth Air Force, I placed under the operational command of Field-Marshal Montgomery and Air Marshal Coningham. . . .

And thereby hung a tale, for Montgomery as usual had a master plan. The very antithesis of the American reaction, which was to attack and never give up any ground as matter of honour, Montgomery, always provided the Germans were not allowed to threaten the—to him—vital area to the north-west of the Meuse, was content to wait until the enemy overstretched themselves, outran their resources, were halted and thus ripe for destruction. So much for the moment for the higher commanders; what about those who were doing the actual fighting?

On the United States side there were many examples of low-level resistance, determined on and executed by young lieutenants and sergeants with a handful of men and without the benefit of either inspiring direction from above or adequate artillery support from behind. In the northern section of the battlefield the village of Lanzenrath lies on the road between Losheimergruben and

Manderfeld, and a small feature to the west of the village dominates an important road junction, whose left and right forks lead respectively to Bullingen and Losheimergruben itself. It will be remembered that it was here, at the so-called Losheim gap, that Dietrich's 6th Panzer Army made a major effort. This road junction lay directly in the path of the 1st SS Panzer Division, and the critical feature was occupied on the morning of 16 December by a weak platoon numbering some eighteen men of the 394 US Infantry Regiment of 99th Division, with a section of tank destroyers from 14th Cavalry Group about a hundred yards away. Shortly before dawn on that day these men were treated to the sight of a mass of German tanks and self-propelled guns moving towards them from the ridge north of Losheim. The enemy artillery preparations so lit up the sky that the panzers were easily distinguishable. Being well dug in with good overhead cover the shelling was a shock to the men's nerves rather than their bodies, and the next sight which greeted them as the barrage moved on and first light improved visibility was hardly calculated either to strengthen their nerves or to give them much confidence that their bodies would remain intact much longer. Their supporting tank destroyers upped-sticks and went off to the west towards Bullingen.

When the platoon commander, whose task was to give warning of enemy movement or attacks in his area, reported on the radio to his regimental headquarters information about the artillery concentrations, he was told to send a patrol to Lanzenrath and report further. Choosing himself as patrol leader, he took three men with him. He found a good OP in a house in the village, and observed columns of infantry heading from the area south of Losheim north-west towards his village. On returning to his platoon position, he again reported to regimental headquarters and called for artillery to 'stonk' the road south of Lanzenrath. The response was disbelief of his report and no artillery. He continued to observe while getting his platoon ready to engage the enemy. With one .5 and two .3 Browning machine-guns and a number of automatic rifles, his firepower was not inconsiderable. What surprised the platoon most when the Germans— they were parachute troops—came into view, was their total lack of tactical deployment. They were marching along in column, close together with no proper vanguard or flank guard, weapons not even at the ready. A perfect target for machine-guns, but the platoon commander decided that rather than engage the leading troops, he would wait for the main body. His interpretation of what constituted a main body was fairly liberal for he allowed no fewer than 300 paratroopers to pass by before deciding to open fire. It was rather the nature of the target—the command group of what seemed to be a battalion—than the numbers which determined him. Yet just as his machine-gunner was about to press the trigger a girl dashed out of a house near the German officers and warned them of the ambush they were running into. By the time the girl had disappeared again, the German commander had dispersed his troops into the ditches with a single urgent order, and the moment was lost. So began an unequal duel between a platoon on the one hand and the best part of a battalion on the other. The snow made it easy for the American troops to observe the strike of their shooting and correct appropriately, and they were well protected from the answering German fire by the depth of their foxholes and the thickness of overhead cover. The platoon commander continued to call for artillery fire which never came and when he asked for instructions was simply told to hold 'at all costs'. Shortly after receiving this uncompromising order, an enemy bullet put an end to his ability to communicate with regimental headquarters by smashing the radio.

The Germans were not lacking in courage—across the snow-covered fields and fences they came with little fire support in an attempt to close with the American platoon, and, of course, were shot down with ease. The fight went on all day with varying degrees of mortar and artillery support for the Germans. The platoon commander estimated that for the eventual loss of his 18 men—killed, wounded, sent to the rear or captured—some hundreds of Germans were put out of action. Only when all their ammunition was expended did the platoon finally stop fighting. By that time the Germans were all round them. The name Lanzenrath is but one among the many villages which made up the story of the Ardennes battle. But it was just such actions as this which determined the battle's outcome—isolated, gallant actions by small groups of American soldiers, which held up and took heavy toll of the advancing German troops.

Another man who was to find himself in Lanzenrath later on 16 December and who had one of the most interesting and at the same time most frustrating parts in the battle was Colonel Jochen

Peiper, commanding 1st Panzer Regiment in 1st SS Panzer Division. It will be remembered that although the bulk of 6th Panzer Army had been held up in the fighting for Monschau, Elsenborn and Malmedy, one *Kampfgruppe* or battle group, did break through south of Bütgenbach—this was Peiper Force, with orders to move west to Stavelot and on to the Meuse at Huy. He was not to worry about his flanks and to leave the evacuation of prisoners to the following infantry divisions. Moving off before dawn on 17 December, and passing through the Lanzenrath road junction heading west, he fell in with a US convoy of vehicles, joined it, surprised and destroyed the US garrison of Honsfeld, captured some 50 vehicles and a dozen anti-tank guns, pressed on to Bullingen, where he had no difficulty in persuading 50 American prisoners to put 50,000 gallons of captured petrol into his own vehicles and pushed on further with little opposition, other than shelling from the US artillery to his north. He reached the cross-roads at Baugnez between Malmedy and Ligneuville shortly after noon, and ran straight into a convoy of lorries from the US 285 Artillery Observation Battalion. Lorries were no match for the leading elements of a panzer group, and after a skirmish, the American soldiers were disarmed and collected together near the cross-roads. Peiper's vanguard drove on westwards, but when the main body of his force arrived, its tanks machine-gunned the American prisoners, killing about 70. This incident became known as the Malmedy massacre. Peiper Force was also guilty of shooting other American prisoners and unarmed Belgian civilians. 'No state at war with another state', wrote Kant, 'should engage in hostilities of such a kind as to render mutual confidence impossible when peace will have been made.' But it was in just such hostilities that Dietrich's SS Panzer Army did engage.

Peiper pushed on to Ligneuville and further west, arriving at the approaches to Stavelot at dusk. Here, in spite of their being no opposition to speak of, he halted, and in doing so broke one of the fundamental rules of blitzkrieg—always to push on, never to halt and so allow yourself to be located, stopped and attacked. At this time on the evening of 17 December, Peiper was about 40 miles from the Meuse. The Stavelot bridge over the River Ambleve was ripe for capture, but Peiper rested his force south of it. Had he taken it there and then and pushed on to the north-west, what further prizes might he not have found for the plucking! Petrol dumps with two *million* gallons of fuel, HQ 1st Army at

Spa and a clear run to the Meuse at Liège. But he did not, and during the night, US reinforcements reached Stavelot so that when the Germans renewed their advance on the morning of 18 December, they found enemy infantry and tank destroyers in their path. This opposition was pushed aside and Peiper advanced his force to Trois Ponts to seize the bridge over the River Salm and move on Werbomont. But the resolute behaviour of a US combat engineer company destroyed the Salm bridge. 'If only we had captured the bridge at Trois Ponts intact,' Peiper commented later, 'and had enough fuel, it would have been a simple matter to drive through to the Meuse early that day.' But it was precisely this ad hoc and just-in-time patchy sort of defensive action by separated groups of US combat troops which stopped him. Thereafter Peiper Force, in spite of re-crossing the Amblève at Stourmont and advancing towards Werbomont, ran into every sort of difficulty. Harassed from the air by fighter aircraft, the Stavelot bridge recaptured behind him, no sign of the rest of 1st SS Panzer Division to reinforce him—they too were caught by Allied fighters during 18 December—the bridge at Neufmoulin over the River Lienne blown in his face—the rest of Peiper's adventures were a combination of petrol shortages, dithering, harassment on all sides from ground and air, and eventually abandonment of his tanks and vehicles in an only partially successful attempt to escape on foot. Peiper's advance had caused a great deal of concern. It had never looked like being a real breakthrough. Nor was Peiper's *Kampfgruppe* the only hostage to fortune.

Colonel von der Heydte's parachute operation, codename *Awk*, which he himself had given a ten per cent chance of success, had even less than this when it was actually launched. His final orders received at Paderborn were telephoned to him by Kraemer, Chief of Staff, 6th Panzer Army, during the day of 16 December. Admitting that progress had been slower than expected and that the American troops were still holding out at Elsenborn, Kraemer gave Heydte the task of dropping behind them at dawn next morning in the area of the Belle-Croix crossroads near the Baraque-Michel in order to block enemy reinforcements moving from the north to Elsenborn, and to assist the drive to the Meuse of the panzers—if they came. He was to hold on for at least two days and to do as much damage to the enemy as possible. Conditions were about as difficult as possible—old, worn-out aircraft, inexperienced pilots and jump controllers, strong, contrary winds, difficult, broken landing zones, von der Heydte himself suffering from injured arms. Almost everything went wrong. Of the 106 Junkers aircraft which were used in the operation—only about a dozen dropped their paratroopers in the right place. The rest were invited to jump either behind their own lines or so that they landed near the forward German positions at Monschau. Radio sets and heavy weapons were haphazardly spread about. Von der Heydte on reaching his rendezvous at the Belle Croix position found a mere 20 men. This grew to 100, and later by scouting the area to 300, but they had very few weapons between them and very little food. The force never took the offensive at all. They lived up to Rosenstock-Huessy's recipe and wandered aimlessly about for three days, capturing some patrolling GIs and recovering one container dropped by a J88 which when opened was found to contain—brandy. After three days of achieving little more than getting tireder and colder and hungrier as each day passed, von der Heydte gave orders that his men would disperse in small groups and try to make their own way back to German lines. On 21 December they started off. Von der Heydte himself was captured the next day. Operation *Awk* had been an unmitigated failure.

The Trojan Horse operations of Skorzeny were not much better. Although about 40 jeeps, full of *Kommandos* did succeed in infiltrating through the American lines during the nights of 16 and 17 December, they achieved little except the creation of confusion. They shot up individual vehicles and some command posts, cut telephone wires, caused traffic to go the wrong way, and one party reached the Meuse. Their main impact was in the security measures which they obliged the Americans to take—even, to Eisenhower's annoyance, encumbering him with special security guards—but their planned purpose of opening the Meuse doors leading towards Antwerp and Brussels to the advancing panzers was achieved in neither sense—the doors were not opened and even if they had been there would have been no one to go through them.

Of infinitely more moment than what happened on Dietrich's front were the operations of Manteuffel's 5th Panzer Army, and before long these operations became a battle for the Quatre Bras of the Ardennes—Bastogne. As early as 12 December, General von Lüttwitz commanding 47 Panzer Corps, and echoing

Manteuffel's remark to Hitler ten days before, had observed to his two panzer divisional commanders that Bastogne must be taken. Once it was cleared their advance could go forward. If it were not, it would be 'like an abscess on our lines of communication'. Such foresight—*Vorhersehung*—was worthy almost of the Führer himself. 17 December was virtually a race for Bastogne—both 101st US Airborne Division and a Combat Command of the US 10th Armoured Division had been ordered there. Von Lüttwitz knew that the Americans were about to reinforce the city because of an intercepted message. But he was confident that his own spearhead—2 Panzer Division and Panzer Lehr—would get there first. Had they acted with the boldness which had once characterized the Wehrmacht's panzer troops, they might have done so. 'If the Germans had won the race for Bastogne,' wrote Chester Wilmot, 'Manteuffel's armour would have had a clear run to Dinant and Namur on December 19th and 20th.' But their armoured spearheads behaved as if they had never heard of cavalry dash. Bayerlein, commanding Panzer Lehr Division, advanced with the utmost circumspection when only a few miles to the east of Bastogne. By 8 p.m. on the evening of 18 December Bayerlein was at Niederwampach, some five miles east of the city. An hour later his leading columns reached Mageret, a mere two or three miles away from the great prize. And there unaccountably he paused, made enquiries from a Belgian civilian, believed the answers, and actually took *defensive* measures, including laying mines. Had he pushed on with the whole of Panzer Lehr, Bastogne must have been his. But he did not, and so allowed the 101st Airborne Division to move into the city from the south protected by detachments of 9th and 10th Armoured Divisions, which were to the east on the high ground at Longvilly commanding the approaches. Once there the Americans tightened their hold on Bastogne, and despite being attacked by three German divisions, they were able to hold it. It became the very thorn in Manteuffel's side that von Lüttwitz had predicted. Nonetheless, the leading panzer elements reached the River Ourthe in two places by 20 December.

So that all in all the first four days had from the German point of view degenerated from the hopes of a quick breakthrough and advance to the Meuse into the facts of failure in the north to make much progress at all except for 1st SS Panzer Division, itself halted west of Stavelot, and failure in the south to capture

St Vith and Bastogne. The American reaction, no matter how spontaneous and haphazard, had succeeded in robbing the Germans of surprise and speed. Even their superiority of strength was beginning to wane as more and more American divisions were directed towards the Ardennes. The problems now facing the two sides were thus that Eisenhower needed to make a plan which would defeat and destroy, as opposed to stopping, the German advance, and Hitler had to make up his mind how to adjust his previously unalterable plan in order to exploit what success had been achieved before all his reserves had been used up and all hope of continuing the advance had gone. For Eisenhower it was largely a problem of command; for Hitler a problem of switching the main effort. Eisenhower could hardly have failed to remember how often he had been urged by Montgomery to put all troops north of the Ardennes under command of one man—Montgomery himself—and it was to this man he now turned to manage the northern part of the battlefield. Montgomery, with his unique system of personal liaison officers, who sped about the battlefield to discover the situation and then report back to their master, was in the extraordinary position of knowing more about what was happening on the 1st and 9th Army fronts than their own commanders, Hodges and Simpson did.

Never was the value of Montgomery's team of liaison officers demonstrated to better advantage than by their activities during the first few days of the Ardennes battle. The importance of liaison officers had been previously emphasized by Napoleon who used generals. Apart from Montgomery's experience with the 47th Division in the First World War which put him on to the track of this particular trick in the first place, it would not have been displeasing to him to follow in the footsteps of the *grand homme de guerre*. In Napoleon's day it was possible to be a general and to be in your twenties at the same time. Montgomery recognized the value of youth without being obliged to promote his team to such exorbitant pay-rolls. 'In addition to all the information reaching him from other sources', wrote Major-General Essame, 'he got a picture of the fighting as seen through the eyes of youth, with practical experience of battle. He was thus able, far earlier than Bradley and the commanders in his Army Group, to make an accurate appreciation of the situation in the Ardennes.'

As a result of this appreciation Montgomery was able to see as

early as 18 December what the threat to his own position was. He
therefore took the steps necessary to safeguard it, that is to say,
to guarantee the integrity of his own forces, to secure the flanks
and vitals of his Army Group. 30 Corps, commanded by Horrocks, on its way from Maastricht to Nijmegen was quickly
diverted to an area west of the Maas between Louvain and St
Trond—where they were suitably positioned to deal with any
German exitings from the Meuse between Namur and Liège.
But he was not satisfied with this. Seeking also to guard the
Meuse crossings themselves, he despatched appropriate garrisons
and reconnaissance parties to them. A complete armoured brigade,
which had been refitting, was instructed to re-equip with the tanks
just handed in and to concentrate at Namur. All these measures
which were rapidly executed meant that by 19 December, the
day before he took over command of the northern part of the
battlefield, Montgomery had a powerful well-located reserve, of
three infantry divisions, one armoured division and several
armoured brigades, totalling nearly 100,000 men with over
1,000 tanks and 500 guns. One of the armoured brigades was
used to secure the Meuse bridges at Givet, Dinant and Namur,
while behind them on the ground to the west, tactically excellent
for fighting a defensive battle, Montgomery was able to deploy the
rest of Horrocks'* Corps in some depth. If the Germans did reach
and attempt to cross the Meuse, there would be a reception
committee worth the name. It was in this way that Montgomery
began his process of tidying up the battlefield.

When ordered, therefore, by Eisenhower on 20 December to
take over command of the northern part of the battle front, he
was ready with a clear plan to hold and destroy the enemy. As
was customary the master mind had a master plan. It was similar
to many of his previous plans from Alam el Halfa onwards—
first the certainty of successful defence; then counter-attack. 'My
policy in the north', he signalled to the CIGS, 'is to get the show
tidied up and to ensure absolute security before passing over to
offensive action and that action will be taken by VII Corps only
when that Corps is fully assembled and ready to deal a hard blow.'
As we have seen the redeployment of 30 Corps was part of the

---

* Montgomery revealed in his *Memoirs* that Horrocks' enthusiasm ran
away with him to the extent of wanting to allow the Germans to cross the
Meuse and then cut them up in what would be the final battle of the war—
at Waterloo.

'heading off' process. Furthermore 9th US Army, by taking over the Aachen front from 1st US Army, would allow 1st US Army generally to concentrate more against the northern flank of the German bulge, and in particular release VII US Corps, commanded by Collins, to prepare for counter-attack. This would complete the 'heading and roping off' and make way for the 'seeing off' and 'writing off' which would follow. This was the broad plan and, like so many of Montgomery's, was more or less what happened.

Since it was on Manteuffel's front that the greatest advances had been made, on the same day that Montgomery assumed command of the Allied forces in the north von Rundstedt was finally allowed by the Führer to switch the main weight of the attack from 6th to 5th Panzer Army. It was already too late. After the first four days, even though further advances and further captures were made, the German drive flagged. It would never regain its initial momentum. What is more, before long another player would enter the arena—the overwhelmingly powerful Allied air forces. In view of all this, could any of Hitler's hopes be said to have survived?

Warlimont recalled that 'Supreme Headquarters'—by which he meant the Führer, for the Führer *was* Supreme Headquarters— 'was carried away by these partial successes and completely the prisoner of his own wishful thinking; it therefore entirely failed to realize that with every day which the enemy was allowed for the movement of his considerable reserves, the prospects of a major victory, getting anywhere near the planned objectives, were becoming more improbable.' In referring to reserves, Warlimont put his finger on what the battle was all about—indeed what all battles, other than walkovers like the campaigns in Poland or Greece, are about. Of all great captains, Montgomery was the greatest exponent of the key role which reserves played in any battle. It was reserves which gave him the balance he always sought and harked back to. It was his reserves which had enabled him to win the battle of Alamein, break the Germans in Normandy, and was now to finish them off in the Ardennes. Hitler too had had his reserves at the start of the battle. But he had refused to commit them early enough in the right place and so both allowed the Americans to regain balance and condemned Army Group B to lose it. 'The Führer commands', Jodl's diary read at this time, 'that the remaining enemy pockets must be broken up from the rear. They must be cut off from the rear so that they cannot be supplied; they will then surrender.' But an enemy pocket like Bastogne could only be broken up by the use of reserves more powerful than those which existed—and Bastogne in any case could be and was supplied from the air. Exhaust your reserves and you can no longer make the enemy react to you. You spend your time reacting to him. It was during the next five days, from 20 December to Christmas Day, that the Germans were to get this lesson rammed home once more.

7
Christmas Present
for the Führer?

On 23 December, Model told me that the offensive had
definitely failed—but that Hitler had ordered it to continue.
Speer

Between 20 and 25 December what remained of the German
initiative was expended. Dietrich's 6th Panzer Army went on with
attacks in the area of Monschau, Bütgenbach and Malmedy, but
the mere fact that a week after the offensive had started they were
still fighting for their very first objectives, ones which Hitler
had hoped would fall at the outset of Day 1, illustrates as surely
as anything that the intended principal *Schwerpunkt*, those
troops who were to have captured Antwerp and rolled up the
whole British position to the north, were simply beating their
heads against a defensive wall which was not going to yield. Only
Peiper's battle group had advanced any distance at all, and in the
end this group was obliged to abandon its guns, tanks and other
vehicles for want of petrol and supplies, and to escape on foot
back to the German lines. To such an ignominious end had come
one of the elite SS Panzer divisions; to such empty ill fortune had
deteriorated the perpetrators of blitzkrieg.

As in the first four or five days of the offensive it was Manteuffel's
5th Panzer Army which had what success there was to be had,
illusory though it proved to be. St Vith was finally taken by them
on 21 December. They did not keep it long.* 2nd Panzer Division
of von Lüttwitz's Panzer Corps even got a glimpse of the Meuse

---

* Roughly a month: St Vith was recaptured by the 7th US Armoured
Division—which had so heroically defended it—on 23 January 1945.

18   *US tanks in battle for St Vith*

19   *St Vith retaken by US 7th Armoured Division*

20 *Bastogne*

21 *US airborne troops near Bastogne*

at Dinant, but it was not much use looking at bridges and possible bridgeheads from the turret of a *Panzerkampfwagen* which had no petrol in its fuel tanks, at a time when the bridges overlooked were in any event powerfully defended by Montgomery's reserves, and when moreover the panzer and other divisions behind them were already blocked by US forces and thus in a state which panzer divisions should never be—stationary. What is more Bastogne held firmly against all efforts to capture it. And then that supposedly neutral agent, the weather, had succumbed to Patton's prayer. On 23 December a fine, clear and dry spell set in with all this meant to Allied air power, both for the air supply of Bastogne and for the fighters to harass and destroy the German columns. Yet the fine weather had not come before rain had turned the Ardennes minor roads, so successfully sought out and exploited by the panzer columns, into quagmires which manacled the German vehicles to the fear and frustration of slow, vulnerable movement.

One of the most curious features of the battle as it now developed was that the three most important parts of it which now were to rage—the German attempts to capture Malmedy, St Vith and Bastogne—had been brought about by Allied reactions which owed their origins not to calculation but to chance. The US 7th Armoured Division had not been directed to St Vith in accordance with some grand design which foresaw that its defence would be critical to the whole operation. It went there by order of a local commander because of the need at that time to meet a local threat. 101st Airborne Division and the Combat Command of 10th Armoured Division went to Bastogne merely, as Eisenhower himself admitted, 'because Bastogne was such an excellent road centre. Troops directed there could later be despatched by the commander on the spot to any region he found desirable.' By such chances, however, are campaigns determined. Yet as far as the battle of the northern shoulder was concerned, the arrival of Montgomery to take charge of it meant above all that from now on there would be a firm grip, a tidy solution, a master plan. Montgomery, it could be safely assumed, would see the battle as a whole.

When Montgomery was put in charge of the northern flank, that is to say took temporary command of two US Armies, the 1st under Hodges and the 9th under Simpson, there was no master plan. Indeed it would have been difficult for Hodges, who had

H

received no directives from Bradley and was out of touch with much of what was happening over his wide incoherent front, to have made one. The measures which Montgomery judged to be immediately necessary, therefore, were to ensure that 'the vital areas were held securely and to create reserves for counter-attack'. When Montgomery entered Hodges' headquarters at Chaudfontaine in the early part of the afternoon of 20 December, 'looking supremely cheerful and confident', as de Guingand, his Chief of Staff, reported, Hodges was anxious to restore some coherence to his front by hanging on firmly to the area Monschau–Stavelot and counter-attacking towards Vielsalm and Houffalize in order to relieve the force under Hasbrouck at St Vith. One of the reasons for this proposal was that Hodges' staff believed that the principal German thrust was directed at Liège, that is north-west through Malmedy. If this were so a counter thrust towards Houffalize and St Vith would not only relieve St Vith itself but take the Germans in the flank.

Montgomery disagreed. Anxious to stabilize first and counter-attack later, and in any case convinced—rightly—that it was not just Liège the Germans were aiming at but also Namur and Huy, he foresaw that Hodges might be faced with further powerful German attacks astride the River Ourthe, directed further west and south. The whole of Montgomery's thinking, coloured by his experiences at Alam el Halfa and in Normandy, was that the enemy should be allowed to outrun his strength, then be halted, then destroyed. To attack prematurely without the prerequisites of firm protection for these critical areas and a force of reserves to preserve balance, was in his view wrong. Yet here he was at odds with American sentiment and pride. For when he proposed that 1st Army should extend their northern defences from Stavelot to Marche and in order to shorten the line and create some reserves, withdraw from certain positions, Hodges refused. He had heard from Hasbrouck, commanding at St Vith, that with his own division, two infantry regiments, and a combat command of 9th Armoured Division he expected to be able to hold on to his horse-shoe line round St Vith for the remainder of 20 December, but that he would be cut off by encircling German formations next day. In spite of his misgivings, Montgomery therefore agreed that the strengthening and straightening of the Allied line would be achieved not by withdrawals, but by an advance. Ridgeway's XVIII Airborne Corps was therefore to re-establish a line

Malmedy–St Vith–Houffalize and 'gain contact with our units in Bastogne'. While there were obvious dangers in such a plan, Montgomery hoped not only that the troops at St Vith would be relieved and withdrawn, but also that it would give him time to extract the VII US Corps from the Aachen area by giving its part of the front to Simpson's 9th Army. It was not long, however, before Montgomery's misgivings were justified.

The truth was that Ridgeway had insufficient strength for his task. By the following morning the circumstances that Montgomery had foreseen had come to pass. Although Ridgeway's forces successfully reached the Salm surrounding Peiper's battle group, and even advanced up to Hasbrouck's western positions, a new German attack by 5th Panzer Army had completely outflanked him and got as far as Hotton, far behind him. From Hotton it would be but a step for the Germans to reach Marche, Dinant and the Meuse. What is more St Vith had fallen.

Hasbrouck's letter of 20 December to Hodges' Chief of Staff had been a model of brevity, informativeness, foresight and resolution:

> My division is defending the line St Vith–Poteau inclusive. Combat Command B, 9th Armoured Division, 424th Infantry Regiment and 112th Infantry Regiment are on my right and hold from St Vith exclusive to Holdinge. Both infantry regiments are in bad shape. My right flank is wide open except for some reconnaissance elements, tank destroyers and stragglers we have collected into defence teams at road centres as far as Chevram inclusive. Two German divisions, 116 Panzer and 560 Volksgrenadier, are just starting to attack north-west with their right on Gouvy. I can delay them the rest of today *maybe* but will be cut off by tomorrow. VIII Corps has ordered me to hold, and I will do so, but need help. An attack from Bastogne to the north-east will relieve the situation, and in turn cut the bastards off in the rear. I also need plenty of air support. Am out of contact with VIII Corps so am sending this to you. Understand 82nd Airborne Division is coming up on my north and the north flank is not critical.

By that evening, however, the whole situation in the St Vith salient had become acute, for no fewer than four German divisions were closing in. That this was so was only made possible by Hitler's tardy decision to switch some of his reserves to

Manteuffel's front. The 2nd and 9th SS Panzer Divisions had been extracted from Dietrich's army and sent to this more promising southern part of the front.

The fight for St Vith was a furious one. Major Boyer, who commanded a battle group of the 38th Armoured Infantry in 7th Armoured Division, has described the fanaticism with which the German forces came on in the face of heavy machine-gun and artillery fire. In depicting the final hours of the struggle on 21 December when the Germans launched three more attacks on the town astride the Schönberg, Malmedy and Prüm roads, he recalled that in his sector of the Schönberg attack the enemy kept advancing no matter how many of their assaulting troops were destroyed. As fast as one wave of enemy infantry was repulsed another would take its place. 'It certainly looked as if the Germans were determined that they were coming through, but their spirit alone was not enough to sustain them against the merciless hail of small arms fire which we were hurling at them.' The Germans seemed set on engaging their enemies more closely and came right up to the American machine-gun positions to lob grenades at the crews or open up with a *Panzerfaust**. One of these machine-gun positions received a direct hit from a *Panzerfaust* rocket, which struck the gun itself on the barrel. 'The gunner fell forward on the gun with half his face torn off; the loader had his left arm torn off at the shoulder and was practically decapitated; while the commander was tossed about 15 feet away from the gun to lie there quite still.' Every time one of Boyer's machine-gun or bazooka teams was put out of action, more men came forward to replace them, and together with the artillery called for, they did the Germans great harm. But 'always there were more Germans, and more Germans! Where they were all coming from I did not know but it looked as if battalion after battalion must have been massed up behind the original assault waves. That's the only way they would be able to keep on attacking, attacking and re-attacking for better than one and half hours.'

Boyer went on fighting as did the other American units, but the weight of Germans was too great. Their combined use of mortars, Tiger and Panther tanks plus infantry saw to it that, before 21 December was over, they had taken St Vith. Yet the battle—much of it in blinding snow storms—fought by Hasbrouck

---

* What was at that time known as a bazooka and what we now call a rocket launcher.

and the mixed group of his own 7th Armoured Division, a combat command of 9th Armoured Division, and two infantry regiments, 112th and 424th, had done on the grand scale what so many smaller actions had done on the same scale. They had taken on an entire German Corps, the 66th. They had stopped and delayed it, with all the consequent slowing down of supplies and reinforcements, and allowed American movement of reserves to stabilize the position further west. In short they had gained *time* and at this point in the battle, time was everything.

The whole of the battle had now resolved itself into two questions. On the Allied side would it be possible to hold the renewed German attacks and at the same time create sufficient reserves to give them a death blow when they had been halted? On the German side could they now continue to reinforce the further success they were beginning to have in such a way that they would not merely pin sufficient Allied strength to the shoulders of the bulge and prevent them from pinching it off, but also drive on to those vital bridges over the Meuse between Liège and Namur—the key to real success—and thus by hanging on to the initiative, continue to force the Allies to react to their own moves without concentrating against them?

Although St Vith was doomed and was taken, Hasbrouck had succeeded in extracting the main part of his force across the Salm. At the same time, following their capture of St Vith, 2nd and 9th SS Panzer Divisions seized control of the roads linking St Vith and Laroche, and while the Germans failed to do the same with the route from Marche to Namur, Manteuffel's spearheads did break through by 23 December to the ridge overlooking the Meuse. During the planning stage, von Rundstedt had expressed his concern that in the face of quick Allied reaction, the whole counter-offensive would turn from an attack into a holding operation to hang on to what ground had been overrun. Would this now be so, or would it rather be the Allied counter-attacking moves which would be forced on to the defensive in a desperate effort to stop a real German breakthrough? The answer would depend on Bastogne.

But at the time when Montgomery was wrestling with the problem on 21 December, this was by no means clear. Montgomery's view all along—and it was a view which highlighted not only the difference in temperament between himself and his American colleagues, but also the difference in experience of fighting battles—was that an advance by the Germans and a withdrawal by the Allies, provided no vital ground was given up, did not matter a bit, was indeed all to the good if in the end it resulted in a decisive defeat of the Germans and brought victory nearer. In other words the primary purpose of fighting a battle was to win it. How and where it was won were secondary. And if by giving ground, forcing the Germans to over-extend themselves and make themselves more vulnerable, it could be won more easily and more decisively, so much the better. The British after all were used to giving ground. They traditionally lost every battle except the last one. The American view was very different. To withdraw was somehow dishonourable, a disgrace, out of tune with national character. The great Jim Gavin, commander of 82nd Airborne Division (described by Dempsey as the greatest combat division in the world), summed up American reluctance to withdraw under *any* circumstances when deprecating such a movement by his own division—because it had never done so before. And when his division had to withdraw, his men did not understand it, criticized the move openly, and allowed it to affect their morale. This totally different approach was echoed by the contrasting attitude to the use of reserves. To Montgomery, as to his great predecessors, Wellington and Marlborough, reserves were what made victory possible and it was by their creation or strengthening *during the battle* that the battle could be won. Such patience and reasoning were entirely foreign to American thinking. To them anything short of a get-up-and-go strategy smacked of pusillanimity. It was thus very difficult for Montgomery to persuade his American subordinate commanders to his way of seeing things. Nor did he ever wholly do so. Yet during these critical four days before Christmas 1944, it was peculiarly necessary that he did.

It will be remembered that most of the roads in the Ardennes lead to the south-west—in other words, as Montgomery saw it, away from the critical routes across the Meuse towards Antwerp. He therefore did not mind particularly when Manteuffel gained control of roads and road junctions which would allow him to extend his panzer forces still further south-west. This would simply make his, Montgomery's, subsequent task easier. In this respect, unlike Montgomery in almost every other way that he was, Patton's earlier comment about letting the Germans go all the way to Paris and then cutting them off and chewing them up reflected Montgomery's thinking. In the matter of the US 7th Armoured Division and 82nd Airborne Division, Montgomery had his way. They withdrew, and not too soon. On 22 December Hasbrouck himself—and his courage and determination to fight were never in question—had answered Ridgeway's order to fight east of the Salm by saying that if he did so it would mean the end of his division. Montgomery's wiser counsels prevailed. The pattern was repeated when Montgomery required 82nd Airborne Division to withdraw to the south of Werbomont. The whole tactical thinking behind these moves of Montgomery was that the Germans should be allowed if necessary to continue their western penetration, while holding the flanks of it firmly by continually shortening the line to be held, until at last the Germans ran out of petrol or strength or both, and once the weather cleared became more and more vulnerable to air attack. In his attempt to pull Collins' VII Corps back to the north of the German salient, Montgomery was less successful and as it turned out this was fortunate, for Collins, by virtue of what was happening at Bastogne, was given a chance he was quick to seize.

By 21 December Bastogne was surrounded by von Lüttwitz's 47 Panzer Corps. Elements of four German divisions were present. 5th Parachute Division blocked the roads to the south; 2nd Panzer, although its main columns had moved on to the west, had left detachments to the north of the town; the main attack on Bastogne was to be delivered by 26th Volksgrenadier Division supported by a Panzergrenadier regiment of Panzer Lehr, the bulk of which had gone to assist 2nd Panzer with its push to the Meuse. The story of Bastogne's siege has been told many times. It is a story on the one hand of German indecision and reluctance to mount an attack of sufficient strength to guarantee success no matter if losses were severe, and on the other hand of a determined and skilful defence carried on by McAuliffe and his mixed force of airborne and armoured troops, with airborne supplies saving a nearly desperate logistic situation and eventual relief by Patton's columns driving up from the south. General Kokott commanding 26th Volksgrenadier Division, unable to see how he could take the town with the forces he had, took the extraordinary step of calling upon the American defenders to surrender. No doubt all Hitler's talk of the Americans being a young nation who would quickly lose heart may have had something to do with it. More likely an explanation is that it was a last resort to break what seemed to him to be a dangerous stalemate, and to win the prize without having to fight for it. Had he attacked with all available forces in as many sectors as possible simultaneously, the defenders' resources might well have been stretched to breaking point.

'Unconditional surrender', read his ultimatum, 'is the only method of avoiding complete annihilation of the surrounded American units. Two hours grace is granted hereby. Should this offer be refused an artillery corps and six groups of heavy anti-aircraft guns stand ready to annihilate the American forces.' Kokott appealed therefore to American humanity to spare the civilian inhabitants further suffering. In fact the 3,500 civilian inhabitants of Bastogne were not suffering unduly except from apprehension. Their food and coal supplies were adequate, their shelters and cellars strong, their courage and morale high. But they could not help asking themselves what would happen to them if the Germans took the town. The determination of American soldiers and the steadiness of civilians acted as a sort of mutual tonic. They must both (the civilians once its meaning had been explained to them) have been considerably heartened by McAuliffe's renowned and monosyllabic reply to the German ultimatum—'Nuts'—surely the most succinct countercheck-quarrelsome in the history of war. On 23 December the Germans broke through on the south-west corner of the town, but after some fierce fighting, the penetration of tanks and infantry was either destroyed or beaten back. What is more that day with its fine clear weather had enabled an airdrop of supplies and ammunition to be delivered to the defending garrison. Even though there was no sight of Patton's much vaunted counter-attack from the south, which, as he had promised, started the day before on 22 December, they were holding on. Bastogne had by now come to figure so large in the German commanders' minds that it prompted them to advocate a complete change of plan. On Christmas Eve Model and Manteuffel put this new plan to Hitler. It was not a Christmas present he relished.

Before we see what it was, it will be as well to summarize the general situation which had come about. By midnight on Christmas Eve, Manteuffel's spearhead, 2nd Panzer Division, was in the area Foy Notre Dame and Celles, short of petrol but overlooking the Meuse at Dinant. The main body of 5th Panzer Army—116th Panzer Division, 9th Panzer and 15th Panzer Grenadier Divisions (Hitler had finally given Manteuffel these last two formations from

OKW reserve on 23 December)—was held up by the US VII Corps which, far from accepting the passive role of holding the northern shoulder of the bulge which Montgomery had foreseen, was bearing down on the extremities of the bulge itself with irresistible strength. In front of 2nd Panzer the Meuse, including the Dinant Bridge, was strongly held by two British brigades. Thus the spearhead of Hitler's offensive had been checked. Further east and south, Bastogne still held out, now being regularly supplied from the air and occupying two or three German divisions. What is more, Allied air power was successfully forestalling all German attempts to re-supply their leading formations. Meanwhile Patton's drive from the south to relieve Bastogne was gathering strength. These last two points require some elaboration.

True to his promise, Patton, in an astonishing demonstration of how to break off one offensive, re-group his Army, give part of it totally different objectives in a direction at right angles to the former one, and get everything moving quickly and dramatically, had begun his drive north from the Saar with the III US Corps in time actually to start attacking the south flank of the German bulge on 22 December. This drive by the III Corps concentrated its main effort on the Arlon–Bastogne road. True to his character, Patton had expected rapid success in reaching Bastogne and even St Vith. His expectations were disappointed. There were good reasons for this. Patton's actual attack (as opposed to his redeploying and making forces available for it) was a masterpiece of bad planning, inadequate preparation, poor tactics, and perhaps the worst blunder that a general can be guilty of—committing illtrained troops to their first battle in conditions wholly unfavourable to their enjoying a tolerable baptism of fire. In addition the Germans knew what was coming and braced themselves to receive it. They may have been surprised by Patton's extraordinary dexterity in swinging his command about. They were not surprised by its actual progress or intentions since the American network of telephones and radio gave them the very information they needed. 'As far as troop movements were concerned, reported Model's Chief of Intelligence, Colonel Michael, 'we were not at all surprised—the American Army traffic net was still working well for us.' It took Patton's III Corps four days to break through to Bastogne, but once they had done so, of course, once the US 4th Armoured Division had actually reached Bastogne on 26 December with its tanks, other weapons and supplies, the battle if not over, was largely a matter of arithmetic. The siege was raised, and the town's survival would now depend on who could reinforce more quickly. Furthermore that same day another of Patton's corps, the XII, had driven back the left flank of Branden-berger's 7th Army and further consolidated the American grip of the bulge's southern shoulder. The siege of Bastogne had already lasted for more than a week and the German failure here was perhaps the most significant and far-reaching of the stumbling blocks which faced the Germans throughout the Ardennes offensive, for it was not only defeat in itself. It caused defeat elsewhere as well.

One of the most marked defeats of all was that of the Luftwaffe. While the Luftwaffe made a major effort—its last—to win tem-porary air superiority over the battle area during its first ten days, they were simply unable to meet the Allied air forces on anything like equal terms. For every sortie the Germans put into the air, the Allies were able to put six.* This meant not only that the Allies were able to supply Bastogne by air, not only that the endless pounding of German concentrations in the forward area by fighter bombers caused heavy losses, not only that the German supply columns were themselves subjected to constant attack and therefore by failing to get forward rendered the panzer spearheads immobile through lack of petrol and therefore even more vulnerable, not only that the Allied heavy bombers were attacking supply dumps, raiding road junctions and bridges further back in German rear areas as far as the Rhine, and so stifling the flow forward of the sinews of war, but also that by virtue of maintaining more or less continuous surveillance of the battlefield by their reconnaissance aircraft, the Allies were able to keep the whole battle area under observation, this itself, plus the resultant target identification and attack, made easier by the fact that most movement was confined to the roads.

No wonder that the Commander of 5th Parachute Division besieging Bastogne, General Hulmann, complained on 24 Decem-ber that although this day was one of intense air activity, it was not the sort they wanted. 'Not a single German aircraft appeared over Bastogne. What had happened to the air support we had been promised for vital sectors?' It was a very different story for the other side. 'When night fell a glow could be seen stretching right

* General Galland, who commanded Germany's fighter force, said that it was in the Ardennes battles that the Luftwaffe received its death blow.

back to the West Wall. The roads were marked by lines of flaming vehicles.' In what was one of the most devastating illustrations of air power that had been seen on the Western front, the Allies dropped more than 30,000 tons of bombs in a sector encircled roughly by the Rhine from Bonn to Koblenz and forward to the western extremities of the bulge—all in ten days. We have seen that in spite of a good road network in the Eifel and Ardennes, many of these roads were twisting and turning between the hills and rivers, ideal for the creation of traffic hold-ups and thus of sitting targets. During it all about 1,600 Luftwaffe aircraft were destroyed whilst the Allies lost less than a quarter of this number. 'The outstanding feature of the air battle', the *Official History* tells us —and this was one of the main success stories of the entire Allied handling of the crisis—'was the ease and harmony with which three American and three British air commands collaborated in complicated actions for which there had been no time for overall planning or preparation.' Air power had often before been credited with flexibility as one of its principal and most deadly characteristics. Never was this cliché shown to be more true.

With the air battle never within their grasp and the ground battle hopelessly bogged down, the senior German commanders, Model and Manteuffel, returned to the charge and tried to persuade Hitler to modify his plans and intentions. The day before the offensive began, a US 1st Army Intelligence report had referred to the possibility of a limited scale offensive to be launched for the purpose of making Aachen a Christmas present for the Führer. Now it was Christmas Eve and once again the question of Aachen as the first prize was put forward.

Model and Manteuffel were fully aware by this time that the offensive had failed. Lack of progress in the north, the ulcer of Bastogne, shortage of fuel, the quick reaction and intervention of US and British reserves, Allied air power—all these had robbed them of the chance to cross the Meuse, let alone drive to Antwerp. Therefore let them return to one of the smaller, more modest plans, establish a firm western defensive base near Dinant, clear the enemy up to the Meuse with Manteuffel directed on Huy and Dietrich on Liège, then turn north and take Aachen. This briefly was Model's proposal. Furthermore if the Führer would give up his idea about a further offensive in the Alsace area, more forces could be assembled to the north for an attack on Maastricht. Hitler as usual was unable to cut his losses and face facts. He

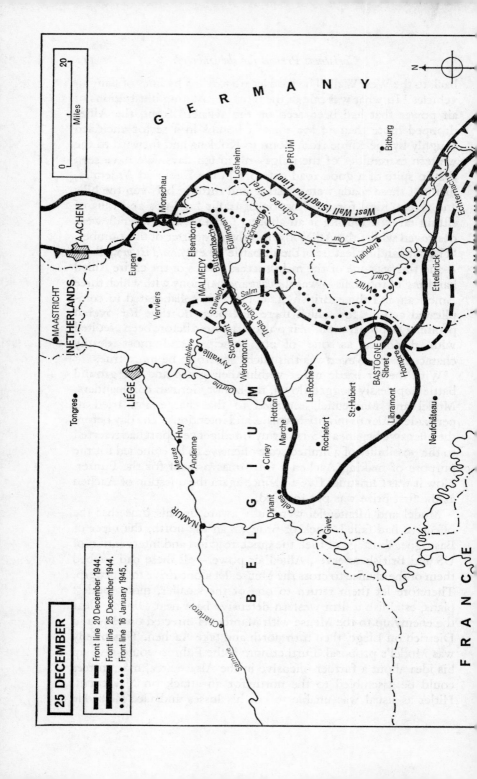

25 DECEMBER

Front line 20 December 1944.
Front line 25 December 1944.
Front line 16 January 1945.

0   20
Miles

N

GERMANY

NETHERLANDS

BELGIUM

FRANCE

MAASTRICHT
Tongres
AACHEN
Eupen
Verviers
LIÉGE
Huy
Andenne
Ciney
Dinant
Givet
NAMUR
Charleroi

Monschau
Elsenborn
Eupen
MALMEDY
Stavelot
Amblève
Trois Ponts
Stoumont
Werbomont
Aywaille
Salm
Ourthe
Hotton
Marche
La Roche
Rochefort
St-Hubert
BASTOGNE
Sibret
Hompre
Libramont
Neufchâteau

Losheim
Büllingen
Bütgenbach
Schönberg
Schnee Eifel
West Wall (Siegfried Line)
PRÜM
Bitburg
Ettelbrück
Echternach
Vianden
Clerf
Wiltz
Our

Meuse
Sambre

would not give up the Alsace attack since this would free Patton to divert more reinforcements to his columns advancing towards Bastogne. On the other hand he did agree to the operation which would clear the area up to the Meuse—not because he accepted Aachen as an ultimate objective but simply because he could not reach Antwerp without crossing the Meuse. Above all Bastogne must be taken first. But in the event not Antwerp, nor Aachen, nor even Bastogne were destined to be Christmas presents for the Führer's last Christmas. Instead he was to be presented with an end to his advance, an end to the whole offensive except for defeat and withdrawal.

On Christmas Day itself at three o'clock in the morning, the Germans attacked Bastogne once more. Manteuffel now had the best part of three divisions for the task, including the newly arrived 15th Panzer Grenadier. The main attack went in at the north-west of the city, one of the strongest points in the defence. Although the assaulting troops penetrated the defences with tanks and infantry, US tank destroyers sited for just such an eventuality knocked out all the German tanks. Without tank support the German infantry were quickly eliminated.

An American newspaperman, Mackenzie, who was in Bastogne throughout the battle, described the action of the 1st Battalion of 502 Airborne Regiment during this assault:

The enemy [about 18 Mark IV panzers and some hundreds of infantry seemed to have taken part in the attack] came on without hesitating, and our forward tank destroyers began to withdraw towards Rolle. The enemy tanks opened up on them and both were wrecked. This success apparently encouraged the attackers; they came plunging directly at C Company's line. The Company Commander did not know he had the support of tank destroyers in the woods behind him, and decided he could best meet the charge by pulling back to the edge of the wood. From the woodside, C Company's machine guns, bazookas and rifles toppled into the snow in large numbers the enemy infantrymen riding on the tanks. The column altered its course unexpectedly then and headed towards Champs. This turning exposed the flank of the tank column to the gunners of the two tank destroyers hidden in the woods. They opened up for the first time. Now the Germans were exposed to fire from four quarters. The tank destroyers pounded three tanks into fiery ruins almost at once. Company B outside Champs hit the column from the front. Company C continued to belabour it from the woods. 502 Regimental Headquarters group itself had the quarry in range and knocked out a Mark IV with a bazooka. Only one enemy tank survived to get into Champs. It was wrecked by A Company bazookas and a 57mm gun. Company C rounded up 35 prisoners. The dead around the smashed tanks numbered 67.

Next day, 26 December, in spite of renewed German attacks, Patton's relieving forces drove into Bastogne.

By 26 December the 4th US Armoured Division had been battling its way forward for four days to reach Bastogne. It had not been easy. That afternoon two of the battalion commanders of Combat Command R, Lieutenant-Colonel Creighton Abrams* and Lieutenant-Colonel George Jaques had reached the high ground overlooking Clochimont. They were still about four miles from Bastogne cross-roads and the task they had been given was to go not for Bastogne but for Sibret, a village to their north-west and roughly the same distance from Bastogne as they were. Directly to the north in their path between themselves and Bastogne was the village of Assenois. Seeing the transport planes re-supplying the besieged city made them determined to drive direct to the garrison's relief and ignore their orders about capturing Sibret. As both Abrams' 37th Tank Battalion and Jaques' 53rd Armoured Infantry Battalion had suffered more than 50 per cent casualties since 4th Armoured Division had begun its battle to reach Bastogne, they could not afford many more. Abrams had only 20 tanks left. They therefore ordered a small tank–infantry team to smash its way through Assenois while the full weight of their artillery suitably occupied the Germans in that village. The team was not to stop until they reached the defenders of Bastogne. And so more or less it transpired. Part of the tank–infantry force broke right through Assenois while the artillery kept the Germans' heads down, and another began a serious fight for the village itself, which included the business of clearing from the road mines scattered by the Germans after the leading tank elements had driven past them. At about 5 p.m. the leading tank crews reached the defence perimeter

* Now General Abrams, who succeeded General Westmoreland in command of all US forces in Vietnam.

of Bastogne. McAuliffe himself went quickly to meet the commander of his relieving force. 'I'm glad to see you', he told Captain Dwight as he shook hands. It now remained for Combat Command R to secure and strengthen the corridor that had been cut through to Bastogne—a process which yielded 400 German prisoners in Assenois alone—and the job was done.

This setback to Manteuffel's struggle for Bastogne was matched by a comparable setback to the leading group of his 2nd Panzer Division. The joint action of the British Guards Armoured Division and 2nd US Armoured Division, put paid to any idea of reaching the Meuse or Dinant. This *Kampfgruppe* of 2nd Panzer Division suffered a crushing defeat west of Rochefort, while Collins' 7th Corps kept Panzer Lehr and 116th Panzer busy and by 27 December, as Chester Wilmot put it, 'the spearhead of Manteuffel's Fifth Panzer Army lay broken in the snow'. One of the most serious things that can possibly happen to one in a battle, Tweedledee had gravely observed to Alice, is to get one's head cut off. It was precisely this fate which had overtaken Model's group of Panzer Armies.

8

Final Fling and Failure

My Führer, in the name of the assembled commanders I wish
to give you the firm assurance on the part of leadership and
troops that everything, absolutely everything, will be done
to make this offensive a success. We ourselves know where
in our first offensive we have made mistakes. We shall
learn from them.

von Rundstedt, 28 December 1944

On 28 December 1944 the two opposing Supreme Commanders
conferred with their subordinates. Both Hitler and Eisenhower
were hungry for attack, an appetite not shared by all those
required to carry it out. The prospects for the Allies were the
more promising, for the German offensive had finally forfeited
two of the indispensable qualities of successful attack—momentum
and manoeuvrability. The seemingly endless draining of their
strength at Bastogne, the *Schwerpunkt's* head cut off at Rochefort,
Allied air power—which as von Rundstedt later declared 'devasta-
tingly contributed to the halting of the Ardennes offensive' since
'the lack of manoeuvrability and the inability to bring supplies
up caused the undertaking to fail'—all these meant that the
offensive had ceased to be one. In other words it seemed that the
classic moment for the Allies to take advantage of the Germans'
floundering about and to counter-attack had arrived. But there
was disagreement as to whether this was in fact the moment.
Bradley's view was that a strong assault in the south by 3rd Army
reinforced to the tune of three divisions from Eisenhower's
SHAEF reserve, together with a comparable push by 1st Army in
the north, making use of the four British divisions which
Montgomery had in reserve, would complete the Germans'
discomfiture and eliminate the Bulge once and for all. Yet the

22   *US artillery in the battle for Bastogne*

23   *Bastogne air supply*

24 *British airborne troops advance*

circumspect Montgomery still wished to wait. He had two reasons for doing so. First he thought—wrongly as it turned out—that the Germans were about to make one more effort in the north, and since their principal strength was there it was a reasonable supposition but that in any event he must allow the enemy finally to exhaust themselves before striking back; secondly he did not believe that there was sufficient strength in the 1st Army to mount a proper counter-attack unless he made use of *all* his British reserves, and these he wished to keep up his sleeve for the coming battle of the Rhine. The American willingness to commit everything they had at once is readily understood when we remember that more and more divisions were still on the way from the United States. For Montgomery, as for Wellington a hundred and forty years earlier, Britain had but one army available for Europe and he was determined that it would not be frittered away before the war was won. Eisenhower, as so often before, accepted Montgomery's arguments. He later recorded the outcome of their meeting.

We agreed that the best thing to do in this situation was to strengthen the front, reorganize units, and get thoroughly ready for a strong counterblow, in the meantime preparing to beat off any German attack that might be launched . . . if no such German attack was launched Montgomery would begin his own offensive on the morning of January 3.

On the same day as this conference, however, Bradley and Patton, reinforced by three reserve divisions, renewed their attack on the south of the Bulge. It was none too soon, for the Germans were now concentrating, far too late, on Bastogne. Both US generals were furious with Montgomery for what they regarded as his excessive caution, and Bradley went so far as to demand the return of 1st and 9th Armies to his command. Yet this was the precise time that Montgomery chose for harping back to his old theme of a single tactical commander in the north. He records in his *Memoirs* that the crisis of the Ardennes battle had obliged Eisenhower to do what he, Montgomery, had always suggested, and it may have been this feeling that he had been right all along (neglecting perhaps that Bradley's unwary deployment and eccentric positioning of his headquarters was what caused the command difficulties in the first place) which prompted him to rub salt in the wound. The language he chose

I

to use to the Supreme Commander bordered on the insolent. Referring to his idea that all forces engaged on the northern thrust to the Ruhr, in his view the critical objective, he wrote that it would be necessary for Eisenhower 'to be very firm on the subject, and any loosely worded statement will be quite useless'. He almost began to write Eisenhower's directive for him and suggested that it should finish by vesting himself, Montgomery, with full operational direction and control of the whole tactical battle on the northern thrust. If this were not done, Montgomery maintained, they would fail. Although, when he realized how ill received it had been, Montgomery subsequently asked Eisenhower to tear up the letter, Eisenhower's reply which enclosed his outline plan for the opening weeks of 1945 made two points which stand out from all the others. Firstly he wrote: 'You disturb me by predictions of "failure" unless your exact opinions in the matter of giving you command over Bradley are met in detail.' Secondly he did not agree, and surely in this he was right for it certainly would not have worked, that one Army Group Commander should fight his own battle and at the same time give orders to another Army Group Commander. He could go no further in the matter than placing a complete US Army under Montgomery's command, because it was militarily necessary. And this is what his plan did.

The plan itself was to destroy enemy forces west of the Rhine, north of the Moselle, and to prepare for crossing the Rhine itself with the main effort north of the Ruhr. The initial tasks were to reduce the Ardennes Bulge, then for 1st and 3rd US Armies both under Bradley to drive to the Rhine via Prüm–Bonn and for 21st Army Group with US 9th Army under command to get ready to attack from the Reichswald Forest and gain possession of all ground west of the Rhine. Bradley's and Montgomery's headquarters were to move close together and any special problems of coordinating boundaries between the two Army Group Commanders would be for Montgomery to arbitrate.

Arbitration was a much easier affair for the Supreme Commander of the Wehrmacht as he made clear in his talk to the generals at Adlershorst on the same day, 28 December, that Eisenhower and Montgomery had met at Hasselt. Von Rundstedt's attempt to persuade Hitler to abandon the offensive, go over to the defensive on a line east of Bastogne and withdraw what was left of the two Panzer Armies to meet the inevitable Allied counter-attack (this was the precise course of German action that Eisenhower most feared and strived most to prevent) was in vain. 'In a military sense,' Hitler declared, 'it is decisive that in the West we are moving from a sterile defence to the offensive. The offensive alone will enable us to give once more a successful turn to this war in the West.' During his long speech Hitler with a mixture of historical rhetoric and military calculation demonstrated once again his endorsement of Henry Adams' point that 'practical politics consists of ignoring facts'.

It is when we consider what it was that Eisenhower most feared and what it was that Hitler determined to do that we may see once more how compromise between intention and capability is indispensable to military operations which are to have some chance of prospering. Hitler could not bear to think of being on the defensive. He might have done well to recall Wellington's definition of it. 'By defensive', he wrote once to a subordinate commander in India, 'I do not mean that you should wait in any particular place till you shall be attacked, but that you should attack any party that may come within your reach.' It was in this respect that there was something to be said for the Small Solution.

The Allied advance on Germany in 1944 might perhaps be compared with the Allied advance on France 130 years earlier. In February 1814 the great Napoleon had given an extraordinary demonstration of what to do in such circumstances, of what could be done with the limited pounce. A. G. Macdonnell has described how the Emperor suddenly

> sprang to life, and showed the world a sight that had not been seen during eighteen years, had been half forgotten, had been obscured by vast events, the sight of the young gunner-general of 1796 handling an army of 50,000 men. For twenty-six days Napoleon wore his 'long boots', whirling his little army up and down the valleys, striking blow after blow, now flinging Blücher back in rout, now appearing miraculously upon the Austrian flank and sending Schwartzenberg spinning back towards the frontier, now cutting off and almost annihilating a Russian Corps.

This was what Wellington meant by the defensive. This was offensive defence indeed. But the Ardennes offensive was not like this. If it needed a Napoleonic parallel, there is one, as Piers

Mackesy* has shown, to hand. It was like Soult's bouncing out of the Pyrenees towards Pamplona in July 1813, dithering, losing a chance, launching his main assault after Wellington had made his arrangements, and being bundled back again. Hitler was not interested in the limited pounce or in the offensive defence. For him it was all or nothing. The German situation, explained the Führer, was very simple. It was a question of whether Germany had the will to continue in being or whether it would be destroyed. There were to be no half measures. The Reich was fighting for its very existence. If Germany lost the war, she would perish.

This was not to be taken as an indication that Hitler 'even remotely' contemplated that the war could in fact be lost by Germany. Capitulation was unthinkable. Difficult situations were nothing new. He had been in far worse situations than the one they were in now. Let the generals be in no doubt therefore that nothing could wear their Supreme Commander down. Nothing could shake his determination to fight on and pursue his objectives with fanaticism until at last the scales came down in their favour. Having made clear that there was no question of abandoning the offensive, Hitler proceeded to analyse what had happened up till then and set the stage for the next series of attacks.

In his analysis of the battle so far, Hitler was able to convince himself that the entire strategic position had been transformed during the foregoing two weeks. While it might be true that the really decisive results he had expected had not been achieved, there had been a 'tremendous easing of the situation'. The enemy had been thrown off balance, had had to abandon all their own offensive plans, commit their reserves, re-group everywhere. The reasons he gave both for what success his offensive had had and for its not being even *more* decisive, while not untrue in themselves, missed the main points—the brilliant adaptability shown by the Americans, the fatal lack of adaptability inspired by himself, and the critical influence of air power. Nor did he mention the ultimately decisive strategic factor that whereas Allied losses could be replaced, his own could not. He put their initial gains down to three causes—the fact that they had succeeded in keeping the operation secret, the fact the weather had been favourable to their assembly and concealment of troops, and the

* Piers Mackesy, 'Wellington: The General', *Wellingtonion Studies,* Ed. Michael Howard, 1959.

fact that the enemy did not believe them capable of mounting an offensive in the first place. In other words Hitler was simply saying that two of the prerequisites for a successful offensive—surprise and concentration—had been realized. The third and fourth requirements, on the other hand, speed and mobility, had been compromised, not by ill-management or faulty planning or lack of leadership, but by 'unlucky moments'. The roads were bad, bridges had taken longer to repair than had been thought and then it had become clear what loss of time could mean. To a panzer division ten hours lost could mean a whole campaign lost. Speed in short was everything. In elaborating on speed's partner, mobility, Hitler touched on a matter which has been puzzling the British and American armies ever since and is no nearer solution; that is to say that if units are over-mechanized, overburdened with vehicles and encumbered with every variety of 'cag', mobility goes out of the window. He recalled a Mountain Division which in 1940 in spite of having very little transport had 'whizzed along like a weasel' and almost outpaced the panzer units. In the recent battle, roads had become so clogged that the armies' full strength could not be deployed. 'Either the artillery, or the infantry or the grenadiers won't get to the front. Actually the battle out front has been fought by quite small spearheads. That happened in the fighting of Army Group Model.'

Hitler used his arguments about the need for speed as one justification for continuing the offensive. They could not allow the enemy to regain his wits. The enemy had been obliged to thin out on other parts of the front, particularly in Alsace, and advantage must be taken of so unique a situation even at the risk of not themselves being quite as strong as they would like to be. As for being ready, 'I have been in this business for eleven years and during those eleven years I have never heard anybody report that everything was completely ready. . . . You are never entirely ready. That is plain.' Ready or not, Model was required to strengthen his grip on the Ardennes, renew his attempts to deal with the American forces at Bastogne and reorganize for yet one more drive to the Meuse. This action would ensure that the Americans were kept busy, and so allow another offensive by the German forces in the Saar to break out at Alsace.

I want to emphasize right away that the aims of all these offensives which will be delivered blow by blow is the elimina-

tion of all American units south of the penetration point* by
annihilating them piece by piece, division by division. . . . The
task of our forces at the penetration point is to tie down as
many enemy forces as possible. . . . I appeal to you to support
this operation with all your force, with all your zest, with all
your energy.

The success of these operations, Hitler maintained, would knock
away half of the enemy's Western front. Then they would see.
'I do not believe that in the long run he will be able to resist
45 German divisions which will then be ready. We shall yet
master fate!'

In spite of von Rundstedt's assurances of doing absolutely
everything to make the offensive a success and of learning from
their former mistakes, instead of Hitler's armies mastering fate,
fate went on to master them. New Year's Day 1945 was the day
that eight German divisions attacked from the Saar to the south,
both west and east of the Vosges. Hitler had predicted, drawing
as usual on German military history, that as in the past New Year's
Day would continue to be a good military omen and that the
German people would put behind them the miseries of 1944 and
see what an excellent beginning 1945 was to have. In fact there
was no tactical surprise this time and very little progress. The
main German attack towards the Saverne Gap was quickly
halted, while east of the Vosges the Germans found themselves
faced by a skilful and resolute withdrawal which ended at the
Maginot Line. Even Himmler, commanding Army Group *Ober-
Rhein* in the attack from the Colmar Pocket, succeeded only in
getting a small bridgehead over the Rhine to the north of
Strasbourg. Throughout the operation Eisenhower was not
obliged to switch reserves from elsewhere. The threat to Strasbourg, however, which was a threat also to what had been salvaged
of France's honour so upset de Gaulle that once more political
sensibilities called the tune for military enterprises.

It was appropriate that the greatest Allied expert at reconciling
political and military contradictions and solving strategic conun-
drums—Churchill—was on parade for the occasion. Initially
Devers, commanding 6th US Army Group, alerted by his
intelligence staff of an impending German offensive into Upper
Alsace, gave orders that while efforts would be made to hold

* That is south of the Ardennes Bulge.

Strasbourg and Mulhouse, these efforts would not be allowed to 'jeopardize the integrity of forces in a withdrawal to a rearward position' that is back to the Vosges. General de Lattre de Tassigny, supported by Marshal Juin and de Gaulle himself, had already interpreted these instructions in such a way to define the defence of Strasbourg as 'unequivocal'. After the German offensive had begun Juin told Bedell-Smith, Eisenhower's Chief of Staff, on 2 January that de Gaulle had ordered de Lattre to defend Strasbourg come what might. Bedell-Smith denounced this action as insubordination and added that the French First Army would get no supplies. In that event, Juin replied, the American forces would be forbidden to use French roads and railways. Because of this confrontation, it was arranged that de Gaulle and Eisenhower would meet next day, 3 January, and in order to reinforce his position, de Gaulle had sent telegrams the evening before to Roosevelt and Churchill stating that the French Government could not accept such a withdrawal from Alsace and asking for their support. Typical of the two recipients were their replies. Roosevelt simply answered that as it was a military affair, he would leave it to Eisenhower. Churchill came in person. Although it is clear that his intervention was decisive, from the accounts left by himself, Eisenhower and de Gaulle, the casual reader would not deduce as much. Both the Prime Minister and the Supreme Commander in their subsequent accounts of the incident refer to the former's being there as—chance. De Gaulle predictably gives himself the credit for Churchill's presence and his own success in getting Eisenhower's former decision reversed.

De Gaulle's account of the affair casts both Churchill and Eisenhower in unusual roles—agreeing with him, de Gaulle:

During the afternoon of 3 January accompanied by Juin, I went to Versailles. Mr Churchill, alerted by my message, had also decided to come, apparently disposed to provide his good offices. General Eisenhower explained the situation, which was certainly a serious one. He did not conceal that the extent and the energy of the German offensive in the Ardennes as well as the sudden appearance of new enemy weapons—robot planes, Panther tanks, etc—had morally shaken the Allied forces and even surprised himself.

So far so good; but when Eisenhower went on to explain that in order to regain lost ground and resume the initiative, it would be necessary to reconstitute a reserve, and that in view of the precarious position in Alsace caused by the enemy's attack there, he had ordered the troops back to a shorter line, de Gaulle was quick to point out that this was not a war-game. Strategy could not be allowed to pull any weight at all when French territory was involved. Alsace was sacred ground. To lose it again would be a national disaster. 'At the present moment we are concerned with Strasbourg. I have ordered the French First Army to defend the city. It will therefore do so, in any case.' Churchill weighed in with a view that the significance of Alsace to the French must be taken into consideration. There were further exchanges before 'finally the Supreme Commander came round to my point of view'.

In any event Devers was told to hold Strasbourg firmly, and he did. This was the story of what Churchill referred to as an 'awkward situation' during the Ardennes battle.*

On the same day as this conference, 3 January, Montgomery began his counter-attack against Houffalize to join up with Patton's 3rd Army attacking from the south. Montgomery's attack was timely for on that day and the next another part of Hitler's directive to the generals was put into effect. The American defences around Bastogne were once more subjected to heavy attack by no fewer than eight German divisions. It was a bitter and costly struggle in weather too bad for Allied air power to come to the rescue. But Patton had sufficient concentrations of artillery and sufficient reserves of infantry to prevent dangerous penetration of his defences. By 5 January Montgomery's pressure from the north obliged Model to slacken his pressure on Bastogne in order to meet this new northern threat. Not that Montgomery's attack made much progress in terms of distance. The strong and well-managed defences in country ideal for defence, together with the Germans' skill at siting weapons, laying mines and fighting a slow withdrawal under winter conditions (much of it acquired in that best or worst of all schools of winter withdrawal, Russia), made the Allied advance expensive and slow.

For a British infantry battalion fighting its way forward to Houffalize against both the Germans and the elements, Mont-

---

* De Gaulle adds that before leaving, Eisenhower confided to him that he was having a lot of trouble with Montgomery—'a general of great ability but a bitter critic and a mistrustful subordinate'. De Gaulle's reply, characteristic of him and magnificent in its way, must have been a poor consolation—'Glory has its price'. Fortunately it was a price Eisenhower was prepared to pay.

gomery's much-heralded counter-attack was no picnic. The country itself—thickly wooded hills and valleys, the trees having such low branches that it was very difficult to see more than a yard or two, steep, narrow, ice-covered tracks and very few of them, movement about as tricky as it could be—was more suitable for jungle warfare than the rapid and wide deployment of tank, infantry and artillery teams. All these problems of movement and observation meant that it was impossible to obtain accurate information as to the enemy's whereabouts, so much so that during the frequent blizzards, British and German troops sometimes found themselves mixed up together without at first realizing it. The impossibility of digging in properly with the ground frozen hard, the question of how to get hot food up when vehicles could not cope with the going, frostbite, exhaustion—it was only when a new broad-tracked vehicle was forthcoming that the problems of supply and evacuation were solved—all these things compounded the difficulties. Major-General Essame, who formerly had commanded the 1st East Lancashire Regiment, describes in his excellent *Battle for Germany* how the battalion fared in one of its many battles:

On the 6th [January] orders arrived to continue the attack on the morrow and take the village of Grimblimont over a mile ahead and, nestling out of view behind the crest, a hill 1,500 yards to their front; both of which dominated the enemy's escape route to La Roche. Patrols during the night and prisoners taken confirmed that the 60th Panzer Grenadier Regiment of 116th Panzer Division was holding the position in strength and was supported by tanks. It snowed steadily for the remainder of the night.

At 11.50 hours on the 7th, the battalion began to form up. The blizzard howled and raged with ever increasing intensity and not even the massive Christmas tree regalia which the fighting soldier dons for battle could in any way relieve the numbing effect of the Arctic wind.

A shell fell on the Advanced Battalion Headquarters, killing the Adjutant and two lance-corporals and wounding 11 of the Commanding Officer's party. Only Lieutenant-Colonel Hill, his Intelligence Officer, and one orderly escaped. A large shell fragment virtually degutted his wireless set, forcing him henceforward to rely on personal contact alone to control his companies. H hour came at noon. At this very moment the support squadron of tanks reported that they could not get across the Rau de Grimblimont.* Nonetheless A and D Companies, punctually on the hour, plunged forward in the snow, followed by the remainder of the battalion across the completely open ground. An immense weight of artillery and mortar fire, as intense as any experienced in Normandy, descended on them, including air-burst shells which exploded with a particularly vindictive bang and produced large clouds of black smoke. The Company wireless sets were soon knocked out; casualties began to mount, but all pressed on.

At last they reached the crest. Now there was a check on the front of the left forward company, D Company—three enemy Mark IV tanks in hull-down positions barred the way; enemy machine guns on their left opened up. The Company went to ground. Without the aid of their own tanks and gunners, further advance seemed suicidal. It was now that Major Macindoe, commanding the battery in support, although wounded, came to their aid. Somehow or other he manoeuvred his half-track forward and [by wirelessing to his regiment's guns] engaged the enemy tanks and machine guns holding up the battalion. At the same time Lieutenant Tuffnell led what remained of his platoon down the reverse slope of the hill. As soon as they got within Piat† range of the nearest tank, Private Wride calmly sited his weapon in full view of the enemy and scored a direct hit with his first shot which jammed the turret of the nearest Mark IV tank. The remaining tanks withdrew.

Major Lake, the Company Commander, now gathered the remnants of his company, formed them into one platoon, and fought his way forward into the houses on the edge of the village of Grimblimont. Meanwhile on his right, A Company disregarding the hold-up on their left had struggled up the hill in the face of fierce machine-gun fire. When they reached their objective, the high ground north-west of the village, only Major Cetre, the Company Commander, and 25 men had survived. The other two companies of the battalion now passed through into the village. The enemy fought well. Every house had to be systematically cleared. How many Germans were killed is not known, as the falling snow obliterated them in a

* Start line for the attack.

† The Piat was a small man-handled infantry anti-tank gun.

few seconds. The battalion's six anti-tank guns now came up. Although they had lost 11 officers and 232 men, nothing could now dislodge the 1st East Lancashires from the village of Grimblimont. After five days exposure, with practically no sleep, to vicious enemy fire and abominable weather, they were nonetheless ready to fight on.

If the infantry had an unpleasant time of it, their discomfort was shared by the armoured regiments supporting them. 29th Armoured Brigade took part with the 6th Airborne Division in what they described as 'one of the toughest little battles in the history of the campaign'—a battle for the village of Bure, to the south of Rochefort and about a kilometre from the River Homme, over which crossings had to be seized in order to continue the advance. The famous Fife and Forfar Yeomanry had a bad time of it on the first day of Montgomery's counter-offensive, 3 January:

'C' Squadron were now ordered to send up a Troop into Bure and a very lively time was had by all. The weather had now become positively savage. Spasmodic blizzards reduced visibility often to a matter of yards, deepening snow made ground conditions nearly impossible, and the cold was most searching. As if these conditions were not enough to be going on with, heavy enemy shelling had to be endured, especially by the airborne troops.

Meantime the Troop from 'C' Squadron that had been sent off to support the attack on Bure was making an adventurous approach to that disputed village. The tanks slithered from side to side on the glassy road. Two hundred yards short of the village the leading tank went up on a mine and this gave the remainder of the Troop some cause for thought. However, a diversion was found, the village was entered from another quarter and another of the tanks was hit, this time by an armour-piercing shell. The unfortunate airborne troops were also meeting trouble from a strong and determined enemy. Major R. L. Leith, who had come up with the 'C' Troop, made liaison with the OC Parachute Battalion, and as darkness was falling the attackers could not hope to make any further progress that night. So, with the British holding one-third of the village and the enemy the rest, a halt was called to the fighting. One Troop of 'C' Squadron remained with the infantry throughout the night, while the remainder of the Squadron proceeded by a series of intoxicated slithers back along the snow-filled road to Tellin.

If a competition were held among the survivors of 2nd Fife and Forfar Yeomanry to-day to decide which was the most perishing period of the whole of the European campaign, 'A' Squadron, Regimental HQ and 'F' Company Rifle Brigade would certainly vote for the nights which were spent on Chapel Hill. This feature, one thousand feet high, was a bastion vital to the success of the operations around Bure. With snow showers howling through the trees, not a solidly built house anywhere in sight, the country was at its mid-winter worst. The men were soaked by their continuous work among snow, and supply vehicles could only be towed up the slopes to a 'thus-far-and-no-further' point, after which they had to be man-handled by the exhausted troops.

From early light on 4th January there was enough excitement to satisfy anyone. All three tanks which had been left in Bure were knocked out by well-directed enemy fire, and when 'C' Squadron, now in position to the south-east of the village, pushed another Troop forward with the intention of out-flanking the village, another tank was lost. There, for hours, the situation remained deadlocked. Each side resorted to heavy shelling. It was certainly remarkable that relatively few casualties were incurred by the Yeomanry, for their position was simply plastered. There were times when it seemed as though the whole Squadron must be out of action. The vehicles looked so shrapnel-scarred and mud-bespattered that they had the appearance of being knocked out. Corporal Gorman and Trooper Lines were killed in this action and Lieutenant Jones and several troopers wounded.

At nightfall 'C' Squadron was withdrawn to Tellin. This village, though right on the edge of the war zone, and fre-quently under German fire, had still a good many civilians in it. And hospitable ones, too! Particularly memorable was the kindness of the nuns who gave food and wine to the tired and shivering tank crews until a direct hit on the convent put an end to the meal. On 5 January the 23rd Hussars were ordered to relieve, while the Regiment moved back to Tellin.

The 23rd Hussars did not fare much better when they tried their hand on 5 January:

'A' Squadron moved out very early indeed with orders to have another crack at Bure. By dint of going across country they reached Tellin, the last village before Bure, by ten o' clock. Now Bure lay at the foot of a very high hill to the south of it and, the original plan having been scratched, or rather failed, 'A' Squadron were ordered to reconnoitre this high ground in order to cover infantry into Bure from the right flank. This hill, steep, wooded and covered in snow, lay half shrouded in mist. The infantry, the 12th Parachute Battalion was contacted, and the plan discussed. 1st Troop was to advance in support of infantry along the main road into and through Bure whilst 3rd and 4th Troop with Squadron Headquarters slowly climbed out of Tellin up a steep and narrow track in an attempt to reach the crest. This track was covered with ice, the visibility barely thirty yards, and the progress murderously slow. But the crest was reached and, Lieutenant Leather leading, Third Troop pushed on to the vital eminence above Bure. Behind them, however, the enemy had laid an ambush. Taking advantage of the mist and snow and of the wooded nature of the ground, the Germans had concealed a party which now laid mines across the track, and brought bazookas into action.

First Sergeant Huthwaite's tank, coming up with 4th Troop, went up on a mine, and immediately behind him Sergeant Roberts was bazooka'd and killed and the Regiment lost one of its most popular and able tank commanders. The tank, however, remained intact and Sergeant Huthwaite, by an act of great daring and enterprise which won for him the MM, gathered the crews of both tanks together and brought them all back on his tank.

That incident in itself was enough to show the hazards of the undertaking. Tanks were not made to fight blindly in fog, up icy mountain tracks, and it soon became obvious that the whole enterprise was doomed, if not to disaster, at least to failure.

By early afternoon it was therefore decided to withdraw and abandon the attack. The mined tank, however, had to be retrieved, and the armoured recovery vehicle, manned by Sergeant Wright and his crew, and protected by 'H' Company, went up to fetch it in.

In the meanwhile 1st Troop was fighting its way through Bure with the remainder of the Battalion. It was found that the Fifes and another Battalion had, in fact, cleared the larger part of it at great cost to themselves and with heavy casualties to the enemy. But the enemy still clung to the eastern edge of the village and some of the remaining ruins. The attack to clear these positions at first went well, and good progress was made towards the river at Grupont.

There, however, the tanks moved forward more warily down the narrow village street. The troop leader, Lieutenant Goss, led with the utmost determination and bravery. But it was all in vain and both his own and the tank following were hit and destroyed. Four of the crews were killed, the wounded having to make their way back under fire. Bure was, in fact, one of the nastiest spots the Squadron had ever been in. The Germans clung to the houses and ruins, hid in cellars and catacombs, fighting and sniping grimly to the end. It wasn't a place for a depleted battalion and half a troop of tanks. Finally the attack was abandoned and our forces withdrawn. 'A' Squadron fell back on Tellin and occupied defensive positions around it for the next few days.

Even out of action, it was no picnic:

The ground was frozen solid and no shelter could be dug. There was nothing for it but to camp out. Everyone did as best he could, but the most desperate measures hardly sufficed to keep one warm, and three nights were more than enough for anything living or human.

Perhaps the worst part of it all were the feeding arrangements. As no fires could be lit, and all visible movement had to be avoided, the food had to come by cook's truck before dawn and after dusk. But the tea froze faster than one could drink it, and the stew turned into iced jelly. No one thought it very funny in the snow, in the cold, and at seven in the morning.

In spite of their stubborn defence the Germans were obliged to abandon Bure in the end. It was not only the spirit of the British infantry and mechanized cavalry, to say nothing of their far more numerous American comrades in arms, which forced the Germans slowly but surely back over all the ground they had re-occupied. It was the fact that this drive of Montgomery's was aimed at Houffalize. This was decisive, for it was a key town and controlled the one good route through which Model's panzer formations to the west of it—there were seven of them—would

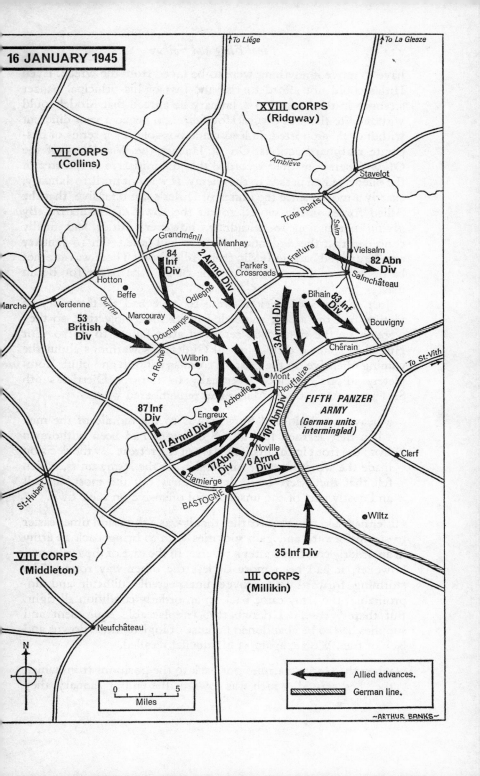

16 JANUARY 1945

↑To Liège   ↑To La Gleaze

XVIII CORPS
(Ridgway)

Amblève

Stavelot

VII CORPS
(Collins)

Trois Points   *Salm*

Grandménil   Manhay

Fraiture   Vielsalm

84 Inf Div   **2 Armd Div**

Parker's Crossroads   **82 Abn Div**

Salmchâteau

Hotton   Odiegne

Beffe   Bihain   **83 Inf Div**

Marche   Verdenne   *Ourthe*   Marcouray

53 British Div   Douchamps   Bouvigny

Cherain

La Roche   Wilbrin   **3 Armd Div**   To St-Vith

Mont   Houffalize

87 Inf Div   Achouffe   **FIFTH PANZER ARMY**
(German units intermingled)

Engreux

11 Armd Div   Noville   Clerf

Hamierge   **17 Abn Div**   **6 Armd Div**

St-Hubert   BASTOGNE

Wiltz

VIII CORPS
(Middleton)   **35 Inf Div**

III CORPS
(Millikin)

Neufchâteau

N

0 ___ 5
Miles

◀━━━━ Allied advances.

▨▨▨▨ German line.

~ARTHUR BANKS~

have to move if anything were to be saved from the wreck. Even Hitler could not afford to risk the loss of his principal panzer strength in the West. On 8 January he agreed that Model could withdraw to the area east of Houffalize. So began a very different withdrawal, supported, indeed made possible, by a series of desperate rearguard actions. On 14 January the War Diary of the OKW Operations Staff recorded that the initiative in the area of the offensive had passed to the enemy. It was not until 16 January, exactly a month since the outset of Hitler's last offensive, that the Allied forces finally closed round the town of Houffalize. By giving permission to withdraw, however, Hitler had finally conceded that the Ardennes offensive had failed. On 16 January also he arrived back in Berlin from Adlershorst There was another battle to be directed—the last one of all—the battle for Berlin itself.

Just as the SS Divisions were to have had all the glory of victory had the attack succeeded in its main objective, so they were to be the first to be removed after failure to do so. For Hitler, in spite of dismissing all Guderian's warnings about the coming offensive on the Eastern front as rubbish and bluff, 'completely idiotic', decided eventually to transfer Dietrich's 6th SS Panzer Army there. Manteuffel remembered what

> a heavy psychological blow it was to the morale of the men when they learned that all SS divisions had been withdrawn from the front in the first few days of the retreat . . . the decision made the worst possible impression on the Army units, which felt that they were being left to carry out the most difficult and costly part of the unsuccessful offensive on their own.

Hitler had said two years earlier that it was a thousand times easier to storm forward and gain victories than to bring back an army in an orderly condition after a reverse. In the case of the Ardennes, however, it had been more or less the other way round. The storming forward had proved unexpectedly difficult and unprofitable; the army came back in an orderly condition all right. But there were fatal drawbacks. Irreplaceable equipment and supplies had to be abandoned because of logistic breakdowns and lack of fuel. Worse, again as Manteuffel recalled,

> when the German armies got back to the positions from which they had started, which was towards the end of January, they

found no arrangements had been made, despite all their requests, to reinforce their diminished battle strength. There were no adequate supplies of ammunition, there was neither equipment nor material to consolidate their positions, and there were no reinforcements of any kind available.

This was not surprising. It had been no mean feat to scrape up 28 divisions for the Ardennes offensive with all the artillery and logistic support that went with it. But in a little month, Hitler had lost 120,000 soldiers, 600 tanks and assault guns, more than 1,600 aircraft, together with endless more equipment and supplies. He had gambled his last reserves. There were no more German armies to be raised.

This melancholy reflection made no difference to the Wehrmacht's Supreme Commander. He had already consoled himself by quoting to General Thomale from the letters of Frederick the Great: 'I started this war with the most wonderful army in Europe; today* I've got a muck heap. I have no leaders any more, my generals are incompetent, the officers are no commanders, the troops are wretched.' The Wehrmacht could by no stretch of the imagination be described as muck-heap. On paper it still contained 260 divisions, and this number was still identifiable with various fronts, but the fronts themselves were so numerous—10 divisions struggling with partisans in Yugoslavia, 30 cut off in the Baltic States, 17 holding down Scandinavia, 24 still conducting a successful defence in Italy, 28 in Hungary, and about 75 each on the two critical Eastern and Western fronts. The priceless asset of concentration had gone for ever. There were leaders galore—some dismissed, some not allowed to exercise leadership properly, but certainly no shortage of them. German generals were as experienced, resolute and competent as any that there have ever been in any army at any time. The officers commanded well; the troops still fought bravely and skilfully. In no respect did Hitler's condition resemble that of Frederick the Great in 1760, save in one. His military condition was without hope. Yet it was from this very paradox that Hitler drew strength. Some people, he told Thomale, give up if things go badly.

One can't make world history that way. World history can only be made if, in addition to continual alertness, a man has fanatical determination and courage of his convictions which

* The letter was written in 1760, fifth year of the Seven Years' War.

K

make him master of himself. That's what matters to the soldier in the last analysis. . . . No one can last for ever. We can't, the other side can't. It's merely a question who can stand it longer. The one who must hold out longer is the one who's got everything at stake. *We've got everything at stake.*

Listening to this must have made clear to Thomale what Hitler had meant two years before when he had declared that if necessary he would fight until five minutes past twelve. By his conduct of the Ardennes offensive he had brought the hands of the clock close to midnight.

9
Balance Sheet

The battle of the Ardennes was won primarily by the staunch fighting qualities of the American soldier. . . . After the battle the Germans gave no serious resistance.

Montgomery

What had Hitler gained and what had he lost by mounting Operation *Herbstnebel*? The smell of death was on the air all right, to the tune of more than 20,000 soldiers killed, of which the bulk were German (12,652) and American (8,497). There were only some 200 British dead. Mr Churchill's declaration in the House of Commons that for every British soldier engaged 30 or 40 Americans had been, and for every British soldier lost, 60 to 80 Americans had been, was sufficient justification for his calling it the greatest American battle of the war and an ever-famous American victory. In addition the Americans lost more than 46,000 wounded, nearly 21,000 missing; the British figures, respectively about 1,000 and some 240, are tiny by comparison. Yet it was the Germans whose losses were heaviest of all—totalling 120,000 or more, of whom 50,000 were taken prisoner by the Allies. The losses, then, leaving aside altogether those of equipment, weapons, material, civilians, their houses and possessions, and excluding too those casualties incurred in the Alsace offensive, *Nordwind,* were formidable. For Germany they were losses which would never be replaced. What about the gains—was there for Hitler a harvest of any sort? Did his claim that the enemy had had to abandon all their plans for attack have any validity? In one sense, of course, it did, in that Bradley's Army Group was obliged to stop attacking both north and south of the Ardennes. But the long-term Allied intentions for a spring campaign to cross the

Rhine and finish off the war were not merely not delayed. Their success was accelerated, for having flung away the last of his reserves, when this final assault on the Third Reich was made, Hitler had nothing left to stop it with. The *Official History* concludes that Hitler did not gain anything of value from all the death and destruction which his Ardennes offensive had wrought.

Some historians and commentators have compared the Ardennes battle with Ludendorff's great attack on the Western front in March 1918. They have been able to draw so close a parallel between these two final offensives, pointing to Hitler's inclination to seek precedents in linking one world historical event with another, and to his actually having taken part in the first of the two offensives as an ordinary soldier, as to suggest that it was this link which principally motivated Hitler in mounting the second one. It is the business of historians to find such parallels, however flimsy the evidence for them. In his book about von Rundstedt, Blumentritt, who was his Chief of Staff for two years, makes just such a claim. He is discussing the argument between Hitler and von Rundstedt as to the small or big solutions of the Ardennes offensive, that is whether to advance to the Meuse and roll up the American positions on the Roer, or to go bald-headed for Antwerp and Brussels: 'When the documents of this period are carefully studied and this bitter struggle between Hitler and Rundstedt is revealed in full one is inclined to believe that perhaps Hitler was thinking in terms of the great Marne offensive of 1918 in the First World War.' This might be true in a historical sense, for after all Ludendorff's offensive did bring something like dismay into Allied counsel chambers; it might also be true in the broadest tactical sense—that of driving a wedge between two Allied armies, severing their communications and reaching the sea; it might even be true in the sense that only an offensive could lead to any alteration of the general strategic situation, since by 1918 the longer the Germans waited, the more American manpower and American material would tip the scales against them.

But there the likenesses end. Amiens, the main objective in 1918, was only some 40 miles away from the German jumping-off point at St Quentin; Antwerp was over 100 miles away from the German panzer assembly areas in 1944. In 1918 the Imperial German armies were able to concentrate on one front only since Russian resistance had been smashed in the previous year; in

1944 the spectre of war on two fronts had become an ever present and crippling reality. Air power had carried little decisive weight in 1918; in 1944 it was of all single factors the most decisive. Almost all circumstances were in fact unlike. The terrain was different; the time of year was different; the weather was different; the frontages were different; the reserves available were different. Ludendorff had had no fewer than 100,000 men under his hand *after* committing the assault forces. Hitler may have asked questions about frontages during First World War battles; movement at night up to assembly positions or deadening the sound of wheels and horses with straw may have been common features. But real evidence that Hitler was himself really thinking of a repetition of 1918 is slim indeed. Indeed in his lecture to the generals on 11 and 12 December he specifically referred to his determination not to be manoeuvred into the sort of defensive stalemate which had so characterized that war. It was not an interlocked struggle of massed infantry formations he had in mind. It was blitzkrieg. Thoughts of 1940 and the greatest of all his victories, yes, for it was of the success in 1940—against all the odds and most professional advice—that Hitler reminded his generals on the battle's eve; thoughts of the Seven Years' War and turning disaster into triumph, yes; but Ludendorff's offensive failed and Hitler was not the man to conjure up past failures to inspire himself and his generals with the prospect of present success. Yet it was in failure that one of the true likenesses existed. The other, a principal cause of this dual failure, was, as Colin Coote has reminded us, the likeness of Allied resistance. 'The five [American] regiments did not disintegrate; nor did the three regiments attacked by four divisions farther south. They resisted manfully—as manfully as the British Fifth Army on 21 March 1918; and praise cannot be higher.'

It is perhaps when we consider numbers that the paucity of German success becomes most remarkable. No fewer than three German *armies* (two of which were panzer armies) totalling nearly twenty divisions (before later commitment of those divisions held back in OKW reserve) had assaulted one US corps of four infantry divisions and one armoured division deployed in poorly knit defensive positions without proper depth over a frontage of more than 50 miles. US divisions were generally speaking stronger in numbers than their German equivalents, but nonetheless some 200,000 fighting troops of the Wehrmacht fell on about 80,000 soldiers of Middleton's Corps; the fire power of nearly 2,000 guns and mortars took on an opposing number of less than 400; 800 panzers and self-propelled guns drove forward to meet about half that number. More or less everywhere and in more or less every type of weapon except tanks, the Germans were able to produce the traditional three to one superiority, normally judged to be a prerequisite of successful attack. Often, at points of particular concentration, the superiority rose to as much as six to one. Yet in spite of getting through the defences in two places, and the fact that it was only two places is itself of great significance, in an area where narrowness of front greatly inhibited the German ability to bring greater panzer and artillery strength to bear, the German armies were prevented from turning these penetrations into real breakthroughs by elements of the very US formations whose forward units had already been brushed aside or outflanked. Then once the race for build up began, it was slowly but surely won by the Americans, for on 2 January, the day before Montgomery mounted his counter-attack, the number of US divisions committed to the battle had grown to 26, including eight armoured divisions, while by that same time the number of German divisions had risen to about 30, including eight panzer divisions. This remarkable American build-up had been achieved by quick shifting of weight and assembly of reserves. The German overall superiority of strength had gone. By the time it had gone their maximum penetration had reached a depth of 60 miles, but its average width had already narrowed to 30 miles, while the most forward troops opposite the Meuse itself were operating on a front of a mere five miles. In short American defence of the shoulders had held, and even the most distant advancing *Schwerpunkt* had been halted short of the Meuse.

Von Rundstedt, with no real faith in the operation, despite his often reiterated avowals of absolute loyalty to it and of maximum efforts to ensure success, was therefore not required to go down on his knees and thank God for reaching that river. The offensive will long be remembered as *his*, even though, leaving aside his opposition to it and his attempts to call it off almost as soon as it had started, he had no influence over its course. 'Each step forward in the Ardennes offensive', he told Liddell Hart after the war, 'prolonged our flanks more dangerously deep, making them more susceptible to Allied counter-strokes. I wanted to stop the offensive at an early stage, when it was plain that it could not

attain its aim, but Hitler furiously insisted that it must go on.'
Thus the conditions for the head-losing operation which
Tweedledee deprecated were created. Why was von Rundstedt so
implacably opposed to the offensive? Fundamentally it was because
he wished to employ the newly formed and strong panzer
reserves in a totally different way. As Cassius had put it to Brutus
before Philippi:

> 'Tis better that the enemy seek us:
> So shall he waste his means, weary his soldiers,
> Doing himself offence; whilst we lying still,
> Are full of rest, defence and nimbleness.

But Hitler would have no truck with the 'barren rot of defence'.
He wanted the initiative. The truth was, however, that Hitler
had asked von Rundstedt for both, had given him two in-
compatible tasks—to hold the Western front at all costs *and* to
prepare and conduct a great offensive. Rundstedt was quick to put
his finger on the faults of Hitler's plan. As soon as it was explained
to him, he pointed the inherent dangers of the plan's *success* or
partial success, let alone its failure. The cost of its failure would
mean that he would be unable to fulfil the first of his tasks and
hold on. But ultimate failure was also intrinsic to limited success.
'I am glad', Rundstedt had told Westphal in October 1944,

> that at last we are to receive more forces in the West. Before the
> beginning of this ordained offensive much water will have
> flowed down the Rhine. From a preliminary glance I can say
> that the distant objective of Antwerp cannot be reached with
> the forces available, for their impossibly long flanks would be
> exposed on both sides of an attacking wedge, and there are
> too few divisions available to cover them. Even if Model were
> to push forward only as far as the Meuse, the result would be a
> front line jutting out towards the West, the holding of which
> would require large forces and which would positively invite
> enemy flank attacks. I am of the opinion that a less ambitious
> objective should be found, whereby strong enemy forces might
> be destroyed without great risk. The entire planning of this
> offensive strikes me as failing to meet the demands of reality.

Here we see the real difference between 1940 and 1944. In 1940
the flanks did not matter for the French defences, short of armour
and mobility, indulging in the 'tired Maginot spirit', could not

react against them; in 1944 facing Allied armies of immense mobility and fire-power the flanks dominated the German commanders' thinking. Model, although by suicide he denied himself the benefit of talking to Liddell Hart after the war, thought as Rundstedt did. Perhaps Manteuffel's comments are the most interesting of all, as it was on his front that the main advances were made, where real chances came to hand and were then chucked away again.

Manteuffel's account of the battle has a recurring theme— Bastogne. As early as 18 December after only two days of fighting, it showed itself to be the main stumbling block to his advance. By 20 December although he had bypassed it, its very screening robbed him of the strength he needed to get on west-wards. Already the beckoning glimpse of opportunism was being replaced by the dull alternative of circumspection. Manteuffel had not the strength both to take Bastogne and to get on. On Christmas Eve he telephoned to Führer headquarters and asked what Hitler wanted—for him to use all his strength to overcome Bastogne or to continue masking it and put his main weight to the Meuse. In Manteuffel's view at that point the most that could be done was to reach the Meuse. He gave five reasons —Bastogne itself, the failure of the German 7th Army to carry out its task of protecting the southern flank properly, the certainty of the Allies being on the Meuse in strength, 6th Panzer Army's dis-appointing progress and the need to fight a battle east of the Meuse. Nevertheless, if he was given both OKW's and 6th Panzer Army's reserves then and there, plus enough petrol, plus air support, he would 'take Bastogne, reach the Meuse, swing north and so help 6th Panzer Army to advance'. But he was not given the reserves in time and when he eventually was, there was no petrol for them. Yet at one point Manteuffel was within an ace, within a few hundred yards of capturing two and a half million gallons of enemy petrol at Andrimont. Even after the war, Manteuffel still thought that had he had what he asked for he would have done what he had promised, while conceding that to have stuck his head out so far might merely have meant that in the end rather more of it would have been cut off. In sum, while agreeing that strategically the offensive was justifiable, Manteuffel concludes that insufficient German strength and supplies, which so inhibited movement together with rapid enemy reaction on the ground and undisputed enemy control of the air, added up to failure.

The inadequacies of movement received a striking illustration from Speer in his report to Hitler of 31 December. He pointed out that since the German vehicles could move with impunity only at night and even then without headlights, their mobility was about one third of the Allies' who could maneouvre freely by day and use lights freely by night. Quite apart from tactical movement, this restriction had a terrible effect on the supply situation. Moreover the condition of the roads in the Eifel and the Ardennes was itself an obstacle. But at Hitler's headquarters where operations were being planned and from which orders were given, no account was taken of all these restrictions. Thus plans and orders hopelessly overestimated both the fighting troops' mobility and their supply. In a battle where movement was everything, such prohibition of German mobility was fatal to them.

Not all the Allied commanders take full account of this point in their recollections, although Eisenhower is not among them. 'Even if the German had possessed', he wrote later, 'as efficient supply system as we—which he did not—he would still have found tremendous difficulty in supplying his spearheads over the miserable roads available . . . lack of supply did become one of von Rundstedt's major difficulties in the prosecution of the offensive.' Patton, in his typically personal approach to war saw the whole offensive as an occasion when the Germans had stuck their heads into a meatgrinder with himself in charge of the handle. Bradley's story is overcast by his dislike of Montgomery, his reluctance to hand over two of his armies to Montgomery's command and his absolute fury at the latter's press conference with his tactless references to 'thinking ahead', coming to the rescue and talk of what an interesting battle it had been.

More objective are the views of historians, and most of them are in agreement, first of all that the basic cause of failure was simply Hitler's belief that the Wehrmacht could under the wholly different conditions of 1944 do what it had done in 1940. Not only was its own strength absurdly overrated, but that of the enemy completely underrated and misunderstood. It was wishful thinking of the first order to suppose merely because winter weather might prevent the full deployment of the Allied air forces that the British and American soldiers would therefore crumble in face of the German attack. He had failed to grasp not only the resolution of the Allied armies facing him, but their very nature, that is their equipment, their firepower (greatly enhanced for example by the new artillery fuses radar-operated by proximity to the target—and therefore particularly deadly in the jammed traffic conditions of the Ardennes), their mobility, their logistic system, let alone what their air forces would do if the weather cleared. He was no longer attacking an Army which 'after the first setbacks would swiftly crack up'. Just the contrary, for the Americans, ever sensitive on a point of military honour, would be hot to avenge a setback, while Montgomery and his Army Group, of all such combinations, were the most practised and most temperamentally conditioned to roll with the punch and then give back as good as they had got. In short the Wehrmacht, unlike 1940, was launching its assault on an enemy stronger both in material and morale.

Nonetheless it delivered a heavy blow. 'If now we can deliver a few more heavy blows,' Hitler had announced on 11 December 1944, 'this artificially bolstered common front may collapse with a gigantic clap of thunder.' The front had not collapsed. What had it suffered and what did the Germans gain to compensate for all their losses? The Allied front had not even split although their command arrangements were put under further strain. On the other hand, the Allies were certainly thrown temporarily on the defensive, put out of balance, the initiative lost. In addition the Germans had inflicted a great deal of actual damage to their armies and air forces. How much damage was in fact done? The difficulty in putting a label on the damage is that as far as equipment and supplies are concerned, the American war machine was so efficient and so prodigal that all the losses were replaced within a matter of weeks. In his meticulously detailed and admirably comprehensive survey* of the battle, Peter Elstob estimates that taking the Ardennes and Alsace battles together, the Allies lost or used up 15–25 per cent of the tanks, guns, vehicles, ammunition, fuel and other supplies which they had in Europe at the start of the offensive. In other words hundreds of aircraft, thousands of tanks and vehicles, more than a million rounds of gun ammunition, several million rounds of small arms ammunition were expended. Manpower was another matter, and here Mr Elstob thinks that the battle robbed the Allies of ten per cent of their strength. As we have seen it was only the Americans who suffered significant losses in men. Nor does a

* *Hitler's Last Offensive*, London, 1971.

mere catalogue of numbers give the full story. Specially trained and battle-experienced technicians were hard to replace—and of them all the most valuable was the infantryman himself. Two US infantry divisions, the 28th and 106th, had been virtually eliminated during the action, another 15 badly mauled. Ridgeway's Airborne Corps, used in an ordinary infantry role, could not quickly be reconstituted as an airborne formation. US armoured divisions too had taken heavy knocks in tanks and crews. But American resources being what they were, no fewer than *nine fresh divisions* reached Europe within a matter of weeks after the offensive was over.

Such rapid and complete replacement was totally beyond the reach of the Germans. Dietrich's 6th SS Panzer Army lost, according to his own record, nearly 40,000 men and three or four hundred tanks. On its way to reinforce the Eastern front this Army received only about half of the men and material which it had lost in the battle. Even then Hitler frittered it away in a fruitless attempt to hold Budapest instead of employing it on the critical central front.

The material damage done to the Allied armies was thus quickly made good whereas that of the Wehrmacht could not be. Morally too the balance sheet was an unequal one. The Alliance had been strained—by Montgomery's press conference, for example, and his constant nagging at the command problem— but had never been in danger of cracking. Besides the Americans' victory, after the prospect of a serious setback, did much to confirm their confidence in themselves and in an early end to the war. For the Germans a disastrous repulse after the promise of victory was simply to add the expectancy of imminent collapse to the reality of immediate despair.

In his history of the 5th Battalion, The Seaforth Highlanders, who, together with the rest of the magnificent 51st Highland Division, fought so successfully in the Ardennes, Alistair Borthwick shows to what depths some members of the Wehrmacht had been reduced:

The postscript to the Ardennes offensive is best given in the words of two Belgian boys, because their description of what they saw during the fortnight of German occupation shows in miniature the whole course of the offensive—the sweeping advance, the first check, the cutting of the supply lines by our planes, the massing of our forces, the final disillusionment.

'They came on Christmas Day,' they said. 'They made a feast and the toast was To Paris, Brussels, Antwerp. But they did not go forward. And when that happened, they knew. In five days, in five days only, the soldiers were saying von Rundstedt was a traitor who had led the Wehrmacht into a trap. Then there was fine weather, and your planes came. By New Year's Day they were slaughtering our beasts because they had no food. Already they had used all our petrol—those vehicles you took, they could not drive them away because of that. They became very miserable. They said they were betrayed by their officers. They knew nothing of the battle. A shell would land, and one would say: That is British. And another would say: No. It is German. They knew nothing, except that the British were creeping in. They stayed in one place, but it was as if the country round them had moved. When you came, they were in great fear and ran to the cellars. They made the old people sit on their knees so that they would be protected by them. Paris, Brussels, Antwerp! Aaah, the bandits, the dirty bandits!'

If the bandits had reason to despair, one man, of course, did not do so—the Führer. On 9 and 10 January in conference at Adlershorst—where Guderian had hurried to persuade Hitler to make his main defensive effort in the East, withdraw forces from the West for this purpose, and also allow Army Group Commanders the flexibility in operations indispensable to tactical withdrawal and the creation of reserves—the Supreme Commander of the Wehrmacht was still talking of keeping the initiative in the West and holding firm in the East. He had at this time Guderian remembered 'a special picture of the world and every fact had to be fitted onto that fancied picture. As he believed, so the world must be: but, in fact, it was a picture of another world.' So he raved about the Wehrmacht's possession of three thousand tanks and guns on the Eastern front and argued that since the Russians did not have three times that number, the necessary superiority for successful attack, they could not break through. Therefore the East would not be reinforced, nor would there be any further withdrawals. About two weeks earlier in his speech to the generals before launching the abortive Alsace

offensive, Hitler had summed up the problem of fighting on two
fronts:

> We are not in a position to put divisions on ice. Every one is
> watched with the eyes of Argus. If there is quiet, or no large-
> scale battle in the East for two weeks, then the commander of
> the Army Group in the West comes and says: 'There are
> unused Panzer units in the East, why do we not get them?'
> If there is quiet momentarily in the West, then the same
> commander, if in the East, would declare immediately: 'There
> is complete quiet in the West; we should get at least 4 to 6
> Panzer divisions over here to the East.' As soon as I have a
> division free anywhere, other sectors are already eyeing it.

Certainly Guderian on 10 January was eyeing the divisions of
Model's Army Group, but was told that the Eastern front must
make do with what it had got. Two days later the Eastern front
collapsed in the face of an assault by one hundred and eighty
Soviet divisions under the command of Marshal Zhukov whose
attacking front extended from the Carpathians to the Balkans.
There was now neither quiet in the East nor the West. On 15
January the day after OKW had finally admitted that in the West
the initiative had passed back to the enemy, and the day before
Hitler returned to Berlin for the last time, Jodl noted that
Guderian telephoned from his headquarters at Zossen for everything to be thrown in to help him against the Russians. Hitler's
gamble in the West was about to reap its reward in the East. It
was in this way that the balance sheet of the Ardennes offensive
revealed the Third Reich as being militarily bankrupt.

Yet its impact should not be underrated. Chester Wilmot
called it the greatest crisis that the Western Allies had known
since 1940. It was never a desperate crisis. It was a spoiling attack
on the grand scale which simply ended by spoiling itself. Model's
Army Group had not merely bitten off more than it could chew.
In Patton's colourful vernacular it put itself in a position where it
was chewed up itself. On the other hand the German's strategic
disease in the winter of 1944 was desperate. So therefore was
Hitler's appliance to relieve it. Given that Hitler's choice was
between defence and attack, given too that it was not so much a
precise strategic objective which was at stake but a general one of
seizing the initiative in order to be able to bargain from a stronger

position in the business of keeping Germany whole, given finally that Hitler's entire granite will-power was at this time harnessed to the single and irrevocable idea of never giving in, never capitulating, never surrendering, so that every straw must be grasped at, every gamble taken, was he right to attack with his very last reserves which he must have known to have been inadequate in relation to the much stronger forces opposed to them? From Hitler's point of view, however unreal the strategic world in which he then lived might have been, had the thing been worth doing?

10

Options of Difficulties

If a thing is worth doing, it is worth doing badly.
G. K. Chesterton

When the war was over the German General Staff got down to the business of showing that Hitler had prevented their winning it. Many were the generals who were able to prove how time after time they had been right as to what should be done about Germany's military position and how the Führer had been wrong. They had forgotten the innumerable occasions when the boot had been on the other foot. Whatever else might be said about the behaviour of Jodl, Chief of Operations at OKW, this sudden reversal of loyalty to the Supreme Commander could not be included. His comments at Nuremberg did not only reiterate this loyalty. They were especially relevant to Hitler's decision to attack in the West in December 1944:

It is often said that Hitler's military advisers ought to have opened his eyes to the fact that the war was lost.* This is a naïve idea. Before any of us, he sensed and knew that the war was lost. But can anyone give up a nation, particularly his own people, for lost if there is any way out? A man like Hitler

* This was an exercise in which Speer was repeatedly engaged, an exercise which was repeatedly futile. For Hitler's response was simply that if the war was to be lost the nation must perish. 'There is no need to consider the basis even of a most primitive existence any longer. On the contrary it is better to destroy that, and to destroy it ourselves. The nation has proved itself weak, and the future belongs solely to the stronger Eastern nation. Besides, those who remain after the battle are of little value; for the good have fallen.' Yet Speer with skill and courage succeeded by out-manoeuvring Hitler's nihilistic scorched-earth policy in ensuring that the basis of an existence did survive for the German people.

certainly could not. . . . He acted as all heroes throughout history have always acted and always will. He buried himself among the ruins and with the hopes of his Reich. Let those who so wish condemn him—personally I cannot.

Throughout his military and political career Hitler had been taking risks. According to Kierkegaard risks may involve two different sorts of danger, one in not taking them, the other in taking them too fully. There was little likelihood of Hitler's falling down on the first. 'By risking too much,' Kierkegaard concluded, 'one turns aside to the fantastic.' Hitler may have risked all on the battle of the Ardennes, but the risk could hardly be said to have been fantastic. Mr Elstob goes so far as to maintain that the risk was justified. 'Hitler made many wrong military decisions,' he writes, 'particularly during the last years of the war, but the Ardennes offensive was not one of them.' He justifies this not universally held judgment by arguing that in the first place to have an offensive at all was strategically correct, second that the objective chosen was appropriate to the circumstances and the risk, for any smaller objective—as Hitler himself so often insisted in the face of von Rundstedt's, Model's and Manteuffel's urging of the small solution—could not have the looked-for strategic results. Mr Elstob subsequently qualifies this last point, but he is giving Hitler high marks in saying that the offensive's timing, placing and target were all right. If the same could have been said of German strategy throughout the Second World War, how different might have been its outcome! Does this claim of Mr Elstob's stand up to examination?

As to timing there can little disagreement, for the offensive certainly could not have been mounted earlier, and had it been left more than a few weeks later, the massive Russian counter-offensive of January 1945 would have quickly sucked in all the reserves which had been put together in the West. Place is hardly more arguable. The attack had to be in the West to have any impact at all, since a mere 30 divisions could not turn the scales on the Red Army with its countless hundreds of divisions and endless space in which to deploy them. And if it had to be in the West then it had to be in the Ardennes. If the attack had been further north or further south, it would have been directed against concentrations of American or British forces and not against the only really weak spot in the whole Western front.

It is when we come to the operation's objective that real controversy sets in. We must not confuse its *aim* with its objective. The aim, that is Hitler's aim, as far as it was ever laid down at all, was so to dismay and split the Western Allies, physically and politically, that stalemate might lead to a separate peace, allowing the Wehrmacht once more to fling its entire weight at Russia, and thereby bring about another pause in hostilities and so leave Germany—if not with the *Lebensraum* which the Second World War had been all about—at least with the territory of the Greater Reich of 1938. It was the old Hitler formula, *so oder so,* two possibilities, this way or that; first smash the West, then turn back and gain a decision in the East. This aim, unlike the risk, was, to use Kierkegaard's expression, turning aside to the fantastic. The objective was only a little less extravagant and illusory.

Antwerp was probably always beyond the reach of Model's Army Group—the distance was simply too great to ensure the security of the flanks even had the panzer divisions quickly reached and crossed the Meuse, capturing all the fuel they needed on the way. The *idea* of taking Antwerp was essentially sound, as its possession was truly vital to Allied operations, but it was just too far in relation to forces available.

If Antwerp were too far, was it after all true that one of the 'small solutions' would have had a greater chance of success than in the event the large one did? It depends which one we think of. Going for Aachen had little to recommend it, for again it would have run up against heavy American concentrations. But to have gone for *the Meuse,* as both Model and Manteuffel at one point proposed, and then, remembering Moltke's insistence that plans must adapt themselves to contact with the enemy, to have exploited somewhere or other might have been to have an objective which everybody would have believed practicable and which would have permitted far greater flexibility in its realization.

As we have seen, in arguing for a small solution, a 'little slam' instead of a 'grand slam', both von Rundstedt and Model had proposed alternatives, which, while differing in detail, had one important stipulation in common, and had this feature found its way into the actual operation, there might have resulted a far greater penetration with all the possibilities this conjures up. They both wanted to concentrate the assaulting Panzer Armies into a single thrust on a narrow front. Von Rundstedt's idea was to destroy the Allied formations east of the Meuse and then see what else might be done. He proposed to use the full strength of the 5th and 6th Panzer Armies on a frontage of about 25 miles astride an axis from Bütgenbach through Trois Ponts to Werbomont, then cross the Ourthe river and so to the Meuse between Huy and Liège. This was a plan which in general brought objectives into line with capabilities, and embraced also a number of elementary and sound tactical principles. To start with a breakthrough was more or less assured, secondly the going was the best available, next there were no river obstacles until the Ourthe was reached, fourth by limiting distance and narrowing the front, more divisions would be available to ensure flank protection, fifth, the two Armies would have been mutually supporting. When we consider what Peiper's* comparatively puny force of one battle group from 1st SS Panzer Division achieved roughly on this very same axis we may legitimately wonder what the whole of 6th SS Panzer Army might have done if it had been so employed instead of battering its head uselessly against Monschau and its environs. Model's alternative plan had a comparable idea of enveloping and rolling up the enemy east of the Meuse, and was like von Rundstedt's also in that it dismissed all notion of two great *Schwerpunkte* and concentrated even more divisions into a single powerful thrust, a little wider than von Rundstedt's aimed breakthrough, between the Hürtgen Forest and Lützkampen. Again, both 5th and 6th Panzer Armies were to be used in one gigantic concentration. If we reflect how late and ineffectually the panzer reserves were employed during the actual operation, the notion of their coming rapidly into action to reinforce the spearheads of leading divisions all in one great drive forward may give us something to think about, and would have given Middleton, Hodges and Bradley even more.

    The controversies which raged round the big and small

---

* Peiper's subsequent comments as to what he would have put right if all were to do again are worth remembering. He named eight improvements, the first seven of which are simple tactical points: rapid fuel supply; no initial artillery bombardments; use mixed tank–infantry teams throughout; more infantry on tanks; each combat team to be self-supporting; attack in more places with shorter columns and then concentrate on the weak spot; a bridging unit to accompany each armoured spearhead. The eighth and final point is the most original and most promising—put a general at each road junction for traffic control. The implication here (road junctions being notorious targets for artillery stonks) was that the number of generals might profitably be reduced in this way. There would, of course, also have been the option, if enemy shelling failed to do the trick, of running them over oneself.

solutions both at the time and in subsequent writings are endless. Manteuffel's impartial account of the battle emphasizes that the key to the whole concept of the operation, whether grand or little slam, was that

> the panzer divisions should not allow themselves to be held up in any way during their advance to the Meuse. They would go round strongly defended places and positions which could not be captured quickly, and they must not allow themselves to be deterred by open flanks. All in all, these were the same tactics that had been used with such success in the Eastern campaign in 1941. However, at the express orders of the Führer, Bastogne was to be taken.

This raises a further point.

While it is true that the essence of successful blitzkrieg is to get on, to outflank opposition, pour ever stronger forces through the breach that has been made, spread out both in depth and width and then as quickly as possible savage the enemy's vitals, his gun areas, his headquarters, his reserves, and so disrupt any possibility of his conducting a coherent defensive battle—that *the Schwerpunkt's chosen axis must be cleared*, in order to guarantee security, reinforcement and supply, is mandatory. It is curious therefore that, in spite of the Führer's expressly ordering the capture of Bastogne, in spite of Model's having realized from the very outset of planning that the operation would resolve itself into a battle for road junctions, in spite of Manteuffel's having actually put his finger on Bastogne as the key to both the German advance and the likely American counter to it, it was not initially laid down at either Army Group or Army level that Bastogne was indispensable to further advance and therefore would on that particular axis be cleared and not bypassed. It is difficult to believe that if Bastogne had been one of Manteuffel's priority objectives and von Lüttzwitz's Corps had made for it at once with strength and speed, it would not have fallen on 18 or 19 December.* It is notable too that had one of the small solutions been adopted, as far as getting to the Meuse goes, Bastogne might never have achieved the critical importance it did, for it

---

* Manteuffel's orders to Lüttwitz contained the following sentence: 'In the case of strong enemy resistance, Bastogne is to be outflanked, its capture is then up to 26th Volksgrenadierdivision.' This was a far cry from ordering its immediate seizure.

was the requirement to reduce it as opposed to neutralizing it that made it figure so large in German calculations after their early failure to bounce their way into the town.

Given any plan, small or large, however, there remained the question of what policy to adopt as far as exploitation was concerned. It was in this respect that Hitler's inflexibility, characterized by his endorsing the operation order in his own handwriting with the explicit '*Nicht abändern!*' 'Not to be altered' proved so crippling and so fatal to the inherent advantages of the whole strategic concept—opportunism added to surprise. Once again, as so often before, Hitler allowed a purely political consideration to cloud and distort his military judgment. His dithering as to which objective to go for in Russia was dictated by political factors. Leningrad and Stalingrad became political objectives out of all proportion to military calculation; his declaration of war on the United States (surely an unthinkable blunder if in military terms he had asked himself how that country was to be defeated) was caused by political commitments to Japan and because he could not bear to think that a world conflict of such historical greatness should not be manipulated by him;* his chucking away 30 precious divisions in the Baltic states was done primarily to preserve his political influence in Sweden. So now again in the Ardennes, when von Rundstedt and Model urged him, in accordance with their alternative plans, to put the *Schwerpunkt* of the attack in the centre for the militarily indisputable reasons that there they would find the enemy at his weakest and the panzer-going at its best, he stuck to his idea that because for the sake of politics the main effort must be made by Dietrich's SS formations and because in turn these could only be committed in the north by virtue of their pre-offensive deployment, the north it must be. As we have seen the north proved to be most unprofitable of all the sectors attacked. Nonetheless it was this area that to start with Hitler insisted on reinforcing. Such a turning upside down of simple military principles and calculations could not be expected to prosper.

Strategic and tactical decisions may be options of difficulties

---

* As late as 1971 Dean Acheson wrote: 'The suicidal Japanese attack on Pearl Harbor, rather than, for instance, subversion in the Dutch East Indies, was one of the supreme errors of history. The German declaration of war against the United States after four days of deliberation, long enough to have enabled Hitler to have seen the advantages to him in abandoning his ally, ranks as a fitting companion piece.'

but there is no justification for adding to them with self-created ones. There was a genuine contradiction between two of blitz-krieg's requirements as to the positioning of Dietrich's 6th Panzer Army before the offensive started. On the one hand surprise was to be maintained by fostering the Allies' belief that it was being held back for counter-attack in the Roer area; on the other hand concentration demanded that it be used where the tactical circumstances of the moment required. One of the elements of surprise is itself concentration and Hitler had already convinced himself that the Allies did not expect an attack. The question therefore becomes whether it would have been possible to maintain surprise and enjoy maximum concentration by beginning to move 6th Panzer Army earlier. In view of all the movement that had already taken place and all the other indications of the German intentions which Allied intelligence staffs chose to misinterpret, the answer is probably yes. Yet having made up his mind to capture Antwerp, to get Dietrich's army to do the capturing, and to take the shorter route to Antwerp, Hitler would not alter his plan and bring this army further south. Once again he found reasons for justifying a course of action already decided on for non-military reasons, rather than find the best course by a process of military reasoning.

It is possible to have sympathy with two of von Rundstedt's comments on the plan. He referred to this last matter, Hitler's insistence on committing Dietrich's army in the north, as 'a fundamental mistake which unbalanced the whole offensive'. This inherent imbalance at the start made it all the more absurd to insist also on distant and specific objectives. Rundstedt's other comment, that all the conditions necessary for success were missing, which is saying a good deal, is more readily understood when we see that instead of choosing between options of difficul-ties, Hitler compounded the difficulties by choosing a combination of options all of which worked to render more difficult the other ones. Thus if it is reasonable to suppose that objectives limited in size and distance would be readily taken, held and logistically supported; that a narrow frontage would have the dual advant-age of offering the most powerful concentration and most secure flank protection; that a general strategic aim would allow maximum tactical flexibility in switching panzer strength to where it was most needed; that immediate and modest success would be much more easily exploited than ponderous and ambitious failure; that to have crossed the Meuse would by itself have constituted a major victory which might really have had the effect of an eagle in a dovecote—if all this is reasonable, then all the stronger is the argument that the relationship between intention and capability must not be ignored.

Yet Hitler broke almost every rule. The objectives were so distant, so substantial, and so widely separated, that leaving aside the question of fuel, they were unattainable in terms of troops allotted to tasks and unholdable in terms of the flanks, which would be exposed even if they were reached. By doubling his purpose, Antwerp and Brussels, Hitler necessarily halved the resources for reaching either; by doubling his frontage, he halved his concentration; by insisting on absolute conformity with a detailed programme, he robbed himself of adaptability; by attacking the Allied shoulders, he pushed against the strongest positions, and so denied himself strength at their weak centre which could otherwise have been overwhelming and perhaps conclusive. In holding back his principal striking force, 6th Panzer Army, he manacled himself to a plan which lacked the one unbreakable principle of blitzkrieg—exploitation of the weakest chink in the enemy's defensive wall. He was circumspect where he should have been bold, and rigid when he should have been flexible, complex where he should have been simple, prodigal when he should have been thrifty, and thrifty where he should have been prodigal. Almost every principle of war and its conduct was contravened. Yet he still believed or acted as if he believed that a really major decision was within his grasp. Self-delusion could go no further. What is more as Guderian put it, he pressed on from 'failure to failure, his head full of stupendous plans, clinging evermore frantically to the last vanishing prospects of victory'. When *Herbstnebel* failed in the Ardennes, he pressed on with *Nordwind* in Alsace. Two failures were to be preferred to one success as long as he could go on attacking. He could not see that in strategic terms one simple realizable plan was always to be preferred to several grandiose and chimerical ones. To go on manipulating the Wehrmacht, indulging in the luxury and illusion of his own will-power, always took priority over sober calculation of the odds. Given therefore that strategically it was sound to take the offensive, we can only justify his actual choice of method by resorting to Chesterton's comment that if a thing is worth doing, it is worth doing badly.

This comment could be applied with equal force to the Allied strategy which made Hitler's offensive possible in the first place, and also to the counter-measures they took when it actually started. The whole philosophy behind Eisenhower's broad-front policy was that it would keep the Germans occupied and stretched *everywhere,* oblige them to go on committing reserves as soon as they were created or, if not commit them, hold them back in readiness and sufficient depth to be committed in order to counter yet one more dangerous salient. In other words, by keeping up the pressure everywhere, Eisenhower would keep the Germans off balance, keep them firmly on the defensive, retain the initiative securely in Allied hands and give the Germans no chance of getting it back. By a curious irony the result of the broad-front strategy was exactly opposite to what was intended. It was the Allies who were stretched, short of reserves, lacking in depth, unbalanced and only nominally in possession of the initiative, which in terms of attack had by the beginning of December lost momentum. On the other hand the Germans while heavily committed were not ruinously overstretched, they were deployed in some depth, they had succeeded in creating substantial reserves, they were tolerably balanced and were about to seize the initiative in a big way.

Bradley, like Montgomery, was allowed considerable latitude by Eisenhower in deploying and employing his Army Group in accordance with the Supreme Commander's general directives, but the way in which he had in fact deployed it spoke up strongly for Montgomery's idea about a single strong thrust in one place and holding operations elsewhere. In any event one of a commander's permanent concerns about the whole of his front, in the sort of tactical conditions which prevailed in the Second World War, is security, and Bradley's front was anything but secure. In his press statement of 9 January, Bradley made a claim (subsequently developed in *A Soldier's Story* to justify his handling of the battle) to the effect that he knew all about the build-up of German forces near Cologne and that he and his staff had carefully considered the possibility of a German attack in the Ardennes, and that he took a calculated risk there in order to concentrate on his attack over the Roer in the north and to the Saar in the south. But as we have seen such a claim would only make sense under two conditions—first if he really was using *all* his other strength to harass and dismay the Germans in his attack areas, second if these measures were effective either in gaining ground and destroying the enemy or requiring all the available German strength to check them. Neither of these conditions prevailed in December 1944. Not only were his so-called offensives not stretching the German defences to breaking point, but some of his own attacking formations were not even committed. Thus his reasons for having left the Ardennes sector without reserves and without depth do not stand up. Chester Wilmot's comment on this aspect of Bradley's strategy—if it can be accorded such a name—is so just, so succinct and so damning that it deserves to be remembered:

> If Bradley really was taking a 'calculated risk', it is strange that neither he nor Eisenhower nor any member of their staffs ever mentioned it to Montgomery; stranger still that Bradley should have had no plan ready to meet a German counter-stroke in the Ardennes, and should have reacted so slowly when the risk became a reality. While it is true that Bradley ordered the movement of two armoured divisions from the flanking armies on the first evening, the German attack had been in progress 36 hours before he called in the SHAEF reserve which Eisenhower had given him; two days before he asked Patton to cancel his pending offensive in the Saar; three days before he began withdrawing divisions from the Roer front-line to reinforce the Ardennes; and even after four days he had produced no overall plan for bringing the situation under control.

Small wonder that Eisenhower handed over part of the battle to Montgomery, and small wonder also that Montgomery should have pronounced that there was no real grip over its conduct and that his first task would be to tidy it up. But Eisenhower himself cannot escape reproof in allowing the situation to develop as it had. He might have ridden his Army Group Commanders on a loose rein. This was no reason for allowing one of them to ignore the demands of security. However great, as Kierkegaard had paradoxically suggested, the dangers of not taking a risk might be, we may suppose that for the Supreme Allied Commander in the winter of 1944 they were smaller than those of taking one, however 'calculated' it might or might not have been. But Eisenhower more than made up for any lack of grip before the Ardennes offensive by his firm handling of it when it was under way.

The risk having been taken and its consequences being upon

them, the other principal Allied commanders had little to con-
gratulate themselves on in their initial reactions to the German
offensive. The sweetness of adversity was by no means quick in
making itself felt. Reactions varied from Bradley's incomprehen-
sion of what was really going on, to Patton's exuberance at the
chance to get at them, to Montgomery's almost censorious
satisfaction that he had been right all along. Bradley judged the
German offensive to be no more than a spoiling attack, designed
purely to relieve the pressure which Patton was exerting in the
Saar. 'If by coming through the Ardennes', he said, 'the enemy can
force us to pull Patton's troops out of the Saar and throw them
against his counter-offensive, he will get what he's after.' Such a
misreading of the real German intentions lends great weight to
Hitler's declaration that the Americans thought in terms only of
their own offensive. Patton was also so obsessed with his own
offensive that when Bradley required him to release the 10th
Armoured Division to go north and counter the German advance,
he replied that to do so would 'be playing into the hands of the
Germans'. It is not a view the Germans themselves would have
shared. They would have preferred Bastogne to have been un-
defended by the 10th Armoured Division. Patton's honesty,
however, compelled him to admit later that so little did he
appreciate the seriousness of the situation that he ordered another
of his Armoured Divisions, the 4th, to get itself heavily engaged
so that it could not also be moved north away from him. In other
words Patton's immediate reaction was to commit his reserves to
another battle. How different was Montgomery's! Once he had
formed an idea of what was happening by use of his unique system
of liaison officers, he moved what reserves he had to 'ensure that
the right flank and right rear of 21st Army Group would be
secure, whatever might happen'.

Yet it is Eisenhower who must take the principal credit for
taking those steps which eventually allowed a successful defensive
battle to be fought. In the first place he overruled Bradley's opinion
as to what sort of attack the Germans were making, and directed
that 7th and 10th Armoured Divisions should be moved to the
threatened areas; then he decided that the formations he had in
reserve, including Ridgeway's Airborne Corps, should be committed, and in particular directed that 101st Airborne Division
should assemble at Bastogne—'perhaps', says Chester Wilmot,
'the most important single decision of the whole battle'. Further-

more, militarily unpopular as it was with Bradley and some other of his countrymen, he did not hesitate to give Montgomery command in the north, when it became clear that the absurd positioning of Bradley's headquarters at Luxembourg simply meant that he could exercise no control over the northern battle; and it must be conceded that even though the piecemeal resistance of American units had already done much to make Model's game go wrong, it was Montgomery's grip, patience and tactical sense which turned the defensive battle from one whose theme was how not to lose it into one of how to win it. Finally Eisenhower saw to it that the broad handling of the situation thereafter took account of the realities. When the choice lay between attacking prematurely without certainty of success and husbanding reserves even at the expense of giving ground in order to guarantee victory, he recognized that the better part of valour, although in a sense wholly different from what Falstaff had in mind, really was discretion. 'In all his career', Wilmot concluded, 'there was perhaps no other time when Eisenhower revealed so clearly the greatness of his qualities.'

This performance was all the more remarkable and all the more admirable because it was Eisenhower who was effectively in charge of strategy. There had been a time when Churchill had had a major, even decisive, influence on both British and Allied strategy. It was he who had reinforced the Middle East at a time when some thought he was thereby putting the United Kingdom at risk; it was he who had badgered the soldiers to take the offensive in the Western desert and insisted on succouring Greece; it was he who had persuaded Roosevelt to adopt the 'Germany First' policy and to land troops in North West Africa in 1942. Roosevelt on the other hand, in spite of being Commander-in-Chief of the United States forces, apart from grand and general decisions, such as the two just mentioned or the faulty concept of invading Southern France, had little or no interest in the actual conduct of campaigns, a matter which so fascinated and at times exasperated Churchill. By 1944 Churchill's influence had greatly declined because by then in comparison with the United States and Russia, he no longer spoke for a great military power. In any event it was Eisenhower as Supreme Allied Commander who did in fact exercise this command without interference from either Roosevelt or Churchill. He had almost as much strategic influence as Hitler himself.

Yet how different were their methods of exercising this influence and how differently was command of the battle and the generalship in it to develop on either side and to determine that the Ardennes bulge was never more than a bulge. 'No reports', wrote Macaulay, 'are more readily believed than those which disparage genius and soothe the envy of conscious mediocrity.' If there were little genius to be detected in the concept and conduct of the Ardennes battle, there was plenty of mediocrity. Nonetheless it is perhaps generalship in the Ardennes which provides us with one of those features of the whole affair most worthy of study.

11

Generalship in the Ardennes

> The Germans can claim no credit for this operation—it was
> not an impressive performance ... neither did any of the
> German Commanders show ability to conduct operations
> successfully in face of Allied unyielding opposition. On the
> Allies' side it is obvious too that they had little to be proud
> of except the determined and effective way in which the
> American troops had fought in most testing circumstances.
> *British Official History*

The first sentence of Chapter 1 suggests that the Ardennes battle
was principally distinguished by the conduct of the high command—and that this was wrong. If the principles of conducting
war are sound, then generally speaking commanders could hardly
do better, while recognizing that in differing circumstances some
principles are always likely to have priority over others, than
observe them. But in December 1944 they were more honoured
in the breach. It is perhaps by examining some of the principles
that the point may be illustrated.

The principles of war may be compared to the demands of a
jealous woman. They are easily satisfied if your resources are
unlimited and your attention to the task in hand is steadfast. At
the same time, neglect them and they are relentless in exacting
retribution. Thus, since in war your resources seldom are unlimited and your attention apt to be distracted, as in so many
other human or mechanical circumstances, priorities are what
determine your behaviour. If we were required to nominate the
master principle of war, we would almost certainly say that it is to
select your purpose correctly, provided always we qualify this
selection by conceding that it presupposes the purpose to be
realizable in purely material terms. This is to say it was no good
Hitler's requiring von Rundstedt to capture the Caucasus in
October 1941, however desirable their possession might have

been, for von Rundstedt simply did not have the strength to do it. Similarly it was absurd for the Allied commanders in Italy to have their eye on Vienna in the summer of 1944 as an achievable objective. When we apply this rule to the Ardennes battle, therefore, we may observe from the very outset not only that Antwerp was too distant and too difficult a target for Model's group of armies, but that in spite of this fact's being pointed out to him repeatedly, energetically and convincingly, Hitler insisted on retaining it as the unalterable aim of the whole operation, and we have seen what retribution awaited this fundamental blunder. This question of the aim, of course, goes hand in hand with another important principle—flexibility, and here too Hitler's rigidity of both concept and execution was in direct conflict with the demands of the moment. Flexibility of ideas came more readily to the Allies, for they had no ideas about the battle before it started and very few when it did.

If Hitler fell down in these two main fields, however, his treatment of some of the lesser principles was far more sound and sensible, even brilliant. The element of surprise, on which he insisted so emphatically and which figures large in any catalogue of strategic tips, he achieved absolutely. It was his failure to harness it to speed and adaptability which robbed it of real dividends. The measure of surprise initially achieved was remarkable, for Hitler had not only persuaded the Allies that a German offensive was as improbable as anything can be in war, but even after he had launched it, several of the most senior Allied commanders refused to believe what was before their eyes. It is never pleasing to find that you have been wrong about something, although fallibility is the prerogative of all commanders. But to persist in claiming that you have been partially right when it has already become clear that you have been wrong in every single detail is to augment fallibility with gullibility.

There were two other principles of war which in the past had danced almost exclusively to Hitler's tune—concentration of force and offensive action. In campaigns of a size comparable with those of the Central fronts in Europe, one had to complement the other if decisive results were to be realized. For the first four years of the war, Hitler, whose adherence to offensive action had never been in question, had been fortunate enough to command such concentrations of machines, firepower and soldiers that his armies had prevailed everywhere except in Russia, and the truth was that in Russia no concentration and no offensive action of a conventional sort which the Third Reich was able to muster, could ever quite have coped with the almost limitless resources of manpower, material and sheer manoeuvrability which Stalin had at his disposal, provided always the will to resist did not falter. Conversely it was the fatal loss of concentration, brought upon the Wehrmacht by the extent of their conquests alone, which made relatively easy the Allied descent on and breach of *Festung Europa* when the time came. Even so it may be doubted, had the Allies not possessed such an overwhelmingly strong concentration of air, sea and land offensive power, whether their foothold in Normandy would have been so rapidly and irreversibly accomplished. After it had been and after the break-out from Normandy, how weary, stale, flat and unprofitable was shown to be their strategy of advance on a broad front which robbed offensive action of the concentration needed to make it effective and rejected a sufficient concentration anywhere to lend opportunity to what offensive action there was. Uneasy equilibrium intervened.

In spite of the Wehrmacht's dissipation, however, the Ardennes battle was the very epitome of offensive action. Nor was the German concentration contemptible. But it was misemployed. Take 28 of your own divisions and hurl them at four enemy divisions and success is as certain as you can ever hope to make it. Yet this would have been impossible in the Ardennes context because it would have ignored completely security of the flanks. Take 28 divisions, use say half of them for flank protection, and hurl the other half at, say, two of those four enemy divisions, and you may be in a position to enjoy both security and the necessary shock effect to guarantee a tactical, even a strategic, victory. But take 28 divisions, fritter away half of them banging their heads against unyielding enemy concentrations, keep one quarter up your sleeve, use merely the other quarter for the offensive action which appears to offer the main chance, then refuse to reinforce it with the quarter still up your sleeve at the moment when appearance takes on the mantle of reality, and you are throwing away the winning cards as soon as play has started. It was thus that Hitler cheated himself of the one tactical condition—concentration—which could properly exploit the opportunities its twin—surprise —had already brought to hand, and by so doing add up to the crushing offensive action which he foresaw as the only way to rescue the Third Reich from the strategic pickle to which his own policies had brought it. As for the Allies, the deadly and devastating concentration of offensive air power which they had so readily available more than compensated for their dithering strategy, which combined the worst of both worlds, in that it lacked the strength of properly mounted attack and incorporated the weakness of ill-coordinated defence.

Concentration has a curious fellow principle in economy of effort, and here perhaps we may say that the Allies won hands down—both at the highest and lowest levels. For as we have seen, some of the major US commanders economized to the maximum extent possible in the effort they made either to understand or to rectify the situation, whereas at the front line the US fighting man, whether in foxhole or tank, behind machine-gun or artillery piece, conducted a series of small economical actions which saved the day for the Allies. Montgomery as usual had the best of it—he did little and gave the world to understand that he had done a great deal. But one thing he did do and in doing so pointed a lesson which holds good down the ages in any military circumstance. No matter how easily you appear to be winning, no matter whether the likelihood of an enemy attack is very high or very low, no matter how convinced you are that the initiative is held firmly and permanently by yourself—never neglect to provide for your own *security*. This can only be done by reaching out to discover the situation and having discovered it,* or even having failed to discover it, make those arrangements to ensure that no enemy moves will take you so much by surprise that you will be pushed off balance. This in its simplest terms is what Montgomery's doctrine of war is all about—gaining and retaining balance by the creation and re-creation of reserves—so that the battlefield is always a tidy one, so that the master plan may be pursued slowly, surely and with a relentless certainty which makes it appear that no other outcome of events was even on the cards.

Apply this formula of security, balance and the master plan to the Ardennes and what do we find? We find on the German side that there is a master plan all right, but the wrong one. As a result balance and thus freedom and speed of action rapidly give

* In the Ardennes, it was Montgomery's use of his liaison officers (the battle being initially in a part of the front other than his own) rather than concentrated reconnaissance operations, which supplied him with a picture of what was happening.

way to an unenviable predicament in which the assaulting troops
may be compared with a tide almost at the end of its flow into an
ever-narrowing bay—the strong banks resisting at the shoulders,
insufficient power left to surge forward, but each little shallow
being sought out and filled, then the whole tide halted for a time
before inevitable ebb sets in. On the Allied side we find no
security worth the name and hence the shock of being surprised,
loss of balance and a sort of frantic, uncoordinated, haphazard
throwing in of unprepared and ill-ordered reserves in order to
restore balance by sheer weight of numbers. Only the cool
Montgomery, by virtue of being unaffected during the initial
German advance, had the time to arrange for security—of an
area which was never seriously threatened—and then by resorting
to his well proved methods of patience, tidying-up, creating
reserves and a step-by-step slogging advance, gave a practical
demonstration of his theory of conducting a successful defensive
action, sealing off and then seeing off the enemy.

No matter what rules and regulations we may care to catalogue
for the conduct of military affairs, no matter what the circumstances, there is one condition indispensable to the proper obser-
vance of any single one or all of them together. It is clarity of
mind, an absolutely overriding conviction that this or that is
what you are trying to do at any particular time. 'Be clear,' said
Napoleon, 'and all the rest will follow.' Had he followed his own
maxim during those most critical few amongst the Hundred Days,
the hundred might have been expanded into two thousand or
more. But the orders that he gave Ney and Soult and Grouchy
were so far from clear that they were consistently misunderstood.
What was needed was unequivocal direction such as 'Take
Quatre Bras', 'Engage the Prussians and prevent their joining
Wellington', 'Capture La Haye Sainte', not such loosely thought
out and worded instructions as 'His Majesty desires you will head
for Wavre in order to draw near to us', when Wavre was in one
direction and the Emperor himself in another. Such orders almost
put one in mind of Raglan's at Balaclava which was capable of all
sorts of interpretation. At the same time since circumstances do
change from hour to hour, no orders can be absolute. There are
two ways to cope with this difficulty. One is to give your subordinates the general strategic idea of the battle and then leave
them to get on with it by whatever tactical methods and
manoeuvres they choose. This way could apply during the

25　*US armoured counter attack*

26   *German prisoners captured by US 4th Armoured Division near Bastogne*

encounter phase of a battle when its precise form is developing and enemy reactions are still unclear. But when the pattern is becoming clear, the other method takes over. Precise objectives and precise instructions are called for, and to give them, you must see for yourself. Thus just as Napoleon's eventual order, that cost what it might, La Haye Sainte must be taken, was far too late by many hours, so the Germans' eventual concentration on the capture of Bastogne, the key, if there was a single key, to the Ardennes battle, was too late by many days. Even when von Manteuffel put the direct question to Führer headquarters—am I to take Bastogne or push on to the Meuse for with my present resources I cannot do both?—he was returned a dusty answer. This was the very reverse of clear thinking and clear direction. It was Mr Micawber all over again.

The requirement for something to turn up is equally applicable if we examine one further principle of war, which may be held partly responsible both for putting the Allies in the strategic posture which made possible the German offensive in the first place, and also for manacling this offensive when it began. Known by the inadequate term, administration,* it comprehends the sinews of war—supply of petrol and ammunition and food, and all the paraphernalia which enable a modern army to march forward on its mechanical stomach and then bite the enemy hard enough to inflict a mortal wound. In this field, once the Ardennes battle had started, while the Allies had a close call here and there, such as the air re-supply of Bastogne in the nick of time, the whole German plan was such that, without the capture of Allied fuel and a far surer system of ammunition supply, it contravened a requirement so fundamental to the fighting of panzer battles— guaranteed petrol to advance and ammunition to shoot—that it was doomed to end in the frustration of panzers with empty petrol tanks and near empty ammunition racks, stranded like whales out of the sea on the high ground overlooking the Meuse. Lack of fuel was a nagging worry for the German commanders at every level; in the end it dominated their tactical thinking.

In equating stability and balance, Robert Bridges, although he

* It would be hard to better Fortescue's summing up of the difference between a good and a bad administrative system. In differentiating between that of the British and French armies in the Peninsula he wrote: 'Wellington's supplies were always hunting for his army; Joseph's army was always hunting for its supplies.'

M

was not discussing military affairs, has reminded us that wisdom lies in masterful administration of the unforeseen. All those concerned with logistic planning would agree with him, while conceding the difficulties of its achievement. But when administrative requirements are eminently foreseeable, as they were if the idea of reaching Antwerp by simple motoring alone was ever to be more than an unrealizable absurdity, *not* to take the necessary steps to minimize the way in which these requirements might interfere with what it is you want to do, was to beckon failure. Yet guaranteed security of administrative resources would from Hitler's point of view have been at odds with surprise and what he hoped would be speed of action. It was not to be expected that a gambler like the Führer, when faced with a choice of priorities, one of which would offer a huge but unlikely dividend, and the other a more probable but more modest one, would choose the latter. As we have seen, neglect altogether a principle of war, and unless you are given luck on an unprecedented scale, Nemesis intervenes. So that in spite of plumping for surprise, offensive action and a good measure of concentration, Hitler's choice of objective and method of reaching it, marred as they were by inflexibility, lack of balance, and shortage of administrative support, did not represent compromise based on a reasoned estimate of what was likely and what was needed to turn likelihood into certainty. It was a throw of the dice with the dice already loaded against him. The history of warfare and the truncated careers of general officers are littered with comparable instances.

In his own *History of Warfare* Montgomery reiterates a good many of these principles of war by grouping them into a list of those factors which he regards as the essence of tactical methods in battle. Those he selects are 'surprise, concentration of effort, cooperation of all arms, control, simplicity, speed of action and the initiative'. Here perhaps is a case of the last being the first, for in that one word, initiative, is contained all the others. It can only be *retained* if all these others continue to be pursued and to work for its retention. It was in this respect that the German commanders failed more than in any other. That Hitler, by launching his offensive, seized the initiative is not in question. The whole strategic situation on the Western front was transformed by the motoring forward of two Panzer Armies. The secret and skilful assembly of the assaulting forces, the admirable cooperation of all participants, in spite of frayed tempers and less than wholehearted confidence in the project itself, the over-whelming concentration of force—all these things made it as certain as anything can be in war that the German attack would achieve notable surprise and therefore give Hitler the initiative he so ardently coveted. But the initiative grows by what it feeds on, it feeds upon itself, it feeds moreover on the ruins which it has brought about. If its appetite is not satisfied, if it does not move from repast to repast, from success to success, if its half-section, exploitation, is absent without leave, it withers, and all that it has achieved up until then falls down to nothing. Thus although it is almost always possible to achieve some sort of local tactical initiative, it can never be decisive unless the other in-gredients of battle management—notably speed of action and speed of reaction—are also there.

Hitler had done more than achieve local tactical surprise by his attack in the Ardennes; he had achieved strategical surprise as well. What a paradox that his doing so should have been brought about by one of the factors which robbed him of the capability, certainly the willingness, to re-group rapidly and so keep the initiative. For, as we have seen, by positioning Dietrich's 6th Panzer Army to the north and east, so that its probable use would remain a question mark for Allied intelligence, Hitler confined its initial operational employment to the least profitable sector and then for political reasons reinforced failure in that sector with his reserves. 'The initiative, once gained', writes Montgomery, 'must never be lost . . . if you lose the initiative against a good enemy you will very soon be made to react to his thrusts; and once this happens you may well lose the battle. In large-scale operations it is very easy to lose the initiative. A firm grip on the battle is necessary to prevent this from happening, combined with a willingness to adjust plans to meet the developing tactical situa-tion.' This is what Montgomery meant by having a 'master' plan, that is not a plan which was unalterable in every detail, but a general tactical idea which one way or another would be achieved. This was what he did at Alamein and in Normandy. The secret of it was having and keeping *balance,* that is sufficient reserves to go on with this general idea without being obliged to take his eye off it by reacting too violently to anything the enemy might do. Obviously there was one prerequisite to this desirable state of affairs, that is that the general idea had to be in itself a good one from the outset. But then, as we have established, to choose your main object correctly is the master rule of strategy, to guarantee its achievement by allotting the necessary forces to it a hardly less important corollary.

Thus we may conclude at once that Hitler's generalship in the Ardennes offensive had two serious flaws right from the start. First the object was not chosen with a precision which went hand in hand with capability, second, his own decree '*Nicht abändern*' contravened the rule for preserving balance and forcing the enemy to react to his moves. We may perhaps contemplate how differently the battle might have gone if the initial objective had been, say, Bastogne or a bridgehead over the Meuse at Namur, and in what a totally different way the 5th and 6th Panzer Armies would have been grouped and committed had these been the objectives. Yet the first of these two initial flaws might not have been fatal to the enterprise provided the other one had been corrected.

The recipe for battle winning, no matter what sort of operation is in hand, is implied by Montgomery in all he writes without his actually putting a name to it. It is, of course, improvisation. The Duke of Wellington was perhaps the best example of an English general who was a master of improvisation. He put his own Peninsular victories down to it. The Napoleonic marshals he fought had made their plans and conducted their campaigns 'just as you might make a splendid set of harness. It looks very well; and answers very well, until it gets broken; and then you are done for. Now I made my campaigns of ropes. If anything went wrong, I tied a knot and went on.' What irony that in the Wehrmacht, in an army which had been fed and bred on improvisation, and whose blitzkrieg methods had given an unparalleled demonstration of its irresistible power, this most telling of qualities, ready and skilful improvisation, had been allowed to wither, indeed had long since been abandoned. Hitler's iron will was no substitute for it. It was an odd contradiction that what he regarded as weakness, that is to say readiness to adjust during a battle's development, is in fact strength, and what he regarded as strength, that is to say fanatical stubbornness in the face of all developments, is in fact weakness. In any event it was this German failure to adjust in accordance with new circumstances that more than anything else robbed them of the initiative. This is all the more surprising in view of the fact that Model, himself a born adapter, who time after time had shown an absolute mastery of improvisation, had stressed in his orders that quick exploitation of progress on the first day would be the key to decisive success and that this in turn would depend on freedom of movement for the panzer divisions. And although except for Peiper's battle group, this freedom of movement was never forthcoming on the front of 6th Panzer Army, it was very rapidly obtained by Manteuffel, but *not exploited*. One of the principal obstacles to this necessary exploitation, this exercise in flexibility which seemed to be lacking, was the very flexibility which *was* shown by the American commanders. It was shown first at the low level by those who quickly improvised small but invaluable rearguard actions which so critically delayed the leading panzers, next by those at the highest levels of command, who put their hand on reinforcements and despatched them to tactically important areas, finally by those middle piece commanders at divisional level, whether at the shoulders of the penetration or in its path, who organized and reorganized the defences. These prompt responses enabled the key to the whole battle—time, and how it was used, that is to say who manipulated his reserves more readily and more agilely to regain or maintain balance—to be turned more firmly by the Allies. 'Ask me for anything but time,' declared Napoleon. Yet even he—when asked by Ney for more troops at the crisis of Waterloo, when he still had fourteen regiments of the Garde Impériale under his hand, at the very moment when he might still have broken Wellington's line and swept on to Brussels—had petulantly sent back the answer 'Troops? Where do you expect me to get them? Do you expect me to make them?' It was because he flung away those two indispensable allies—time and balance—that he lost the last of his battles.

For Manteuffel the story was not dissimilar. Throughout his own account of the battle two themes persist—loss of time and lack of flexibility. He, like Mr Elstob, finds that the sector chosen for launching the offensive was correct; he also concedes that 5th Panzer Army (his own) attacked at the right time and in the right way, and concludes that both strategic and tactical surprise was achieved. What then caused the attack to fail? The mistakes he ascribes to the German High Command are essentially mistakes of adaptability in time to meet or take advantage of changing conditions. Thus, not shifting the weight of the attack from 6th to 5th Panzer Army in time to exploit the latter's success was in his view the supreme error. In spite of Model's recommendation that the reserve panzer divisions, 2nd SS and 12th SS, should go to Manteuffel, *as early as 18 December* (a significant day when we recall it was at dawn on the following morning that 101 US Airborne Division reached Bastogne), Hitler insisted on Dietrich's being allowed another chance. This stubborn refusal to reinforce success at the right time, to maintain momentum, to keep the enemy off balance, and so retain the all important initiative was to cost the Germans dear. There are times when the odds may be ignored. Hitler's rejection of them in 1936 when he reoccupied the Rhineland is an example, so are Churchill's and the Royal Air Force's rejection of them in 1940, or Wavell's rejection of them in his great desert offensive, and the Royal Navy's rejection of them on countless occasions. On such occasions gambling yields great dividends. But for the Germans, December 1944 was not a time for rejecting all the odds. Given the initial decision to gamble, it was a time for backing certainties, a time for obeying all the established military rules, for being conventional, not eccentric, for taking what fleeting tides there were at the flood. Hitler would have none of it, and once this opportunity was missed, once rigid adherence to an unalterable plan was allowed to overrule military common sense, all chances of the offensive's prospering were chucked aside.

It was this refusal of Hitler's to face facts which was perhaps his own main shortcoming as a commander. He had, of course, so often ignored facts in the past and had so often won in spite of them that he was ill-disposed to consider any facts or any opinions when they ran counter to his own preconceived estimate of a situation. It was because of this that in planning and executing the Wehrmacht's operations, intuition so often took the place of military intelligence. Hitler had a low opinion of his Intelligence staff in any case and never listened to their reports, indeed condemned them as twaddle and forbade them to be read out at all, when they failed to support his intuition. That Hitler had an uncanny strategic and tactical instinct on certain occasions is clear enough, and his instinct was once more demonstrated in the Ardennes battle. On this occasion he combined his intuitive choice of the plan to attack with most stringent security measures—even to the point of not allowing the forward troops to know what was in the wind until the day before it started.

In any event German failure in the Ardennes could not be put

down to poor Intelligence. On the other hand Allied unpreparedness for it could and was. In his book* about Intelligence failures
of the last war, Mr Kirkpatrick has shown how close were the
views of the senior German commanders and the Allied Intelligence staffs in considering that a major offensive by the Wehrmacht
could not be undertaken on the Western front in the winter of
1944 with any real chance of success. An Intelligence staff's
business, of course, is not to say whether a possible operation is
or is not sensible, but whether or not it is likely. The reason that
the Allies thought it unlikely was really that they rightly judged
that no German attack could be strong enough to defeat the
Allies; it could gain but a temporary success and, because of the
hitherto terrible attrition of German manpower, would simply
exhaust their enemy's last reserves and speed up his collapse.

It is strange that after all this time when the Allied military
leaders had been given an uninterrupted demonstration of the
way in which the Wehrmacht was in fact controlled—that is to
say by the eccentric and fanatical will of a single man who could
recognize no limits to his power, no curb on his own ability to
impose that will and power on the rest of the world—they
should suddenly assume that military calculation and reason
would be the order of the day. It seemed that the lessons of
Moscow, Stalingrad, Kursk, Cherbourg and Mortain had gone
for nothing. Even Montgomery, who proved right in his bet with
Eisenhower that the war would not be over by Christmas 1944,
had judged as late as two weeks before Christmas that the Germans could not stage major offensive operations. He writes in his
History of Warfare that in order to understand the mind of his
opponent, he would study a photograph of him. Perhaps if he
had had Hitler's photograph instead of Rommel's or von
Rundstedt's he would have revised his estimate.

The failure of Allied Intelligence in this case was aggravated
by their system of command. To start with although Eisenhower
was the Supreme Commander, his subordinates, Bradley and
Montgomery, never hesitated to say if they thought he was
wrong. When Eisenhower expressed his doubts about Bradley's
weakness in the Ardennes sector, he allowed himself against his
own judgment to be persuaded that all would be well—even if
the Germans did attack there. Within the broadest directives,
Eisenhower largely allowed them both, Bradley and Montgomery,

* *Captains without Eyes*, Lyman B. Kirkpatrick Jr, Hart-Davis, 1970.

to go their own ways. Their own ways in the battle of the Ardennes did little to enhance the reputation of either.

It was not so much what they did as what they said they did which showed them in a poor light. Montgomery's claims at his subsequent press conference contained two statements which were perilously close to untruths and it is difficult to imagine any justification for them other than that the Field Marshal wished no one to be in doubt as to his own contribution to winning the battle. At best it was a poor illustration of its supposed purpose— to underline the team-work, the cooperation—one of Montgomery's own chosen battle-winning factors—so necessary during a crisis. The first of these two statements was:

> As soon as I saw what was happening I took certain steps myself to ensure that *if* the Germans got to the Meuse they would certainly not get over that river. And I carried out certain movements so as to provide balanced dispositions to meet the threatened danger; these were, at the time, merely precautions, i.e., I was thinking ahead.

The trouble with this statement is that it implies that he, Montgomery, was the only one who was thinking ahead, yet in fact what happened next was as unforeseen by Montgomery as the attack itself, and the dispositions he made were simply to secure his own communications and then wait and see.

'The great art of generalship', Montgomery wrote in his book about leadership, 'is to simplify a problem and to expose the fundamentals on which all action must be based—followed by decisions and action. The sum total of simplicity, decisions and action is the hall-mark of military genius.' By this token Hitler was a military genius indeed for he was never thrifty of decisions and action and did have the gift of reducing problems to their simplest terms. What Montgomery should have added perhaps is that when the odds are overwhelmingly against you, even these supremely important qualities are not enough to win battles for you. With all the cards in your hand it is a different matter. Nor is it possible to concentrate the art of generalship within a few words. Clarity of mind, opportunism, boldness, intuition, swiftness, sensing the right time and place, concentrating at the point of decision, and the robustness never to give up, never to despair —all these are just as important. What is generalship but the determination of battles? What are battles but the illustration of generalship? As we have seen Montgomery did not determine the outcome of the Ardennes battle. If any single man did that it was Hitler. But how did the Ardennes illustrate Montgomery? What did he do that was important?

What he did was to discover the situation, place a screen of armour and infantry to cover the Meuse crossings, and by moving 30 Corps to the area between Liège and Brussels give the whole northern position some much needed depth. Montgomery's proper contribution to the battle came when he was put in command of the 1st and 9th US Armies. It was then that he was able to impose a general pattern of operations on a series of uncoordinated actions. Furthermore by his patience and insistence on being ready before committing himself to counter-attack, he provided the firmness, balance and depth to Allied defences in the north, which ensured first that the Germans would be halted, and second that they would be pushed back. Yet in the second of the two statements whose veracity was so questionable he talked of employing 'the whole available power of the British Group of Armies'. Since only little more than one division of British troops had in fact been engaged in the Allied counter-attack, compared with an eventual total of 27 US divisions, and since the defensive phase of the battle had been almost totally absorbed by American soldiers, this distortion was really unforgivable, nor was it forgiven by many Americans. The handling of sensitive Allies had been a job inherited by British generals for several centuries— William III, Marlborough, Wellington, Raglan and Haig had all found it difficult. None had succeeded in offending their allies quite as bitterly as Montgomery. This was not generalship. Although Montgomery was right in summing up the battle as one which involved heading off and seeing off the enemy, he implied that it was himself who had done both when in fact most of the heading off had been done before he even entered the battle. He even compared it to the Battle of Alam el Halfa. 'They came on in the old style', he had echoed Wellington, 'and we drove them back in the old style.' He could claim perhaps half the credit for seeing them off—with American troops. Patton and Bradley could claim the other half.

'Chance and luck', concludes Mr Elstob, 'not military reasoning, ruled the battlefield.' In other words, generalship played but a small part in its resolution. Neither Patton nor Bradley showed much generalship if by that word we mean the imposition of a single will, a single pattern on the battle, which then proceeded to develop along the lines conceived by a single mind. Patton's great contribution was one of organization and deployment in that he rapidly extracted two corps of his Army from one part of the front and committed them to another. But his commitment of them—without thorough reconnaissance, without proper preparation, without concentration, without a single coherent design— does much to explain why his greatly superior strength supported by powerful air forces took so long, no less than five days, to advance some 20 miles and reach Bastogne against greatly outnumbered and overstretched opposition. It was the eventual *weight* of the intervention, not Patton's handling of it, which turned the scales on the southern flank. The southern flank was Bradley's too—indeed the whole front had been Bradley's until Eisenhower handed over the north to Montgomery on 20 December. This meant that with two out of his three armies under Montgomery, Bradley was left in charge of Patton, never the easiest of sub-ordinates. Bradley's part in the Ardennes battle may be sum-marized like this—his initial dispositions were such that the German offensive was made possible in the first place; his com-mand arrangements were such that once the battle started he lost control of it; his loyalty to Eisenhower was such that he attempted to undermine Montgomery's authority over Hodges and even threatened to resign his command if there was any question of Montgomery's being given full control in the north for the subsequent operations. On the other hand, his rapid reinforcement of St Vith and Bastogne, after conferring with Eisenhower on 16 December, did have a major effect on the battle. This was a matter of good fortune rather than generalship.

Perhaps the only man who displayed real generalship on the Allied side was the one from whom it was most expected and required—Eisenhower. He was able to think 'big', immediately sensing that it was a major crisis, overriding the objections of his subordinates as to command arrangements, getting priorities right as to when to concentrate, calling off other battles, com-mitting reserves and generally behaving with the calm and judgment called for. At his conference on 19 December he at once demanded that there would be only cheerful faces at the table, and contended that the German offensive, far from being a moment of disaster for the Allies, was one of opportunity, in that the Germans, having abandoned their fixed defences, could now be destroyed. Eisenhower's overall grip of the battle never wavered, his courage in making decisions unpopular with his military subordinates and political masters alike was of the highest order, and his actual strategy of shoring up the bulge's shoulders, stopping its spearheads and then subjecting it to irresistible pressure from either flank was the right one. The Supreme Commander lived up to his name literally and figuratively.

In the tactical field there was plenty of brilliant leadership and plenty of crass blundering on either side. We may perhaps examine this proposition in relation to the various phases of war. One of the main requirements in defence is that ground vital to the fighting of a successful battle must be held. Both in the initial phases of the offensive and throughout its course, it was from the American, indeed the whole Allied, point of view indispensable that the shoulders of the enemy penetration held firm. If they had cracked, Dietrich's Panzer Army in the north and Manteuffel's in the south would have been able to race forward on a broad front, improvising here, destroying there, outflanking some-where else. Opportunity would not have been confined, as it was in the event, to a few lone narrow ventures like Peiper's or 2nd Panzer Division or Panzer Lehr. There would have been a chance for Model to have done in 1944 what Guderian did in 1940, to have crossed the Meuse on a broad front, and have got into the innards of the Allied armies before they knew what it was all about. Hitler's prediction of collapse and panic might have come to pass. The panzer columns really might have driven through the middle of the Allies, got in behind the communica-tions of 21st Army Group, and if not encircled the entire English Army, have done it incalculable harm, even to the point actually of reaching Antwerp. What would the Allied commanders have done with their reserves and reinforcements if their front had been collapsing everywhere?

But the shoulders held. The relatively small-scale actions near Monschau, Elsenborn, Bütgenbach, Stavelot and Stourmont in the north, near Echternach, Waldbillig, Diekirch and Wiltz in the south were in their way decisive. For they squeezed the German offensive into a narrow bulging shape which gave the battle its name; they allowed what reserves were readily available to move to those places whose defence would itself further restrict the Bulge in pace and extent, and in their turn become equally vital. Thus the American defence of St Vith during the first days, and of Bastogne throughout the period of German offensive operations were in their turn critical. What is more, junior American commanders like Hasbrouck and McAuliffe, both in their grasp of this point and in their conduct of actual operations, acquitted themselves admirably. The effect of these two separate yet complementary patterns of defence—the shoulders and the key communication centres between the shoulders—was first to limit the width of the Germans' drive and then to limit its depth. However much chance or pride, hesitancy, ill-judgment or sheer inspired leadership may have influenced affairs, to have limited the enemy attack in this way was to have obeyed the classic rules for conducting a defensive battle after the enemy has effected a penetration of your defences. Locate it, slow it down, pin it if you can, hammer it, confine it, stop it altogether and then subject it to such a coalition of firepower and manoeuvre that it has no choice but to withdraw, perish or be taken. This is the final phase of a defensive battle—counter-attack to destroy the enemy's offensive, before resuming the offensive yourself. Some high marks were gained here by the Americans. It was not because the high command had designed it this way. The high command was not in control of events, but was constantly reacting to them. That this was so is explained if we go to the other end of a defensive battle's phases—the preparatory phase. For here their score was lamentably low.

Equally fundamental to fighting a defensive battle properly is the ability to reach out in order to discover the situation, to get early warning of enemy approach, to avoid being surprised, to ensure—by a vigorous and continuous programme of patrolling and reconnaissance, by the taking of prisoners and their interrogation, by intensive study of the pattern of enemy behaviour opposite you—that you deduce broadly what he is up to. This is not information that will come to you—without your stir. It has to be planned for, fought for, got by all and every means available to that most versatile, skilled and precious of men at arms—the infantryman. It is easy to be lulled into a sense of false security because the enemy is not badgering you. It is easy to say to yourself that you will not upset or annoy the enemy if only he too will play the game and leave you alone, doubly easy in December, in snow and rain and cold. Easy, but full of peril. Had the proper sort of patrolling and information-seeking been done even in an elementary fashion by Middleton's VIII Corps in the middle week of December 1944, the offensive could never have achieved the surprise it did, for the German preparations must have become known, and once known, all the Allied Intelligence staff's talk of no enemy offensive capability or intention would have been shown up for the trash it was. So much for defence.

As for withdrawal, there was a curious misunderstanding of its nature on the part of the Americans. To Montgomery, withdrawal in a battle you intended to win was as natural as for a boxer to go to his corner of the ring when the bell rang at the end of a round. Withdrawal to concentrate, to deceive, to preserve balance, to create new strength, to give the enemy the very rope he needed to hang himself—these were well tried, well understood and well accepted moves in the tactical game. To the Americans withdrawal was somehow shameful, a wrecker of morale, an admission of defeat. It was un-American. Premature, costly, even disastrous attack was to be preferred to withdrawal. It should perhaps here be added that generally speaking withdrawal seemed somehow less shameful to those being subjected to an endless weight of mortar shells and machine-gun bullets than to those doing the planning from the comfort and safety of command posts. The truth was that the Americans confused tactical withdrawal with strategic defeat. In the Ardennes they were obliged to conduct tactical withdrawal. They did not suffer a strategic defeat. Yet this very confusion and their reluctance to consider the possibility of being required to withdraw meant that at the higher command levels they had not mastered its principles, nor at the fighting echelons had they practised its mechanics.

One of the master rules of withdrawal is that the next line* to which the army is retiring (and where a further defensive battle may be fought, prior, it is hoped, to returning to the attack) should be prepared as fully as it can be before the leading troops quit the defensive line at that time being contested. This is to say, reconnaissance will be done, areas selected, weapons sited, defensive stores like mines and wire assembled, and some troops actually positioned. In short one leg is put firmly on the ground before the other one is picked up. You are establishing line number two before abandoning line number one. You have no wish

---

* The word 'line' is sometimes ridiculed by armchair strategists for no real defensive position is in fact a line. But those who tried to penetrate the Mareth Line or the Gothic Line or the Siegfried Line respect the term.

to be involved in a running fight without a firm base. Yet as we have seen from von Manteuffel's evidence, in spite of their unrivalled skill and experience at withdrawal operations, the Germans fell down badly in this respect, in that when 5th Panzer Army returned to its positions after the offensive's failure, nothing was ready for them. On the other hand low-level leadership during the initial American withdrawal in the face of 1st SS Panzer and 2nd Panzer Divisions was in many instances a model of what it should have been. Small combat groups showed a true appreciation of another major factor in withdrawal—timing. They obliged the Germans to deploy for full scale attacks, and still withdrew to do the same again further back. So, when the roles were reversed, did the rearguard troops of Manteuffel's Army. This brings us to the business of advancing.

The essence of the advance is early seizure of really important objectives together with flexibility in switching the main effort. Here the tactical instinct of Army Group and Army commanders on the German side was thwarted by the Führer. Right at the outset Model tried to persuade Hitler to switch the main panzer strength under Dietrich to reinforce and exploit the success being enjoyed further south by von Manteuffel. Manteuffel too pressed strenuously for the extra strength which he felt, both at the time and with the advantage of hindsight years later, would have enabled him both to have captured Bastogne and reached the Meuse. But the Führer would have none of it until such time as the sheer weight of Allied reinforcements was such that the tactical opportunity was gone, never to reappear. In spite of Manteuffel's personal leadership and his insistence—also fundamental to the conduct of an advance and a point Hitler never grasped—on seeing it all at the sharp end, the vital objectives were either not taken at all or taken too late. Real flexibility in switching the main effort was almost totally lacking. Nor were the Allied efforts at advancing distinguished by speed, concentration or adaptability. Of course the conditions were different; of course they were up against skilled and brave soldiers; of course there was a need for improvisation and the proper cooperation of all arms. But this was no excuse for the ill-prepared, haphazard and eccentric way in which Patton launched inadequate, piecemeal and unnecessarily costly counter-attacks, thereby sacrificing forces, equipment and time, instead of adorning sheer superiority of numbers with patience—a combination which would have done much to guarantee quicker and cheaper success. The adage, 'More haste, less speed', was rarely shown to be more true.

The secret of successful attack is to maintain momentum by the most effective concentration and combination of firepower and movement which you can lay your hands on and by the timely commitment of reserves. It was Napoleon's failure to commit his reserves at the bloody encounter of Borodino which allowed the Russian Army to escape and so not only robbed him of victory, but brought about the utter dissipation of the Grande Armée and thus the loss of his throne. Untypically he was not even close enough to the front line to see that by sending forward the Old Guard, he could have crushed the Russians once and for all. 'What the blazing hell is he doing so far behind,' yelled Ney. 'If he is no longer a general, let him clear off back to the Tuileries and leave us to do the commanding for him.' It's a thought, however wordless, that must have occurred a thousand times to the Army commanders of the Wehrmacht, while Hitler continued to give the orders and control the reserves from Adlershorst or his other Führer Headquarters. Yet all this cannot explain why von Lüttwitz and von Manteuffel, realizing as they both so thoroughly did, that Bastogne *had* to be taken, did not turn on to it the full concentration of firepower and fighting forces which they had at their disposal to ensure its capture before it could be relieved. Their neglect remains a puzzle.

Throughout the battle another hallmark of modern generalship—the management and use of air power—worked almost exclusively in favour of the Allies. The Luftwaffe simply failed either to support the panzer columns in a direct sense or to ensure that they were uninterfered with by American and British aircraft. For the Allies, however, their almost unrestricted and admirably coordinated use of air power was a success story without parallel in the whole Ardennes campaign.

It was this omnipresent and unchallenged command of the air which enabled them to maintain the offensive spirit. The offensive spirit has been applied to that greatest exponent of it in British military history, Nelson, as his ace of trumps among the four aces of leadership. It was an ace which never deserted Hitler. But for Hitler, the Ardennes offensive would never have taken place at all. Oddly enough when we think how different their characters were, he held most, but not all, of Nelson's aces, although in a very different manner. He was able to inspire both officers and soldiers of the Wehrmacht in a way that the generals never could. During the battle signed photographs of von Rundstedt, which had been distributed to the soldiers as marks of confidence and esteem, were returned by the recipients as being absolutely useless for the maintenance of morale. Even the third ace—creative imagination in planning battles—was held by Hitler, particularly in the days when the Wehrmacht had the initiative, but Hitler never took it to the lengths which Nelson did, that is to say anticipating all the contingencies, all the twists and turns that a battle might take, and then preparing for, even rehearsing, them. It was no good Hitler's shouting at Guderian that he had studied Clausewitz and Moltke and the rest of them, and then refusing to adapt his plan to changing conditions as Moltke had so strenuously advocated.

It was this last point—with which was so bound up also the fact that Hitler's subordinate generals were not allowed to take decisions at the moment when they had to be taken—which underlines Hitler's complete deficiency of the fourth ace. He would have done well to remember Joshua Reynolds' contention that if you refuse ever to ransack any mind but your own, you will soon be reduced to the poorest of all imitations. You will be obliged to imitate yourself, and to repeat what has often before been repeated. Thus 1944 was a poor imitation of 1940. Hitler could not, as Nelson could, make use of his subordinates' ideas when they ran counter to his own. Above all he could not separate what was possible from what was probable. 'Nothing is impossible', Macaulay has reminded us, 'which does not involve contradiction.' It was possible that the Meuse would be reached on the first or second day of the advance; it was possible that all the 'bank clerks and Jewish hoodlums' who made up the American armies would fling down their arms and run off bawling for quarter; it was possible that the weather would be so bad for so long that not a single Allied aircraft would be able to take to the skies for the duration of the offensive, but that in this same bad weather the panzer groups would have no difficulty in getting forward; it was possible that Model's armies would find in their path all the petrol to make up for the untold thousands of gallons which Keitel had failed to make provision for; it was even possible that 5th and 6th Panzer Armies would reach Brussels and Antwerp, split the Allied armies, roll up 21st Army Group and maintain their positions without their exposed flanks being

27 *US air power: Cause . . .*

28 *. . . and effect on German horse transport*

29   *Me 109 begins its death dive*

30   *Execution of German spies wearing US uniform*

hammered and destroyed by counter-attacking forces. All these things were possible. But they were so immeasurably improbable that they were but poor premises for undertaking a military operation. Politics may be the art of the possible. War is more the science of the probable. Throughout the operation Hitler refused to acknowledge probability, refused to learn by mistakes or events. This characteristic deficiency in his tactical adaptability was matched by the illusion of his strategic instinct. He either ignored realities or dismissed them. At a time when of all times his strategic policy and his practical conduct of war should have been based on balanced reasoning and a shrewd calculation of the military odds, it relied instead on eccentricity, stubbornness and misjudgment. The requirement and the reality were too far apart to be reconciled.

The main influence that high command can exercise in a battle of the Ardennes sort, once its shape, because of initial contacts, is beginning to be determined, is to position and commit reserves at the right time and right place.* In the actual Ardennes battle, it was the failure of the German high command to do this, together with the actual slowness and narrowness of the spearheads which more than anything else robbed them of the initiative. On the other side of the hill, it was the unexpected stubbornness of the American defenders and the rapid release of reserves by the American high command which complemented and aggravated the German failure, even though the American defensive and reinforcement moves were notably haphazard.

In his great work on the Second World War, Churchill concludes a chapter on the Ardennes counter-offensive by quoting from his speech on 18 January 1945 in the House of Commons. After describing how Eisenhower had given command of the north to Montgomery and the south to Bradley, he declared: 'In the result both these highly skilled commanders handled the very large forces at their disposal in a manner which I think I may say without exaggeration may become the model for military students in the future. . . .' To which we might add— the model perhaps, but if so, the model of how *not* to do it.

* Marmont, the great friend and ultimate betrayer of Napoleon, observed: 'With 12,000 men one fights; with 30,000 one commands; but in great armies the commander is only a sort of Providence which can only intervene to ward off great accidents.' Eisenhower would probably have endorsed this view; Hitler would certainly have rejected it.

12

A House of Cards

It is one of the ironies of history that the long-term result of
Hitler's attempt to keep Germany intact is that today East
Germany's frontier lies about a hundred miles further west
than it would have done had the Ardennes Offensive never
been launched.
Peter Elstob

On 9 January 1945 the Supreme Commander of the Wehrmacht
was at Adlershorst discussing the military situation with Guderian,
Chief of the General Staff. Guderian was anxious to adjust the
fronts of both General Hanke's Army Group A (formerly known
as Army Group North Ukraine) and General Reinhardt's Army
Group Centre. The moves proposed by the two Army Group
Commanders were modest. Hanke wished to shorten his line,
improve his defensive position and reform some reserves by
pulling back about 12 miles. Reinhardt's plan was similar—to
withdraw to a shorter line at the East Prussian border and
reconstitute a reserve. But Guderian wanted more than this. He
wanted Hitler to transform his entire defensive strategy, to get
out of Italy and the Balkans, Norway and the Baltic, and to
concentrate the whole strength of the Wehrmacht on the defence
of Germany—more particularly to keep the Russians out. Most of
all he wanted to switch immediately the main defensive effort from
West to East. He could not have had much confidence in his
ability to persuade Hitler to do any of these things, but with his
customary sense of duty and perseverance, he tried. Hitler's
behaviour was equally characteristic. He lost his temper. Having
heard what Guderian's staff thought about the military situation,
he pronounced it to be completely idiotic and that the officer who
had prepared the estimate of the Red Army's strength and
deployment should be shut up in a lunatic asylum. He reverted

to his old accusations that for generals, military operations meant simply a retreat to the next position in rear.

When the Duke of Wellington was asked what was the best test of a great general, he answered: 'To know when to retreat, and to dare to do it.' It was a lesson Hitler never learned, and although it may be doubted whether Guderian pointed it out to him, at least he himself was never one to retreat in the face of the Führer's outbursts of anger. Guderian recorded that OKW refused to contemplate the creation of reserves on the Eastern front because they stuck to the belief that the Russian preparations for an offensive were nothing more than bluff. He added that 'Hitler and Jodl knew perfectly well that if the expected attack should materialize, the Eastern front was quite incapable of holding it with the resources available.' Nevertheless Hitler refused to hear of any withdrawal. 'I get an attack of the horrors whenever I hear that there must be a withdrawal somewhere or other. . . . I've heard that sort of thing for the past two years and the results have always been appalling.' Not only would there be no withdrawal, therefore, but there would be no reinforcements for the East either. Priority would continue to be given to the West 'so that we may keep the initiative there'—an initiative already lost. Self-delusion could hardly go further however, than when Hitler assured Guderian at the end of this conference on 9 January: 'The Eastern front has never before possessed such a strong reserve as now. That is your doing. I thank you for it.' Guderian replied that the Eastern front was like a house of cards and that, if the front were pierced at any point, all the rest would collapse.

At this time the critical portion of the Eastern front between the Baltic and the Carpathians was manned by some 75 German divisions, of which about 12 were in reserve. On the same front Stalin had assembled for the greatest offensive of the whole war some 180 divisions with no fewer than four tank armies, each of which mustered about 1,200 tanks, giving the Russians a six-to-one superiority in men and material—double the conventional three-to-one required for attack—over the German forces. No wonder that when on the morning of 12 January Koniev's Army Group broke out of its bridgehead on the Upper Vistula and swept across the frozen ground, the German defences, as Guderian had predicted, went down like a house of cards. By the end of January Zhukov's offensive had rolled forward everywhere—and his armies were within striking distance of Berlin itself. If future students of military history (particularly students from Western countries) require a model of how to conduct an offensive, it is to Zhukov's, rather than to Eisenhower's, that they might well turn their attention.

One of the effects of Zhukov's success was the political use made of it by Stalin at Yalta when he was able to contrast the huge gains of the Red Army with the paper plans of the Western Allies. It was not for nothing, however great the over-simplification, that Chester Wilmot called Yalta Stalin's greatest victory. Roughly a month before Yalta, on 6 January 1945, Churchill had sent a message to Stalin. He did so, according to his own account, in response to a request from Eisenhower to discover whether Russian plans for an offensive in the East would be likely to take pressure off his own armies in the West. Churchill's message was:

> The battle in the West is very heavy and at any time large decisions may be called for from the Supreme Command. You know yourself from your own experience how very anxious the position is when a very broad front has to be defended after the temporary loss of the initiative. It is Eisenhower's great desire and need to know in outline what you plan to do, as this obviously affects all his and our major decisions. . . . I shall be grateful if you can tell me whether we can count on a major Russian offensive on the Vistula front, or elsewhere during January. . . .

Stalin's prompt reply was that, in spite of unfavourable weather which inhibited Russian exploitation of their air and artillery superiority, the Russian Supreme Command had decided to speed up their preparations and start offensive operations along the entire Central front not later than the second half of January. We have seen that in fact they started on 12 January and met with rapid and spectacular success. The question then becomes—was the Ardennes offensive finally defeated in the West because of the Russian offensive, as the Russians themselves claimed, or was the Russian offensive immediately and strikingly successful because the Ardennes battle was keeping so many German divisions busy? When we remember, first Hitler's absolute refusal to listen to all Guderian's arguments about the weakness of the Eastern front; second his insistence that it was in the West that the initiative was to be had; third that by 12 January the failure of the Ardennes offensive had been recognized by the Germans themselves who were by that time everywhere on the defensive although still fighting stubbornly; fourth that Dietrich's 6th SS Panzer Army was not ordered east until 22 January, and then to Hungary—we may draw two conclusions. We may conclude that it was the Ardennes offensive which assisted the Russian attack to be so fast and furious, and we may conclude that it was, of course, the inter-relation of both fronts which finally defeated the Wehrmacht. That so much of the Wehrmacht's strength was in the West in January 1945, and so much of it was written off in the battle, merely made certain that a good deal of the German Reich would be occupied by the Red Army.

Thus we may perhaps set the Ardennes offensive in its true strategic context. Within just over three months of its conclusion the war itself was over. Did it then end the war more quickly than some different strategy on the part of the Germans might have done or would the result have been the same? There are those who argue, Mr Elstob among them, that the Ardennes offensive, designed by Hitler to keep Germany whole, merely ensured that Germany was more divided than it would have been if the offensive had not been mounted. If by this he means that had German strategy been—as many of the generals, and particularly Guderian, wanted—to give in the West and hold on in the East, then it is possible that—undertakings at Yalta notwithstanding—the meeting place of the British and American forces with the Red Army would have been further east, say, the Oder–Neisse line instead of the Elbe–Mulde. But if, on the other hand, von Rundstedt had had his way in the West—that is to hold tight, hold on and use the 6th Panzer Army and the other reserves for shoring up the West Wall—while not substantially reinforcing the East, then we may imagine a very different result. We may even imagine a Germany intact. But a more successfully defended Siegfried Line in the West and a collapsed house of cards in the East could have added up to a rendezvous between the British–American forces and the Red Army *on the Rhine*. Germany would have been intact all right, but there would have been no *Bundesrepublik*. All of it would have been a huge *Deutsche-demokratischerepublik*. In any case short of an absolute give-West/hold-East strategy on the part of the Germans, it was not so much the Ardennes offensive which caused Germany to be divided, it was the Yalta agreement and Allied strategy thereafter, a strategy compounded and confused by political and military

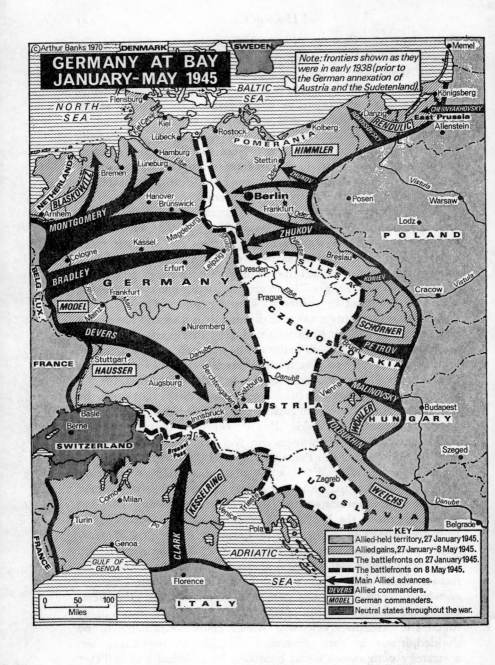

disagreement among the Allies themselves and aggravated by the sinister intransigence of Stalin.

That the purely military part of Allied strategy should not have been clearer, bolder and more forcefully pursued was all the more extraordinary because after the Ardennes battles, Hitler—as usual painting pictures and believing that at least two months would pass before the Allies would have recovered sufficiently from those battles to resume their offensive in the West—gave absolute priority of reinforcement to the East. After all the threat to Berlin was both serious and imminent. In February 1945 for example whereas the best part of 2,000 tanks and assault guns were despatched to the Eastern front, less than 100 went to the West. Yet the determination for resistance on both fronts, emanating as it did from the top, was in no way lessened. Although Speer had written a memorandum to Hitler explaining that after the loss of Upper Silesia, and with the Ruhr in ruins, the armaments industry simply could not meet requirements of tanks, ammunition and guns, and that German soldiers' bravery could not alone compensate for these material deficiencies, the Führer countered by declaring that he and he alone was entitled to draw conclusions from the armaments situation. The three leaders at Yalta, Stalin, Roosevelt and Churchill, might be insisting on Unconditional Surrender. But even with the hands of the clock at five past twelve, Hitler had his answer:

> Those war mongers in Yalta must be denounced—so insulted and attacked that they will have no chance to make an offer to the German people. Under no circumstances must there be an offer. That gang only wants to separate the German people from their leadership. I've always said surrender is absolutely out of the question. History is not going to be repeated.

Two such uncompromising positions meant that the war could not be over until either the Soviet armies met those of the West somewhere in the centre of Europe or the Almighty 'released the Führer from his duty of representing the interest of his people'. In the event the two occurred more or less simultaneously. The exact linking-up point would be determined by the precise courses of military action taken respectively by the Germans, the Russians and the Western Allies. Towards the end of January 1945, well after the Ardennes offensive was over, the Western armies were roughly closed up to the Siegfried Line. The Russians had overrun much of East Prussia and were also fighting on German soil in Silesia and Pomerania. They were in fact within 100 miles of Berlin. If all the Western Allies' talk of capturing this great prize were to be more than talk, *now*—when the Wehrmacht was concentrating its strength in the East and weakening the West in the last of the great robbing Peter to pay Paul processes which had characterized Hitler's strategy ever since he had lost the overall initiative in the autumn of 1942—was the moment for them to forget their differences and make a final and concentrated move forward.

Yet at this very time Allied counsels were once again disturbed by old controversies. Which was right—a broad-front advance or a narrow thrust across the Rhine? And what were to be the final objectives? Eisenhower predictably stuck to his broad-front strategy. In the north Montgomery's group of armies was to drive across the Lower Rhine and into the North German plain in order to make best use of that area's suitability for mobile operations and to deny Germany use of the Ruhr. Bradley, further south, was to attack towards Kassel, complete the envelopment of the Ruhr and drive on to link up with the Russians. The British Chiefs of Staff doubted whether there would be sufficient strength for both operations and feared that the Red Army would reach the North Sea before them. The British also went to the extraordinary length of renewing their arguments about having one land battle Commander-in-Chief under Eisenhower. Montgomery's appointment to this position might well have caused the resignation of Bradley and Patton, although it was Alexander whom Churchill had in mind for the job, so that he could direct Allied land operations in accordance with his, Churchill's, view of what British political objectives should be. American opposition to such an idea persuaded the British to drop it.

The outcome of this controversy, that is to say the outcome of the Rhine battles themselves, showed Eisenhower once more to be right both in his strategic plan and in his command arrangements. By this time he had complete confidence in his own judgment and had, as Chester Wilmot put it, 'learned the need for firm command to ensure concentration and for a central reserve to maintain flexibility'. If the Ardennes battles had done nothing else, they had provided the Supreme Allied Commander with personal evidence of the soundness of these two rules. The measure of his success is best illustrated by the fact that, whereas at the time of Yalta the Allied armies in the West were stuck, while the Red Army had even then been sweeping forward, now, after the crossing of the Rhine in March, it was in the East that the German armies were holding firm on the Oder–Neisse line, while for Eisenhower's armies the roads to Berlin and to most of Germany were open. After Model's armies had been encircled in the Ruhr, a gap of 200 miles had been created in the German Western defences. Eisenhower had the operational and logistic resources to motor to Berlin. Only political considerations could prevent him.

By this time, however, distrust of Soviet Russia had been steadily growing among the counsellors of both Roosevelt and Churchill. Indeed Churchill was equally alarmed by his own enduring suspicion of Stalin's aims and the Americans' refusal to acknowledge the reality of these aims. What is more the misunderstandings aroused by the projected meeting at Berne between Allied representatives and General Wolff, Chief of the SS in Italy, to discuss an end of hostilities on the Italian front, produced a telegram to Roosevelt from Stalin which implied that the Western Powers were about to make a separate peace with Hitler, that Kesselring (since March, Commander-in-Chief, West) had agreed to lay down his arms on the Western front and so allow Anglo-American troops to advance into Germany from the West, while the German armies continued to fight against the Russians in the East. All these things further compromised Allied unanimity of strategic purpose.

Eisenhower's final arrangements for completing the campaign were based on his compelling wish to end the war quickly with the minimum casualties. Convinced, rightly, that there would be no surrender while Hitler remained at the head of affairs, and persuaded, wrongly, by his Intelligence staff that Hitler's most likely final course of action would be to put himself at the head of a fanatical group of die-hards, personally direct defence of the so called National Redoubt or Alpine Fortress in the mountains surrounding Berchtesgaden, and hold out there, supported by secret weapons and guerrilla bands, Eisenhower took his eye off Berlin. 'Military factors,' he concluded, 'when the enemy was on the brink of final defeat, were more important in my eyes than the political considerations involved in an Allied capture of the capital . . . [which] no longer represented a military objective of major importance.' What irony that in fact Berlin itself held until the very end the military objective *par excellence,* the only thing which kept the war machinery of Germany turning over at all, the key to the whole situation—the Führer himself.* Not comprehending that *Götterdämmerung* in the capital was to be the grand finale of the 12-year tragedy of the Third Reich, Eisenhower made his plans. These were that Bradley, with the bulk of Allied strength concentrated under his command, would make a huge central drive towards Leipzig–Dresden to split Germany in half, and join up with the Red Army. Then the Allied armies would branch out with two thrusts north-east and south-west, the former to the Baltic, the latter to seize the National Redoubt. Churchill took an instant dislike to this plan. Not only did it rob the British of a leading part in the final advance, but far more grave, it did not cater for the seizing of Berlin, which in Churchill's eyes had become a political objective of first importance. Churchill was one of the first to recognize, as Hitler himself did, that the future struggle for Europe would be between Soviet Russia and the United States, and that the destruction of German military power would completely change the relationship of the wartime Allies who had brought about that destruction. Only a common enemy could unite them. Take away that enemy and they would become enemies themselves. Therefore, argued Churchill, *well before the event,* since there would be a new front between these new enemies, this front must be as far east in Europe as possible, and therefore Berlin was a 'prime and true objective of the Anglo-American armies'. Those seeking to perpetuate the present status quo in Europe would do well to ask themselves whether the aims of Soviet Russia in 1972 are very different from what they were in 1945. Churchill put his views to the British Chiefs of Staff thus:

> It seems to me that the chief criticism of the new Eisenhower plan is that it shifts the axis of the main advance upon Berlin to the direction through Leipzig to Dresden, and thus raises the question of whether the Twenty-first Army Group will not be so stretched as to lose its offensive power, especially after it has

* The amount of detective work that Professor Trevor-Roper would have been saved if the British had got to Berlin first hardly bears thinking of. Indeed his enquiry which led to publication of *The Last Days of Hitler* might never have been necessary, and we would have been robbed of an incomparable work.

been deprived of the Ninth United States Army. Thus we might be condemned to an almost static role in the north and virtually prevented from crossing the Elbe until an altogether later stage in the operations has been reached. All prospect of the British entering Berlin with the Americans is ruled out . . . it also seems that General Eisenhower may be wrong in supposing Berlin to be largely devoid of military and political importance. Even though German Government departments have to a great extent moved to the south, the dominating fact on German minds of the fall of Berlin should not be overlooked. The idea of neglecting Berlin and leaving it to the Russians to take at a later stage does not appear to me correct. As long as Berlin holds out and withstands a siege in the ruins, as it may easily do, German resistance will be stimulated. The fall of Berlin might cause nearly all Germans to despair. . . .

There was perhaps one German, who had repeatedly called himself simply the first soldier of the Third Reich, for whom, as for Frederick the Great, even the fall of Berlin would not have caused despair. For despair was not in Hitler's makeup. But by the time Berlin did fall, Hitler had caught an everlasting cold. It was the reaction of the only other Supreme Commander, who really did wield supreme power—Stalin—to Eisenhower's plan that redoubled Churchill's instinctive strategic fear of allowing Berlin to fall into Russian hands. For Stalin welcomed this new plan, which 'entirely coincides with the plan of the Soviet High Command'. Berlin, Stalin declared, had lost its former strategic importance, and therefore only secondary Soviet forces would be directed against it. Churchill's comment was that this statement was not borne out by events. When we recall that Berlin has remained in the centre of the international diplomatic stage for more than a quarter of a century, we may perhaps concede that it was only on rare occasions that Churchill's shrewd strategic grip foresook him. Nor was Churchill proposing great changes in what Eisenhower proposed to do. He was simply arguing for pursuing a plan already agreed upon. 'I should greatly prefer', his message of 31 March to the Supreme Commander read,

persistence in the plan on which we crossed the Rhine, namely, that the Ninth US Army should march with the Twenty-first Army Group to the Elbe and beyond Berlin. This would not be in any way inconsistent with the great central thrust which you are now so rightly developing as the result of the brilliant operations of your armies south of the Ruhr. It only shifts the weight of one army to the northern flank.

Nonetheless Eisenhower's views prevailed. Indeed he too went so far as to claim that he was reverting to his original strategic idea—to make one great thrust to the East after the Ruhr had been taken and to capture first, the bulk of what was left of the enemy's industrial capacity, second, the area to which as it had transpired the German administrative machinery was moving. In other words he was still thinking in terms of the *defeat* of Germany, how to end the war. It was not the defeat of Germany that Churchill was concerned with. This to his way of thinking had been accomplished, even though the final act of surrender was still to come. It was the link-up with Russia *after* the war which worried Churchill. 'Who is to have Constantinople?' Napoleon had once asked. 'Who was to have the Baltic, who was to control the Atlantic ports?' Churchill was now asking. So it could be argued that at the very end when Eisenhower at last went for the single powerful thrust—he did so with the wrong objective. At long last he had got the tactics right—and the strategy wrong. He had many supporters, Marshall and Bradley amongst them. The latter spoke contemptuously of the British wish to 'complicate the war with political foresight and non-military objectives'. To the simple soldier, destruction of what remained of the German armed forces was everything. It may be questioned whether Bradley was familiar with the works of von Clausewitz. Yet as late as the first week of April 1945 Eisenhower in a signal to Marshall admitted that the purpose of war was the realization of political aims and that he would change his plans to take Berlin if the Combined Chiefs of Staff thought it proper. That he could have done so is not in doubt, for on 11 April the armoured spearheads of the US 9th Army were over the Elbe near Magdeburg, a mere fifty miles from Berlin, while Zhukov's forces had still not crossed the Oder. At this late, but not too late, hour while the British, Churchill and his military men alike, tried once more to impress on American Chiefs of Staff the incalculable importance of the German capital, and Churchill even appealed to the dying Roosevelt*, Marshall and his colleagues, still concerned about the mythical Redoubt and unwilling to issue

* The President died on the afternoon of 12 April.

political directives, had their way. Eisenhower's final orders required Allied forces to halt on the general line of the Elbe and Mulde except for Montgomery's group of armies which pressed on to the Baltic. The glittering prize, the great political plum of Berlin, would not be plucked by Eisenhower's armies, but by Zhukov's.

We must be wary of over-simplification. No single event, certainly not, as Mr Elstob suggests, the Ardennes offensive, determined the present frontier between the two Germanies. Here we may rather subscribe to the determinist view of history, and put it down to the capricious coalition of many events. This much is clear. But it brings us full circle to the more speculative, and in our context more pertinent, question—was there any alternative course open to Hitler in the autumn of 1944 which would have made more sense than staking so much on a single and final throw of the dice?

Even without an exhaustive examination of how Hitler might have deployed and developed his full defensive strength in a *Festung Deutschland* strategy, with all the delaying action which might have been made possible by a real drawing in of horns, an abandonment of the by then irrelevant Scandinavian north and Balkan–Italian south, we may perhaps agree that to have defended Germany against a three- or even four-front assaulting strategy by the Allies could not have made any difference to the early defeat of Germany. Allied manpower would have continued to rise. No doubt *all* Hitler's former friends would have turned against him. Russian, British and American air power would have been on the Reich's front, back and side doorsteps and able finally to pulverise both industrial and military sources of power. The sinews of war at Speer's disposal would simply have run out. And then the atomic bomb was within the Allies' grasp. Would they have used it against a *European* power if *in extremis*? It may be doubted. Kant's point about not indulging in military activity which would make subsequent dealings impossible might have carried little conviction in relation to the National Socialist régime; but in relation to the German people Allied counsels, nay, United States counsels, would hardly have been unanimous.

Even without its use the Allies ended the war in May 1945, little more than three months after the Ardennes offensive came to an end. The squandering of a dozen divisions may have hastened the verdict. Could their husbanding or even the different use of all thirty divisions that Hitler had mustered have reversed it, have made any difference at all? This too may be doubted. But not to play the last card in the pack was simply not in Hitler's nature. That it was not high enough is beside the point. It had to be played. Claudius, King of Denmark, put the Ardennes offensive into its proper context with his contention that:

> Diseases desperate grown
> By desperate appliance are reliev'd,
> Or not at all.

The particular disease from which the Third Reich was suffering was too desperate—short of possessing, before the Allies did, a nuclear weapon or its equal—for any relief, but this was no reason for not trying the desperate appliance. Therefore it was tried. Hitler's question, which he asked on 27 January 1945— 'Do you think that deep down inside the English are enthusiastic about all the Russian developments'—that is their swift advance into Eastern Europe, would probably have been answered by Churchill with the same words as it was answered by Jodl— 'No, certainly not!' But Hitler's strategic error to cause all other strategic errors to fade into insignificance was first to take on three of the potentially strongest military powers in the world simultaneously, and then having done so to suppose that their will power to defeat him would be less than his to defeat them.

The lessons of the Ardennes offensive are negative lessons as the whole operation was itself negative. Don't commit untrained troops to a serious battle; don't assume security exists without reconnaissance; don't undertake an operation which demands extensive tactical advances without the necessary logistic resources; don't assume that you can neutralize overwhelmingly superior air power by reliance on the caprices of weather; don't attempt to command a battle when you have no idea of what is happening; don't, when playing the last card out of a house of cards, take it from the bottom; don't set yourself unachievable targets; don't dither; don't fling away the most telling of all military options—improvisation; above all, don't dismiss probability. Speer was no doubt speaking the truth when he confessed at Nuremberg that 'Hitler deceived us all'. But even Hitler was unable to deceive himself in April 1945 that the Third Reich was not cracking in ruins. So he made his quietus with a bare bodkin. Of the other principal commanders in the Ardennes offensive, only Model did the same. Dietrich, in spite of all his SS-ness escaped the hangman's noose. Von Rundstedt provided historians with some ammunition for analysis, Manteuffel too. Patton provided material for an extravagant film. Bradley went on to be one of the longest lived 5-star generals the US Army has ever known. Eisenhower applied his military technique of compromise to the business of being President. Montgomery went on to write military history and to discover that he had almost always been right in the conduct of his battles.

Some battles are necessary for determining the shape of history. The Ardennes offensive was not one of them. It was a strategic irrelevance, for the war had already been lost and won. Its effect was to make a gloomy outlook still more gloomy. For all the participants, for the Germans and the Western Allies alike, the winter of 1944 was one of discontent. Stalin alone perhaps was able to take comfort from the reflection that whoever might be the loser in what Nobécourt called *Le Dernier Coup de Dés de Hitler,* it would not be himself.

Epilogue

A man cannot be too careful in his choice of enemies.
Oscar Wilde

The final battles of any great and lengthy conflict are a mixture of triumph and tragedy. The triumph is short-lived, the tragedy prolonged. This was perhaps more true of the Second World War than a number of others, for once Eisenhower's armies were firmly established in Western France, the issue was no longer in doubt. It was just a question of timing. How different were some of the other European conflicts. Who would have cared to predict the decline and elimination of Charles XII before the battle of Poltava? Who would have supposed in 1702 that the humbling of the Sun King would be accomplished with a few battles like Blenheim and Ramillies, the French withdrawal from Italy and Madrid's fall? As we have seen the great Frederick's fortunes positively somersaulted in 1762; but who would have thought it? Most of the world, himself included, looked upon Bonaparte as invincible. Leipzig and Waterloo did for him. Yet Waterloo was in the balance until late in the day. Had Napoleon won this last battle, even bringing about Wellington's death in the process, is it not arguable that the Allies might have given up and let him keep his throne within the boundaries of pre-revolutionary France? A hundred years or so later Ludendorff's last offensive might have succeeded before American weight could tell. In all these cases, the world was required to hold its breath like the ringside watchers at a close-run boxing match, and await the outcome. Waiting did not lessen the triumph of such men as Blücher or Clemenceau. Wellington and Churchill preferred to remember the tragedy.

1944 was quite different from 1762, 1814 or 1918. Arthur
Bryant's perceptive article published on Trafalgar Day, which we
glanced at in the prologue, was reflected by all the planning for a
post-war Europe that had been going on in Washington and
London and Moscow. Discord at Yalta did not alter the military
facts. The question of who was going to win was not in doubt,
never really had been in doubt as far back as 1941. As soon as
Hitler had elected to add Russia and the United States, two world
giants, to his relatively pygmy-like enemies before that time, and
short of possessing some weapon with the war-stopping
characteristics of a nuclear bomb, there was no strategic recipe
which could have enabled the Third Reich to overcome these
enemies. The tragedy of 1944 was accordingly greater and the
triumph proportionately less. 1944 and 1945 were not simply
years of bitterness between enemies. They were years of bitterness
between allies as well.

Hitler who had poured such scorn on the political leaders and
strategists of the First World War had got his own Germany in
far worse a mess than had the Kaiser, Ludendorff and Hindenburg.
He had not chosen his enemies with that care which Oscar
Wilde had advocated and he himself had guaranteed. England
had been written off as impotent, the Americans dismissed as
bank clerks and Jewish hoodlums and Russia brushed aside as a
race of Slav *Untermenschen,* as a structure rotten and decayed.
Events were to show each in a somewhat different light—
England and her Empire virtually unconquerable no matter how
numerous or disastrous their military defeats in the field outside
Great Britain; the United States an unexpectedly energetic source
of boundless invention, inexhaustible reserves and aggressive
strategy; the Soviet Union the graveyard of the Wehrmacht. It
had not quite worked out as the Führer had predicted.

Having failed to learn or at least profit by some of the major
strategic lessons of the First World War, it was not to be imagined
that Hitler would change his spots when it came to the battle for
Germany. Haskins made the point that the man who is too old to
learn probably always was too old to learn. The Stuart Kings, for
example, except for Charles II, powerfully personified this
proverb. It is curious how further reinforced it is when we think
of Hitler, in spite of all the new methods of warfare that he
developed and introduced. His strategic ideas were not altered by
all the new weapons and tactics; these latter were simply made to

o

conform to his strategic ideas. Thus his talk to Rauschning in the early 1930s, even before coming to power, of great annihilating blows which with a single, all-powerful combination of violence and speed would obliterate the enemy's will to resist, all the talk of supremacy in the air, of restoring freedom of manoeuvre to military operations—everything had been decided upon before the creation of the Wehrmacht and the practice of blitzkrieg. When, after coming to power, he saw Guderian at work with his panzer teams and exultantly cried out that this was just what he wanted, it was not that Guderian's work and ideas were inspiring the Führer's strategic vision. It was that he saw that his own imagination and ideas coming true in front of his eyes. If ever there was a military leader with an *idée toute faite,* it was Hitler. And the idea did not change. 1944 was simply to be 1940 all over again. He could not see that the circumstances had themselves so altered, circumstances over which he had little control, that the same formula could not be made to work twice.

It may be an interesting exercise to ask ourselves what might have occurred if Rommel rather than von Rundstedt or Model had been in charge of the Ardennes offensive, if Rommel had survived the *Attentat* revenge and had been in command of the Western front in the autumn of 1944; Rommel, acknowledged master of the spoiling attack, which was what the Ardennes battle essentially was; Rommel, the arch-deceiver, the expert juggler of reserves who had confounded the British in the desert, the Americans at Kasserine and who if he had had his way might have taken his revenge on Montgomery in Normandy. We may be sure of one thing. He would not have frittered away his strength banging on at unprofitable portions of the front, but would have done what he always did in attack—his first shot at Tobruk excepted—find a weak spot quickly and smash the whole of his panzer strength through it with all the speed, violence and cunning of which he was capable. Not for Rommel, we may conclude, the bumbling and dithering which marred, albeit by the Führer's orders, the so-called Rundstedt offensive.

There was, of course, one other great panzer soldier, still alive, still in harness at the time of the battle. But he was not in direct command of armies. He was Chief of the German General Staff and doing his best to keep the creaking door of the Eastern front from bursting wide open. There was still Guderian. When Churchill discussed the Ardennes offensive with Stalin, the

Generalissimo made two comments of enduring interest, and one
of them was about Guderian:

> When I asked Stalin what he thought of Rundstedt's offensive
> against the Americans he called it a stupid manoeuvre which
> had harmed Germany and was done for prestige. The German
> military body was sick and could not be cured by such methods.
> The best generals had gone and only Guderian was left, and
> he was an adventurer. If the German divisions cut off in East
> Prussia had been withdrawn in time they might have been used
> to defend Berlin, but the Germans were foolish. They still had
> eleven armoured divisions at Budapest, but they had failed to
> realise that they were no longer a world-power and could not
> have forces wherever they wished. They would understand in
> due time, but it would be too late.

Guderian an adventurer? When he was striving in vain to withdraw those very divisions about to be cut off in strategically
irrelevant places so that he could muster the mightiest possible
effort for the vital battle of Germany? Guderian an adventurer,
when he was aiming to pull back the Wehrmacht from all distant
adventures, fight a holding battle on the Western front, and
concentrate every available element of offensive strength to hold
back the eastern enemy? No, it was Hitler who was the adventurer, not Guderian, Hitler, who was determined on one more
gamble, one more adventure. Guderian had taken part in some
military adventures in the past which put most others in the
shade—notably the encirclement of Poland, the crushing of
France, the overrunning of Russia—but he was far from being
an adventurer now. Indeed his whole policy was one of conserva-
tion, of sticking to those well-tried rules of defensive warfare
which were likely to leave the German military leaders with some
chance of improvising to meet circumstances outside their control.
It was Germany he was thinking of, and when he told Hitler so it
produced one more paroxysm of rage from the man who was so
well practised in them.

The other comment of Stalin's which we might do well to note
is that you cannot have forces wherever you wish. Just so. It is a
point brought home sharply to those without the initiative at
the beginning of a major conflict and much later to those whose
initial possession of the initiative has resulted in success so
widespread, conquests so numerous, territories to defend so

unlimited that once their peak of power and expansion is reached, decline and fall set in. It was this way with the Roman Empire. It was in this way that the British found they could not both hold on in the West in 1940 and 1941 and keep control of their Eastern territories. Even with all the Far East gone, and the British Isles themselves but precariously sustained, all their early efforts to clear North Africa or intervene in southern Europe failed, and it was only when the United States* added their numbers and machines that the Axis powers were driven back into *Festung Europa*. Then later when Hitler's conquests, like Macbeth's murders, were sticking on his hands, he tried to hold on everywhere with the result that bit by bit he lost his power everywhere. It might give us pause to wonder what would have happened if Hitler had recognized one supreme tip that history has constantly been touting—that all military conquerors have to give ground sooner or later. If, say in the autumn of 1941, before the battles for Moscow or Leningrad took such toll of the Wehrmacht, with so many of the Russian armies smashed and all of Western Russia in ruins, with the great power of his own armies still intact, and the United States not even in the contest— if then Hitler had decided that the time had come to prepare for a long war, had drawn in his horns, made Europe from the Vistula to the Atlantic and the Alps a real *Festung*; if he had done that and had one last glorious gamble with Raeder and Rommel to dominate the Mediterranean and capture the Middle East oil, then concentrate on fighting a war of attrition with U-boat and bomber, whilst employing Speer to produce the secret weapons which would really pay off, would he then have been defeatable?

It was by trying to have forces everywhere that he brought about his own destruction. He refused to grasp Goldsmith's point about running away at the right moment. The British and French have learned the lesson. The United States and Russia are learning it. In short, Stalin had said a mouthful.

The Battle of the Ardennes may thus be seen as the outcome of Hitler's eventual realization that he could not have forces everywhere. He himself made the admission that it was necessary only for a single panzer division to be idle for a week or two and all his subordinate commanders on other fronts would try and get their hands on it. So in a final concentration of effort under his own hand, he tried to do away with the need to have forces everywhere,

* Now even the United States finds it impossible to have forces everywhere.

to kick the English out of Europe once more, dismay the New World into leaving the Old to stew in its own juice and come back to his great, his original, his enduring mission—to erase Russia for good and all. In one sense, therefore, Stalin missed the point. What do you do, as a hunted wild beast when your enemies are closing in? Lie down and let them bite you to death, put chains on you, if you refuse to die? Or turn on your tormentors and attempt a last desperate throw to savage them into fear or flight? We should not overlook Hitler's saying to Speer— 'if it does not succeed, I no longer see any possibility of ending the war well'. Moreover, if it were done when 'tis done, then 'twere well it were done quickly. If the assassination of the American and English armies could catch success and trammel up the consequences, all might yet be well. Hitler's strategic problem had been that there was always one more enemy to defeat. His Europe was never whole as the marble, founded as the rock. It was never as clear and general as the casing air, but even at its greatest extent, was cabined, cribbed and confined by the sea and air power of the Allies. He would not, of course, play the Roman fool until the final chance was gone. While he saw lives, the gashes did better upon them. By mounting the Ardennes offensive, even though all else had failed him, Hitler would try the last and see who would first call a halt. In the end it was Hitler who cried 'Hold, enough!' And it was Hitler who was damned.

BIBLIOGRAPHY

Acheson, Dean, *The Eclipse of the State Department* in *Foreign Affairs*, Publishing Council on Foreign Relations Inc., July 1971

Ayer, Fred, Jr, *Before the Colours Fade*, Houghton Mifflin Co., Boston, 1964

Blumentritt, Günther, *Von Rundstedt, The Soldier and the Man*, Odhams Press, London, 1952

Borthwick, Alistair, *History of the 5th Battalion, The Seaforth Highlanders*, William Blackwood, Edinburgh

Bradley, Omar N., *A Soldier's Story*, Eyre and Spottiswoode, London, 1951

Bryant, Arthur, *Triumph in the West*, Collins, London, 1959; *The Lion and the Unicorn*, Collins, London, 1969

Bullock, Alan, *Hitler, A Study in Tyranny*, Revised edition, Penguin London, 1962

Churchill, Winston S., *Triumph and Tragedy*, (*The Second World War*, Vol. VI), Cassell, London, 1954

Cole, Hugh M., *The Ardennes: Battle of the Bulge*, Office of the Chief of Military History, Department of the Army, Washington DC, 1965

Ehrman, John, *Grand Strategy* (Vol. VI), H.M.S.O., London, 1956

Eisenhower, Dwight D., *Crusade in Europe*, Heinemann, London, 1949

Eisenhower, John S. D., *The Bitter Woods*, G. P. Putnam's Sons, New York

Ellis, L. F., *Victory in the West* (Vol. II), H.M.S.O., London, 1969

Elstob, Peter, *Hitler's Last Offensive*, Secker and Warburg, London, 1971

Essame, H., *The 43rd Wessex Division at War 1944–1945*, William Clowes and Sons Ltd., London, 1952; *The Battle for Germany*, Batsford, London, 1969

de Gaulle, Charles, *Salvation 1944–46*, Simon and Schuster, New York, 1960

Gilbert, Felix, Ed., *Hitler Directs His War*, O.U.P., 1950

Guderian, Heinz, *Panzer Leader*, Michael Joseph, London, 1952

De Guingand, Sir Francis, *Operation Victory*, Hodder and Stoughton, London, 1947

Hitler, Adolf, *Mein Kampf*, Houghton Mifflin Co., Boston, 1947

*Jacobsen, H. A. and Rohwer, J., Eds, *Decisive Battles of World War II: The German View*, G. P. Putnam's Sons, New York, 1965

Keitel, Wilhelm, *Memoirs*, William Kimber and Co. Ltd, London, 1965

Liddell Hart, B. H., *The Other Side of the Hill*, Cassell and Co., London, 1948

Mackenzie, Fred, *The Men of Bastogne*, David McKay Co. Inc., New York, 1968

Majdalany, Fred, *Cassino, Portrait of a Battle*, Longmans, Green and Co., London, 1957

Manteuffel, Hasso von, *The Battle of the Ardennes 1944–45*, (in * above)

Marshall, S. L. A., and others, *Bastogne: The First Eight Days*, Infantry Journal Press, Washington, 1946

Merriam, Robert E., *The Battle of the Ardennes*, Souvenir Press, London, 1958

Mitford, Nancy, *Frederick the Great*, Hamish Hamilton, London, 1970

Montgomery, Viscount, *Memoirs*, Collins, London, 1958; *A History of Warfare*, Collins, London, 1968

Nobécourt, Jacques, *Le Dernier Coup de Dés de Hitler*, Robert Laffort, Paris, 1962; [*Hitler's Last Gamble*, Chatto and Windus Ltd, London, 1967]

Patton, George S., Jr., *War As I Knew It*, Houghton Mifflin Co., Boston, 1967

Rauschning, Hermann, *Hitler Speaks*, Thornton Butterworth Press Ltd, New York, 1939

Salmond, J. B., *History of the 51st Highland Division, 1939–45*, William Blackwood and Sons Ltd, Edinburgh, 1953

Sellar, R. J. B., *The Fife and Forfar Yeomanry, 1919–1956*, William Blackwood and Sons Ltd, Edinburgh, 1960

Shulmann, Milton, *Defeat in the West*, Secker and Warburg, London, 1951

Speer, Albert, *Inside the Third Reich*, Weidenfeld and Nicolson, London, 1970

The Story of the 23rd Hussars, published privately by Members of the Regiment, 1946

Taylor, A. J. P., *English History 1914–1945*, Clarendon Press, Oxford, 1965

Toland, John, *Battle: The Story of the Bulge*, Muller, London, 1960

Trevor-Roper, H. R., *The Last Days of Hitler*, Third edition, Macmillan, London, 1956; Ed. *Hitler's War Directives, 1939–1945*, Sidgwick and Jackson, London, 1964

Warlimont, Walter, *Inside Hitler's Headquarters, 1939–1945* (translated R. H. Barry), Weidenfeld and Nicolson, London, 1964

Westphal, Siegfried, *The German Army in the West*, Cassell and Co. Ltd, London, 1951

Wilmot, Chester, *The Struggle for Europe*, Collins, London, 1952

INDEX

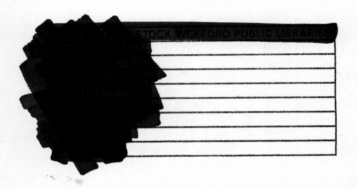